C000263286

DESTROYING ANGEL
STEVE BLOOMER
ENGLAND'S FIRST FOOTBALL HERO

DESTROYING ANGEL
STEVE BLOOMER
ENGLAND'S FIRST FOOTBALL HERO

PETER SEDDON

First published in Great Britain in 1999 by The Breedon Books Publishing Company Limited, Breedon House, 44 Friar Gate, Derby, DE1 1DA.

Paperback edition first published in Great Britain in 2010 by The Derby Books Publishing Company Limited, 3 Parker Centre, Mansfield Road, Derby, DE21 4SZ.

ISBN 978-1-85983-777-1

Printed and bound by Cromwell Press Group, Trowbridge, Wiltshire.

CONTENTS

This book is dedicated to the
memory of Steve Bloomer and
family and to all lovers of
football through the ages.

FOREWORD

AND now, at last, the book!

In today's common vernacular, Steve Bloomer could now claim to have 'done it all', even if it has taken around 100 years to get there.

He's scored the goals (some of them still records), won the England caps, coached overseas, survived four years of civilian PoW camp life in Germany, merited various memorials in Derby and in his birthplace of Cradley, been the subject of a video and finally the book too... the first written exclusively about him in a century.

Thankfully, it is far-removed from being a mere collection of football phraseology, achievements and statistics; it reflects, as much, the gradual development of our national sport and part of society in the late 19th and early 20th centuries, witnessing the enthronement of its first 'superstar' with less grandiose trimmings than we are used to in these Millennium days, when even one goal can sometimes signal a premature award of 'greatness'.

Being too young to have seen my grandfather (or 'pop' as I called him) play, I had to be content with the other 'goals' he scored for me in my parents' home in the 1930s... producing threepenny bits from his waistcoat pocket for me to buy aniseed balls, or some other such luxury for a seven-year-old, after I had cheekily interrupted his morning read of the then broadsheet *Daily Mail*, with spectacles on the end of his nose, a smile teasingly withheld.

While the Bloomer scoring records are inescapable in Derby football talk, his biography should serve to cement the wider stature and fame which his lasting greatness continues to promote over 70 years after his passing.

Steve Richards
Dorking
Surrey

ACKNOWLEDGEMENTS

Many people have helped in making both the first edition and current edition of this book possible. I would particularly like to thank Steve Bloomer's grandson Steve Richards for showing the initial enthusiasm which enabled a mere suggestion to proceed to publication. His subsequent help and guidance proved invaluable.

In the time-honoured spirit I express my thanks in alphabetical order to the following further helpers. Peter Barnsley, Julie Bunyan, Jim Clark, Phil Crossley, Michael Dexter, Claire Foley, David Holmes, Denise Holmes, Michael Knighton, Robert Lindsay, Rebecca Marshall, Richard Marshall, Ian Methven, Jeanne Minchin, Norman Shiel, Lorna Spare and Steve Swanwick. My sincere apologies and thanks also to anyone inadvertently omitted here.

I would like to express particular gratitude to the publishers for taking the initial manuscript through to fruition, and to all members of my family for their interest and support. Finally a special 'thanks' to my partner Kate Ibbitson for a continued willingness to accommodate my impulsive forays into the world of books and vintage sport.

INTRODUCTION

This is an updated edition of a book initially published in 1999. Although since then Steve Bloomer has become much better known to a wider audience, the reasons behind my writing the life story of such a gifted footballer and remarkable character remain unchanged. So here again is my explanation – this time addressed to what I hope will be an extended readership, perhaps enjoying a more intimate acquaintance with the 'Destroying Angel' for the very first time.

My first encounter with Steve Bloomer must have been about 40 years ago. In those heady days before the football heritage industry had found its feet, the Derby County match programme or the Saturday evening *Football Special* would occasionally give this ghostly figure from a bygone age a passing mention.

There was usually a photograph – invariably the same one – and a brief overview of Bloomer's credentials. Namely, that he remained Derby County's record goalscorer and had once held the same coveted honour for England.

Being only 13 years old at the time this did not make a great impression on me. In the late 1960s and early 70s my attention was grabbed instead by the dynamic duo Brian Clough and Peter Taylor. They were winning things for my team in a colourful 'here and now' which seemed to me light years away from a monochrome age I knew very little about.

As for heroic strikers, there was only one man in the frame for me – Kevin Hector. 'King Kev' ultimately graced the Rams' starting line up 581 times and scored 201 goals in the process. Only in the fullness of time – and after cultivating an interest in sporting history – did I consciously register that Steve Bloomer topped Hector's own impressive goal haul by a considerable margin.

Bloomer bagged 332 for the Rams in 525 appearances – 131 more goals than 'The King' but in 56 fewer outings. Now that really did impress me – having witnessed for myself the prolific talent of Hector, I began for the first time to seriously wonder about 'that man Bloomer'. So I resolved to find out more.

But thereby lay a problem. Although routinely dubbed 'Derby County's most famous player', little apart from the standard pen-picture was ever presented. As such I began to realise how little was known of this 'legendary footballer' – he remained a rather two-dimensional figure who might almost have been a cartoon hero or someone who inhabited the same misty reaches of human consciousness as Robin Hood and Sherlock Holmes. Where was the flesh and blood?

Nor did a search beyond Derby's own archives bear any more fruit. It emerged that no biography of Steve Bloomer had been published anywhere; indeed, not a single full-length biography of any English-born professional footballer from the Victorian era had ever been written. So I resolved to make Steve Bloomer – indisputably pre-eminent in his time – the very first. I felt he deserved it – not least because, with the passing generations, there seemed a very real danger that his star would eventually fade to almost nothing.

When I contacted Bloomer's grandson Steve Richards to propose the suggestion, he responded positively and with great enthusiasm. But any hope I harboured that he would present me with Bloomer's life story 'on a plate' was quickly banished. The retained family records were useful but worryingly scant. And it soon became apparent that there was a great deal about his illustrious grandfather's life and career that Steve Richards, like the rest of the world, simply did not know – but certainly wanted to.

That being the case, I set about the task of painstakingly reconstructing Bloomer's life from disparate early sources. And as the pieces of the jigsaw were slowly slotted together, a much fuller picture emerged. That is the one presented within the pages of this book. It makes no claim to be complete in every sense, but I hope it brings new life to both the 'sporting hero' and the man himself.

Just as Steve Bloomer did, the book aims unashamedly to entertain, although it doubtless falls well short of the marksmanship standards set by the incomparable 'Paleface'. But if it can put just a hint of colour into those sepia-toned photographs that for so long epitomised Bloomer's established persona, then I hope it has achieved its other main goal – that of giving due recognition to a diminutive yet charismatic man blessed with the legendary talent that made him truly 'England's first football hero'.

Peter Seddon
Derby, 2010.

BLACK COUNTRY BOY 1874-1879

"It has nailshops past my counting,
Where men and women toil,
Making 'roundheads', 'forties' and 'clinkers'
For the tillers of the soil"
Thomas Crofts

TUESDAY, 20 January 1874 is not a date that is universally remembered for any special reason; in fact it marked just another ordinary day in the lives of the teeming millions, going about their daily routine, getting on with the serious business of survival in a rapidly changing mid-Victorian world. The Queen embarked on her 37th year on the throne, William Gladstone clung precariously to Prime Ministerial office and Caleb Bloomer, a 24-year-old 'puddler', trudged through the biting cold to the burning hot forge that was his daily bread. Yet if Caleb seemed slightly distracted on such an ordinary day, he had good reason. With his young wife Merab at home due to give birth to their first child any day now, this was an important time in the Bloomer household.

Exactly how important in a much wider sporting sense, only time has told, for on that very day, 20 January 1874, the baby boy that arrived on a humble Cradley stage was destined to become one of the greatest names that Association Football has ever known. Welcome to the world, little legs kicking… Stephen Bloomer.

Cradley Roots
Both Caleb and Merab were themselves Cradley-born and shared a common family background; their own fathers, Edward Bloomer and Andrew Dunn, were makers of nails for horseshoes, a thriving cottage industry in the mid-19th century Black Country. Their environment would certainly have been a tough one, as a popular and macabre anecdote of that era humorously suggests: "A visitor to town pokes his head into a nailmaker's shop and asks the time; scarcely looking up from his anvil, the hardy nailer lands a bludgeoning blow with his hammer on the visitor's skull, adding with a wicked smile, 'It's just struck one.'" This is not to suggest that the Bloomer antecedents were a murderous lot, but it's a fair bet they were no softies…the nailmakers were described by the contemporary press as 'the white slaves of the Black Country' and were renowned for working long hours in appalling insanitary conditions for very low pay.

By the late 1860s both the Bloomers and the Dunns had made the short move from Cradley to Dudley, the nail-making capital of England. There, young Caleb and Merab met and courted and finally married in the Parish Church on 1 April 1872. Denied anything akin to a formal education, neither was able to sign their own name on the marriage certificate. They settled back in their native Cradley where Caleb, progressive enough to break with tradition, took the opportunity to leave behind the repetitive grind of the sharply declining nail trade in favour of work at the rapidly expanding heavier end of the market as an iron worker.

Thus settled, almost two years into the marriage, 21-year-old Merab gave birth to Stephen not in the atmosphere of pastoral rusticity that the Biblical names of her and her husband might suggest, but at their rented terraced home in Bridge Street, Cradley, in the county of Worcestershire, England. If Caleb had troubled to hasten home from his workplace that day in anticipation of the impending new arrival, the anxious father- to-be might well have had something of an uphill run to get there on time. Bridge Street made its way up the slope from the narrow cut of the River Stour, a short row of artisans 'cottages' on its right-hand side. Despite some scholarly research having been undertaken by a number of Bloomer enthusiasts, there is as yet no conclusive evidence identifying the exact house in which Stephen made his debut. The 'Bloomer Row', as it has been called by some of the proud and sportingly inclined locals, was demolished soon after the onset of the progressive 1970s, all but obliterated by the industrial units and attendant sprawling development which now characterise much of the area.

In fact, over the many years in which Bloomer's career has been covered by journalists and admirers, even his exact place of origin has been the subject of some confusion. Most of the modern sources state his birthplace as Cradley Heath and even as early as 1922 such an august publication as *Burke's Who's Who of Sport and Sporting Records* made the same assumption. Such things become perpetuated over time, but in truth the correct place of birth was Cradley... if only by a few yards!

The River Stour, which snakes its murky way through the adjoining communities of Cradley and Cradley Heath to the west of Birmingham, marks the boundary between the two. In 1874, a full century before Local Government reorganisation began to confuse matters further, the river also marked the county boundary between Worcestershire and Staffordshire. Stephen was certainly born just south of the river, which makes him not only a Cradley lad but a Worcestershire one too. Do I hear cries of "What does it matter?" Well, the residents of Cradley and Cradley Heath, rightly proud of their heritage, are liable to engage in a bit of friendly banter and local rivalry from time to time, and confusing the two is rather like saying that The Beatles hailed from Manchester or that Danny Blanchflower was an Arsenal hero; to people who care deeply, these things can rightly assume an importance entirely beyond the comprehension of those on the outside... just ask the natives of Dudley about their own favourite son, the dear departed Duncan Edwards.

A photograph of the top end of the 'Bloomer Row' shows what locals claim to be 'the' house, known as the 'Old Toll House' or 'Round House', a simple corner terraced cottage with a curved frontage standing at the top of the hill at the junction of Bridge Street and Lyde Green. It is very likely that this is absolutely correct, but unless concrete documentary evidence is unearthed, and in the absence of Sherlock Holmes, 'the mystery of Bloomer's cottage' must remain in the unsolved cases file for now. Meanwhile, the site is occupied by a small modern industrial unit, only a few bricks of the back wall of the original dwelling remaining.

It is rather easier, though, to put the record straight on a number of alternative and incorrect Bloomer theories that have reached the press or been bandied about by fans over the years. When Merab Bloomer went to register her child's birth on 10 February 1874, the name Stourbridge appeared boldly at the top of the birth certificate and this has suggested to some that Stephen was a native of that town which, in truth, was merely the Registration District which covered the Cradley area. The birth certificate also includes the wording 'in the County of Worcester' and as it happens that there is a small village named Cradley not far from the delightful spa town of Malvern, Worcestershire, some people have even suggested that Stephen was a country boy at heart. But not for the first time two and two have been put together to make anything but four. The image of young Stephen gambolling with the lambs on a verdant pasture, dribbling a ball around a static defence of poppies and wild orchids, only pausing to take a drink of crystal clear water from a babbling brook, is an appealing one, not least to the pasty-faced lad himself, but alas an incorrect one. In any case, that particular Cradley is just over the border in Herefordshire, so perchance the riddle of the birthplace can be laid to rest at last.

The 'Black Country' Cradley was, as its name suggests, a touch more industrial. The immediate area in which Stephen was to spend the first five years of his life was a higgledy-piggledy mass of rooftops and chimneys... houses and workshops, mills and factories, belching out smoke, echoing to the sound of cold metal on hot, jostling for space along the banks of the Stour which once provided the water power to turn the wheels, which made the whole place work and grow. Day after day the rhythmic grind of incessant work wore on. There was open space, too, and certain elements of traditional village life, but much of the nearby countryside and heathland was rapidly being eaten up by ongoing development, so the environment was essentially a hard and industrial one, even if softened by a rural fringe.

Stephen's working class roots, then, injected not a hint of privilege into his early upbringing. Indeed, the very name Bloomer rings with the sound of the iron works. It is what the genealogists call a metonymic derivation, one which substitutes a name for an action or occupation, like Baker or Butcher. In Middle English a 'blome' was an impure ingot of iron, later known as a 'bloom'. It had to be passed through a refining process in the room known as a 'bloomery' and the man in charge of that activity was, not entirely surprisingly, a 'Bloomer'. The name first crops up as a surname in the Sussex area, where iron-making was the greatest of all their industries until the end of the 18th century. When that work gradually spread into the Midlands, reaching its frenzied peak in the massive industrialisation of the region throughout the 19th century, the surname came too. There were several hundred people named Bloomer in the Cradley area when Stephen was born – and scarcely a handful in the whole of Derbyshire, placing the family origins firmly in the West Midlands and leading the man himself, on one occasion long after his retirement from football, to admit to – whisper it quietly – 'a sneaking regard for the Villa!'

Young Stephen was baptised in the Parish Church of St Peter's on 5 October 1874 and as he struggled through his first few years of family life he was typical of the mass of ordinary folk who made up the industrial labouring classes of that era; working to live was what it was all about and comfort and luxury were not words which the Bloomer family would have associated with themselves. Caleb continued to toil at an iron foundry, generically a blacksmith but specifically a 'puddler', someone who worked to convert unrefined pig iron into wrought iron. Cramped living conditions and a complete lack of 'modern' conveniences were the lot of the Bloomers and their ilk in the 1870s, a pungent mix of the earlier gloomy world of Dickensian fiction, mildly sweetened by the first stirrings of social progress and a genuine family warmth, then soured afresh by the harsh and bitter truths of real daily life.

Yet by the time of Queen Victoria's death in 1901, England would become a highly industrialised, fairer and far more sophisticated society in which the early motor car, telephones, electric power, increased leisure time and basic wireless telegraphy were forming the beginnings of a hugely different modern age. But novice father Caleb had no idea of the great leap forward which society and all its attendant paraphernalia would make in the 30 years which followed the birth of his son. All he knew was that he must keep working, do the best he could for his wife and family, and hope that Stephen would develop the strength, sinew and lung capacity that would make him into a good 'smith', a healthy 'bloomer' and a chip off the old block.

Football to 1879
It wasn't that Caleb lacked ambition for his son; merely that his hopes and fears were hidebound by the constraints of his own background and the limitations of realistic opportunity.

Nowadays, many a father expresses the wish that one day his son might make a living out of sport. Whether it be football, rugby, golf, tennis, snooker or any of a host of other potentially lucrative activities, 'being a professional sportsman' is today both an ambition and a viable career option for those special few who have the desire and ability to make the dream come true. Yet Caleb Bloomer could not possibly have harboured any such hopes for Stephen, battling his way through the toddler years towards a future which only the most perceptive football administrator might have had a chance of predicting. Caleb would certainly have known the game of football, but to have suggested to his work colleagues then that 'one day my son will play professional football for Derby County' was truly in the realms of fantasy. It wouldn't, and indeed couldn't, have been said; Derby County were not formed until 1884, and paid 'professionalism' was only legalised a year later, so the future that lay in store for young Stephen really was 'the future' in every sense of the word.

He would become what, during the first few years of his life, simply didn't then exist. So to fully appreciate how and why a boy born in 1874 could achieve what Stephen did, we really need to understand something of the development of football up to and including the 1870s. Many thousands of words, indeed entire volumes, have been written on this aspect of the evolution of the game, constantly being added to by new academic and historical research. Within the narrative of the Bloomer life story, though, a generalised summary of the 'prehistoric' game will place Stephen's birth into its relevant football context.

Middle Ages to 1845

Football, in one form or another, had existed for at least 700 years before Stephen's birth. As early as 1174 the chronicler William Fitz Stephen penned his account of the game in London: 'After dinner all the youth of the City goes out into the fields for the very popular game of ball, the elders and the men of wealth coming on horseback to view the contests of their juniors, arousing in them a stirring of natural heat by viewing so much activity and by participation in the joys of unrestrained youth.'

Many a football player and supporter since has surely felt that very same 'stirring of natural heat'. Such hearty early 'skirmishes', which ensued almost everywhere in the land until the middle of the 19th century, were really akin to mini-battles, variously described in the football history books as 'folk' football, 'street' football or 'mob' football. Wherever there was an open field, a suitably enclosed space, or even an entire townscape in which a 'blown bladder' or 'leathern orb' could be kicked or tossed around, there would gather crowds of youths and excited onlookers all intent on letting off steam and causing general mayhem into the bargain.

Serious injuries were common and deaths by no means rare, as Phillip Stubbes made graphically clear in this archaic description from 1583: "As concerning football playing I protest unto you that it may rather be called a friendlie kinde of fyghte, a bloody practice than a felowly sport. For does not everyone lye in waight for his adversarie, seeking to overthrow him, so that by this means their necks, backs, arms and legs are broken and their noses gush out with blood? And when 'tis one betwixt two they dash him against the hart with their elbowes, and butt him under the short ribs with their gripped fists, and hereof groweth envy, malice, brawling and sometimes homicide, with great effusion of blood."

Although it may sound very reminiscent of Leeds United at the Baseball Ground in the 1970s, it was to be many years before this unlawful activity labelled the 'rude and manly game' could metamorphose itself into 'the beautiful game'. Over the centuries most of the reigning monarchs and their administrators issued damning proclamations 'forbiddinge ye foteballe playe' but it took years and years of such killjoying before the great British public at large began to accept that their riotous footballing days were numbered.

Only by the 1840s were most of the annual 'festival' games, usually played at Shrovetide, finally quelled. The famous Pancake Tuesday game at Derby, in its day the most celebrated of them all, eventually bit the dust in 1845; only the rare and watered down survivors, like the world-famous Ashbourne game, would live to see the 20th century and beyond. For the ancient mass football game to ferment into something more palatable across the social spectrum required an ongoing refinement. But rough cloudy ale to clear amber brew, tart cider to the sweetest champagne perry, is no easy transformation. It took some timely input from the educated classes to ensure football's survival and slake a thirst still raging in the throats of the people.

Ten vital years – 1845 to 1855

Seeing off the pre-planned festival games didn't stop the more spontaneous street and field games entirely… lads still got together, kicked lumps out of each other, terrorised passers-by and caused wilful damage to property. Then, as now, such behaviour certainly worried the educated lawmakers, politicians and church types intent on making their own little patches 'a better place to live'. As a result, from the late 1840s and into the next decade, the notion began to develop that, if 'boys will be boys', it might be wiser to let them play but to do so in a more controlled environment with rules and administration to keep them on the straight and narrow. The churchmen particularly favoured this type of approach, seeking to mould the aggression of youth into the virtuous concept which became known as 'muscular Christianity'.

But, above all, it was the Public Schools and then their 'Old Boys' which truly developed organised football through the middle decades of the 19th century. Westminster, Harrow, Charterhouse and their ilk had all played their own special brands of football for years… Eton football existed from at least 1747. But until 1840 or so, it too had been very much a disorganised rough and tumble; it wouldn't be too far from the mark simply to give it the label of 'posh' street football, a designer version of the common game, football for rich kids who still kicked lumps out of each other but wore nice stripy costumes to do it in and said 'sorry old chap' when they broke someone's leg.

But then came school reform and by 1850 or so the cult of 'organised' games had begun to creep into the curriculum. Same time each day or week, let's pick proper sides, make sure a master supervises and, above all boys, 'stick to the rules'. 'But what are the rules, sir?' chirps a shrill voice from among the chasing pack. And once that so obvious question had been asked, the laws began to be written down. Different schools played to different rules, but then when they played each other they soon tumbled to the fact that they must unify the rules into a common code; either that or they'd stick to their guns and play to a different code altogether... the handling code or the kicking code, gentlemen make your choice. Hence Rugby Football and Association Football, later to be dubbed 'the real football' by a leading writer of the day. I can't possibly disagree with his observation; whoever heard of an oval 'ball'?

As football began to crystallise in the quality schools into a form much closer to the game we know now, one more vital step had to be completed. The modified and newly respectable game needed to be taken out of the privileged cloisters and into the real world, and when a group of schoolboys left their classrooms to became the young men about town of 1855, they took that step.

Let's form a football club – 1855 to 1879

Most groups leaving school like to keep in touch and carry on the old traditions, be it cricket, drinking or football. The former pupils of Sheffield Collegiate School were no different... it was just that they had a new craze to keep them amused. Thus the Sheffield Club, originally formed by a nucleus of old boys in 1855, became what is now regarded as the world's first-ever football club. This was quickly followed by Sheffield Hallam (1857) and the Forest Club (1859), a team of Old Harrovians who played at Snaresbrook near Epping Forest. Excellent early photographs of these sides survive, some showing 11 men and a ball, the first visual evidence that the game as we know it was on its way. 1862 saw the first stirrings of the Notts County club and by 1863 the kicking game had forged its identity well enough to be able to form its own association, the first of its kind anywhere in the world, and as such forever known not as the 'English' Football Association but simply 'The' Football Association. Thus it was, only 11 years before the birth of Stephen, that Association Football was itself born after a gestation period of many centuries.

From 1863 it developed rapidly but remained a game largely for the gentlemen who both created and administrated it. Many more clubs were formed and friendly or invitation games were arranged. England played Scotland in an 'unofficial' international in 1870 and won the first official contest in 1872. A knockout contest, the FA Cup, was suggested and implemented in 1871-72, just 15 clubs taking part in that first historic year. The players' garb was amusingly quaint, pitch markings and many rules were different, no one played officially for money and silver spoons were the order of the day, as educated chaps, privileged all, learnt to play the new game. It didn't take long, though, for it to become a wider craze, if only a minor one at first, and the working man, with newly acquired half-holidays at his disposal on Saturday afternoons, boosted by improving wages, was not in the mood to be left out. Cricket clubs, public houses, churches and neighbourhood districts all began to form football clubs. Sheffield Wednesday (1867), Stoke (1868), Aston Villa (1874), Preston North End and Wolverhampton Wanderers (1879) and a myriad of local clubs gradually followed. In this way, working class local lads with the necessary aptitude could instinctively learn how to kick and master a ball equally as well as the public school types who they were soon destined to play alongside at the highest level.

So, by the time of Stephen's birth in 1874, football had taken on a form which, although different, we would certainly recognise and be able to take part in were we to possess a time machine. It is possible that some might query what on earth all this has to do with the Bloomer life story, but in truth this diversion away from Cradley back into the fields and streets of mediaeval England, the cloisters of public schools and the panelled London offices of FA committee men is absolutely central to an understanding and explanation of the Bloomer legend. It is quite impossible to divorce the growth of 'Steve' from that of the game itself. Had he been born 30 years earlier he would not have become a professional footballer. Or 20 years later, the tidal wave of robust turn of the century 'soccer wanabees' might have engulfed his nimble frame completely. Quite simply, by making his entrance in 1874, Stephen had unwittingly displayed for the very first time the attribute of timing which was to bring him so much of his success in the future.

Years after Bloomer's final game in 1914, an old Derby County sage was to remark: "My lasting image of 'Steve' will always be of him hovering on the fringe of the mêlée while others tried to make something of a situation; then, just as the time was right, out he'd pop and away he'd go with not a chance of a mortal soul catching him."

That could almost be a metaphor for the events of 20 January 1874 as Stephen took his first gulps of air and set off on life's relentless pursuit. From that first moment the infant Bloomer was to grow up chronologically in close synchronisation with the infant football. Whether he would embrace it or not depended first on his close and constant exposure to it, second on his capacity to enjoy it and third on his ability to take a chance if it presented itself to him. Whether the lad had such a hat-trick in him, only time would tell. It might be argued that Cradley, being close to the Villas, Wolves and Throstles of this football world, was a fine centre of excellence in which to give a youngster a football education, but with his father Caleb later unreservedly admitting to his own thorough early disinterest in the game, one suspects that Stephen needed the sort of special environment and tutoring which might only be available in a real 'football town'.

Transfer Talks

Those first steps towards his illustrious future in a veritable 'university of soccer' were to be taken courtesy of his father. Caleb was well aware of the need to move in search of work if necessary and, as the 1870s wore on, he turned his thoughts to that very option. When he was only one-year-old himself, he had been bundled off to Belper when his parents travelled there seeking employment at that time in the early 1850s when the small Derbyshire town produced a staggering two million nails a week. In the event, his father and mother Jemima (née Harper) stayed there some time while Caleb and his brothers and sister were sent back to Cradley to be cared for by their grandfather, Edward Harper, and aunt Elizabeth. Caleb would be only too aware, therefore, of the sort of difficulties and disruption which the uncertainty of irregular or seasonal work could cause. Yet he was aware too that, just as his job was to turn the crude into the refined, so that process of betterment could be mirrored in life itself.

As the 1880s approached, there was an increasing concentration of heavy industry, with the prospect of regular work, in the larger Midlands towns. Although by 1878 Caleb had secured a more skilled position as an anchor smith, it seemed likely that his own route to the land of opportunity lay beyond Cradley. The birth of Stephen's brother, Phillip, in 1875 followed by a sister, Alice, in 1878 meant there were now five hungry mouths to feed. Taking an apparent lead from his Biblical namesake, who went in search of the promised land with Joshua, Caleb gathered his wife and children together for a journey of their own. Sometime in 1879 the Bloomers made a bold move in the direction of progress which was truly to shape their five-year-old son's destiny... they took a train journey and disembarked at Derby.

A DERBY LAD
1879-1886

"The little boys of Derby, sir,
They came to beg his eyes,
To kick about the street sir
For they were football size.

Indeed, sir, this is true, sir
I never was taught to lie,
And had you come to Derby, sir
You'd have seen it as well as I."
Ballad of The Derby Ram

THE Bloomers were far from being the only family who decamped to Derby in search of a better life; the historic town described by *Robinson Crusoe* author Daniel Defoe early in the 18th century as 'one of gentry rather than of trade' had changed so significantly 150 years later as to become a veritable hive of trade and industry which attracted many families seeking work and advancement. When young Stephen disembarked the train which had brought him from the Black Country to the East Midlands, it was a journey of much greater significance than the modest mileage and noticeable dialect change might merely suggest. He had left behind a Cradley with its industrial heritage then firmly rooted in the past and landed in a forward-looking 'new' town in both senses of the word. Although none of the Bloomer clan could possibly be sure of it then, their arrival in the rapidly expanding Derby township known as Litchurch was a timely one indeed.

Litchurch – land of opportunity
Although milk and honey didn't come on tap and 'land of opportunity' wasn't a slogan which industrialists actually used to attract new employees to the increasingly productive southern confines of Derby, it might well have been. In 1801 Litchurch was a mere hamlet outside the Borough of Derby with an attributed population of just 30 rustic souls and in 1840 it was said to be 'a pleasant country settlement consisting chiefly of fertile meads and inhabited by numerous cattle'. But the break-up of the landed estates in that locality, predominantly in the ownership of the Dixies of Market Bosworth, enabled Derby to expand southwards on the axes of two roads whose names, prophetically, would one day come to have an altogether different significance to Stephen and his followers... Normanton and Osmaston.

That expansion would not have been necesssary, though, but for the coming of the railways to the town in the 1830s and the establishment of no less than three railway company headquarters there, which subsequently merged to form the hugely successful Midland Railway Company. Derby truly became a thriving industrial centre on the back of that, with a huge expansion in all manner of core and ancilliary industries, and it was the hamlet of Litchurch which afforded much of the space for that expansion to take place. By 1866 it had grown to 53,200 people and been given its own local government – indeed it was as big as Derby itself and effectively a separate town contiguous to the ancient borough. In 1877 it was finally incorporated into the borough and by the time the Bloomers arrived in 1879 its population was over 70,000.

Into that bustling environment, clamouring with the noise of men at work and kids at play amid the ever-present smell of the foundries, the Bloomers were thrust. While the area now is predominantly covered in 'old' housing stock and dilapidated industrial buildings, most of what the new arrivals saw for the first time was itself relatively modern. Housing, shops, public houses, schools, churches, parks… all were created apace to meet the demands of a 'young' community in what today's planners and developers would assuredly market as a 'new town'.

Judged against such a backdrop, the Bloomers were a modern and progressive family for their time and Caleb deserves full credit for having the initiative to make the move. Their first home was a rented terraced house at 44 Yates Street, now demolished but then just off Pear Tree Road on the fringe of New Normanton, only a few minutes walk from the open fields which were later to become the Baseball Ground. While much of the housing in the mediaeval heart of Derby was insanitary in the extreme, the Bloomer's abode was spanking new by comparison, only two years old when they moved in, built to more exacting building regulations and part of a well-planned urban expansion. While it was only a simple property it certainly wasn't squalid in the imagined sense that word now evokes, and in that respect young Stephen's upbringing, though it continued to be hard and 'working class', was for the first time tinged with a relative privilege never enjoyed by any of his forebears.

In the hurly-burly which accompanied the arrival of so many new inhabitants, though, it was a privilege made dubious by the fact that it initially had to be shared; construction simply couldn't keep pace with demand, and as a result of that, and initial financial uncertainty, the Bloomers had to content themselves with the use of only half a house, probably the first floor, sharing the building with Burton-born labourer Joseph Harlow, his blind wife Phoebe and their three teenage children. While it was no picnic, therefore, the main aim of the move was fulfilled in that Caleb found work, calling on his old 'puddling' skills to secure a place at nearby Ley's foundry, founded in 1874 by Francis Ley and later to play more than a passing role in Stephen's own working, football and sporting future.

As Litchurch expanded, successive tracts of ancient open land were consumed block by block in a red-brick frenzy but in Stephen's pre-teen years there were still fields only a stone's throw away on land now centred around Goodale Street and the reminiscently named Dairy House Road. It wasn't a rural idyll but it is easy to imagine that there was a certain charm, freedom and excitement attached to this new world for a growing lad. In later years Steve never much referred to his boyhood, but he was to live most of his life on that childhood playground, one of his later adult homes occupying the very fields on which he once must have roamed, so it is fair to conjecture that the area had pleasant associations for him and that his tender years were not unhappy ones. And if he needed the company of other children with whom to share those relatively carefree days, he certainly had a good pick... the area was simply riddled with them. But all play it wasn't. In the newly enlightened educational environment then beginning to prevail, a five-year-old lad had to think of school!

A right little 'Roadite'

Caleb Bloomer might have had no specific aspirations beyond the foundry for his oldest son but in the short term was no doubt grateful enough that Stephen and his young brother and sister looked set for a better educational start in life than he himself had enjoyed. Through Forster's Education Act of 1870, a Liberal government, increasingly concerned that many males newly-entitled to the vote could neither read or write, had decreed that all areas had to provide sufficient school places for all children between the ages of five and 12 who chose to attend; and by 1880, Mundella's Education Act of that year had further defined the boundaries by making attendance compulsory for all five to ten-year-olds. Young Stephen hadn't a clue as to the significance of this for his future development and well-being, but what it meant to him in practical terms was that on his arrival in Derby he was bundled off by his mother Merab to something called 'school'. Regrettably nothing but tantalising fragments of secondary evidence survive from Stephen's schooldays. While some of us still have examples of even our earliest work, he was never a hoarder and not a jot of primary documentary evidence has come down to us.

What we do have is retrospective material from the 1920s Derby press, written after Bloomer had made his name, which outlines the early years of our young 'scholar'. As a five-year-old Stephen went to Pear Tree School, then just a tiny Church of England Mission School on the corner of Pear Tree Street and Portland Street, still there today, but now the premises of a clothing manufacturer. He stayed there less than a year and perhaps the only observation of note to make about that time, and a mildly spooky one for any fatalists out there, is the name of his first teacher, Miss Goodall – some years later he was to come under the tutelage of another gentle persuader of the same name but opposite gender who he would one day describe as 'the greatest influence any young man could ever wish for'. Whatever progress the young Miss Goodall made with her infant charge she lost him to the 'big school' not long after his sixth birthday in 1880.

Wherever the provision of voluntarily-run schools could not meet the desired capacity, the Education Acts provided for the setting up of publicly-elected school boards to set up grant and rate-aided Board Schools aimed at giving a standardised elementary education to the masses. Many of these schools were built to lavish and well equipped standards and often several storeys high in urban areas where building land was at a premium. They were a new animal indeed, once described by someone with quite a quick brain of his own, one Sherlock Holmes, as 'rather like lighthouses... beacons of the future'. Stephen was fortunate indeed, just six years down the line from the nailshop world of Cradley, to be guided by such a beacon. Although standard football texts have for the last 15 years or so simply stated that Bloomer was 'educated at St James's School', that in itself is too vague as there were several schools with St James in their titles at that time. The school Stephen actually attended between the ages of six and 12, from 1880 to 1886, and for which Caleb might well have had to pay a small weekly fee known as 'school pence', was the newly-constructed St James's Road Board School, specifically erected to cater for the huge influx of youngsters into the area and designed to take 1,500 pupils at full capacity. Situated and still standing, but under a different name, towards the bottom of St James's Road on land bounded by Hastings Street and Wright Street (now Dover Street) it was just a few hundred yards from his Yates Street home.

Critics of the system argued that Board Schools were too lavishly appointed, but for the children fortunate enough to be in at the start of the new regime that was a blessing. Although many of Stephen's lessons were conducted to a somewhat repetitive daily pattern, the teaching methodology and equipment provided was generally sound and, as far as the teaching standard was concerned, Derby became rather a centre of excellence by virtue of the teacher training college for school mistresses established in the 1850s on Uttoxeter New Road. While rote learning, copy books and object lessons were the order of the day, all lessons were centred around achieving the childrens' proficiency in the three R's, Reading, wRiting and aRithmetic, so by the time Stephen left school aged 12, although by no means academically gifted, he had achieved all the desired 'standards' to send him out into the world well equipped. Certainly he acquired beautiful copper-plate handwriting and considering neither his father or mother could write at all, that is illustrative of the great leap forward achieved in education at that time.

While most of his teachers were young women not then inclined to become involved in the hurly burly of football, the headmaster Mr James E. Kaye and one of the young 'assistants', Mr Surman, provided a balance in the regime which enabled the new 'big ball' craze to figure with the longer standing cricket in the timetable. Six-a-side contests, very popular at the time, were played, and by 1885 the 'Roadites' certainly had their own football team which played against other local sides on Saturday mornings. Years later Mr Surman had good reason to remember one of his earliest charges:

"When Steve Bloomer was at St James's Road School, I well remember his ability with a ball, even when only in the playground. He was so nippy that he could leave all the other lads of his own age standing."

So even at the tender age of 11 or so, it seems that a certain natural ability was beginning to emerge. No photographs of Stephen as a child are known to survive, but we know he was small and skinny, a typical 'urchin', and it seems likely that this lack of physical robustness was responsible for the development of the skill and control he cultivated, and indeed needed, to be able to survive against boys far superior in physique. Football was still in the evolutionary stage during Stephen's time at school and games at that schoolboy level were invariably disorganised affairs lacking discipline and played by a chasing pack, with limited knowledge of the rules and techniques, among whom the heavyweights generally held sway. Even at a very young age there is suggestive evidence that Stephen took things rather seriously, liked to do things properly and was something of a thinker in the matter of technique and he later confessed that the boisterous nature of his early footballing experiences very nearly put him off for life:

"I settled down in the great Midlands town of Derby at quite a tender age and I have a vivid recollection of those days when I first took to football and found out for myself that it was the healthiest, if the most strenuous, of all British pastimes. It was when I was a very small boy at school that I first developed a fondness for the game and I must have met with a fair measure of success judging by the manner in which my youthful opponents fastened themselves upon me and did their utmost to upset my tactics; indeed so attentive were those opponents, and so vicious their kicks, that more than once I decided to abandon the game altogether."

As discussed in the opening chapter of Stephen's story, two of the pre-requisites for his advancement in the game of football were his capacity to enjoy it and his close and constant exposure to it. With the first of those under undoubted threat from the 'happy hackers' it was the special relationship which the town of Derby had with the game which ensured the second and encouraged one of its eager but bruised young citizens to stick at it.

Derby – 'a real football town'.

Whenever any new manager has arrived at Derby County Football Club in the modern era, their first media interview invariably cites as one of their reasons for coming the observation that 'Derby is a real football town.' While we all know that to be true, the significance of that rather trite little phrase is historically far more deep-seated than might be imagined. Ever since mediaeval times Derby had been the scene of one of the most celebrated of street football games, fought out annually on Shrove Tuesday and Ash Wednesday between the rival parish camps of All Saints' and St Peter's (we still refer to a game anywhere between two local rivals as a 'derby'). And such was the tradition which attached to this ritual that Derby families down the centuries became steeped in the old form of football and as a consequence far more receptive to soaking up the heady essence of 'new' football than they might have been had they lived elsewhere.

Once the Shrovetide games were officially ended by proclamation in 1845, there was a token gesture at continuation for a couple of years thereafter but by 1847 the throwing up of the ball in Derby Market Place, and the consequent boisterous mayhem which ensued, passed into history. But the spirit of football which was such a powerful part of Derby's folklore lived on, and informal games continued to be played whenever and wherever time, space and the constabulary allowed. As a consequence, the development of Derbyshire football after the formation of the Football Association in 1863 followed the pattern displayed elsewhere in the country but in a more pronounced and accelerated fashion than in many areas. Repton School, Long Eaton's Trent College and Derby School all took to games based on Association Rules in the 1860s, the latter school's team being described at that time as 'probably the best side in the county' and in and around the town itself clubs of enthusiasts began to be formed. One of the first of these, late in the 1860s, was St Andrew's, whose founder, Mr C. W. Houseman, became secretary of a body formed in 1872 which titled itself the Derbyshire Football Association, an unofficial forerunner of the 'bona fide' affiliated Derbyshire Football Association which was formed at a meeting at the Midland Hotel in September 1883.

Thus it was that by the time Stephen was nine years old, a locally based body was actively engaged in encouraging the development of the game throughout the town and county. As it happened, Derbeians needed little pushing, and club formations, many based on church, school or works organisations, continued to gather pace. It was in 1883, too, when Stephen was at just that impressionable age when boys begin to look up to heroes, that the Cup Final of that year threw up an event of national significance for the game's evolution from 'toff's game' to 'people's game'.

In that year Blackburn Olympic, a side composed of 'paid' professionals in all but name, became the first northern working class club to wrest the Cup from the Old School brigade with a sensational 2-1 victory over Old Etonians. That was a pivotal moment in football history and Blackburn and the North simply went football crazy…the weavers, spinners, moulders and machine operators who made up most of the Olympic team gave ordinary men and boys a surrogate hope that they too could strike a blow for the masses.

The effect of that Blackburn victory was inevitably felt most strongly in Lancashire, where Blackburn Rovers took up the cudgels to dominate the Cup in the next few years, but it was echoed in most of the industrial centres of the North and Midlands. Derby and the township of Litchurch were affected more than most and men, boys and some women embraced the game with real fervour. As J. B. Priestley once so memorably put it, football provided an escape from 'the clanking machinery of this lesser life'.

If 1883 was an important year for Derbyshire football as a whole, then 1884 was a massive one for Derby itself. Before that date, from the late 1870s, a side called Derby Town had gained a degree of supremacy in local circles but their position was ever vulnerable, as they found out to their cost… when the railway-based Derby Midland formed in the early 1880s, Town lost most of their best players to them and it was the death-knell to a club that might otherwise have existed to this day. But vulnerability is no respecter of reputation and in late-summer 1884 it was Midland themselves who began to look over their shoulders as another newcomer arrived on the scene from an unexpected quarter.

Derbyshire County Cricket Club were having an awful time of it. Their finances were in a mess and their performances at the wicket in 1884 were equally sloppy and unbalanced. Their committee men were mightily impressed, though, by the pulling power of football, a record 7,000 spectators paying to enter the club's own County Ground itself to witness the first Derbyshire Cup Final, in March 1884, between Midland and Staveley. The cricket men quickly resolved to set up a football section and the matter was first seriously debated at a meeting at the Bell Hotel in Sadler Gate in May. By September 1884 the *Derby Daily Telegraph* was able to make the following announcement:

'The Derbyshire County Cricket Club has decided on the formation of a football club under Association Rules and desires to render football worthy of the patronage bestowed upon it by the public by endeavouring to arrange matches with first-class clubs which will enable the public to witness matches of a higher order than have hitherto been played in Derby. The subscription for the Derbyshire County Football Club is fixed at five shillings, which we think will be thought sufficiently moderate.'

The club soon to shorten their name to something less unwieldy, and one which the fusspots of the Derbyshire FA were happier to sanction, took the field for the first time on 13 September 1884 against Great Lever for a friendly match in Bolton. Derby County Football Club was born. A 6-0 defeat, with five scored by a certain John Goodall on his debut in English football, was not an auspicious start but, their ranks boosted by the defection of a number of Midland and other rival local clubs' men, they made rapid headway and lost only 11 of their 34 matches in that first season. At the start of the 1885-86 campaign, they truly arrived on the national scene, staggering the admittedly small football world of the time by beating mighty Aston Villa 2-0 at the County Ground in the second round of the FA Cup; it was 14 November 1885 and when the final whistle sounded, hats and umbrellas went up in the air and 'the magnificent piece of turf' which was the scene of this triumph was duly invaded. Incurable football fever had come to Derby and the first 'Rams' heroes were feted.

Eleven-year-old boys were particularly prone to catch the bug and long after Bloomer had become 'a working class hero' in his own right, he remembered this heady time, recognising what was effectively a defining moment in his life and that of Derby's subsequent football history:

"Such was the roughness of many of the boys' games I played in, I would surely have given the game up altogether if I had not, at a most opportune moment, gone to see a match between two great League teams. I was absolutely thrilled by the excitement and surprised by the amount of science displayed; yet, in spite of the huge difference in 'class', I firmly made up my mind that I would become a first-class player and perhaps represent my country."

Whether it was quite such a visionary experience at the time, one must obviously ponder with some scepticism, but what that reminiscence illustrates in terms of the character of young Stephen is a supreme single-mindedness and determination which stayed with him right throughout his life. Other boys may have 'dreamed' of 'becoming' footballers but Stephen 'resolved' that he 'would' be one...there is a world of difference and it is a difference that, even now, so often separates the successful from the 'nearly' men in any walk of life, but especially sport.

We can't be certain of the two teams which so inspired Stephen. Although he referred to them as 'League' teams it seems likely that his use of that term is retrospective, as the Football League was not formed until 1888. Certainly Derby versus Villa would be a good bet for a boy originally from the West Midlands and a possible alternative would be the 1886 FA Cup Final replay between Blackburn Rovers and West Bromwich Albion, again played at the County Ground. On that occasion 12,000 saw Blackburn win 2-0 and it seems likely that Stephen either paid his threepence or wriggled in for free. Whichever his first big game was, by 1886 he was hooked and he had made passing acquaintance with his future employers.

So much had happened to football since Stephen's birth in 1874 and that progress opened up doors which simply hadn't existed only a dozen years earlier. When professionalism, 'playing for money', was officially sanctioned in 1885, after some years of 'brown envelope' and 'money in boots' shenanigans, an 11-year-old Stephen finding himself in the right place at the right time could truly say for the first time what many have articulated since... "I want to be a professional footballer."

Into the wide world
That ambition, of course, had to wait. Derby County and their 'professionalism' in both name and approach might just as well have been light years away. In the meantime the schoolboy player had simply to try to hone his craft in invariably shambolic games against the likes of 'Mr Titterton's XI', 'All Saints' Band of Hope', 'Nine of Mr Percival's School' and the Dog's Home, who inevitably played under the name of 'Rovers'. Many of the games were as bizarre as the team names, often played on pitches of dubious quality. Without nets and crossbars, disputes as to whether the ball had 'gone through' were regular affairs and although the offside rule had been implemented as early as 1866, most of the games Stephen played in before his teens were conducted without offside which led to a complete lack of structure in the play and some overwhelming scorelines on occasions when a forceful team came up against a more timid bunch. Incidents of sides arriving late, walking off mid-match or turning up

men short and without a ball were almost to be expected. It was football, but all too often it was farce as well. One imagines that Stephen, rapidly becoming a rather earnest 'Master Precise' in matters of football procedure, despite his youth, was extremely irritated by such prevailing 'amateurism' but he had to bide his time and simply hope to upgrade himself if the opportunity arose.

In the meantime those fearsome words 'responsibility' and 'future' had to be faced. The Bloomer family had continued to grow during Stephen's schooldays by the addition of 'one of each' – Emma in 1882 and David in 1884. As a result of that expansion, Caleb and Merab, still only in their early 30s at the time of David's birth, had moved over the road with their five children to 87 Yates Street. But more mouths to feed, and higher rent to pay for their 'own' accommodation, simply meant more money to find.

And as the oldest son, and with an education behind him, there was an expectation that Stephen should start to contribute to the family budget. He ceased to be a little 'Roadite' in 1886, leaving the school as a diminutive 12-year-old to make his way in the world, a world which, if his father had anything to do with it, would not encompass that potentially crippling game of football. Caleb never expected great things for his lad… just a regular job and good health would surely do; but there was a strength of will developing in that bony young frame and sharp brain, and with it just a hint of a chance that he might live up to his Christian name… while Stephen had undoubtedly by now become a local Derby boy, little may he or his father have known that the plain ordinary 'Stephen' came from the noble ancient Greek. Would it bode well for the future that it was a name traditionally bestowed on 'he who wears the victor's crown'?

TEENAGE PRODIGY 1886-1892

"The 'prentice quits his shop, to join the crew,
Increasing crowds the flying game pursue…"
John Gay

D ESPITE a solid enough education, it would be a mistake to imagine that this gave Stephen a passport to non-manual work. Although a significant number of his classmates achieved success in business and public life, including future Mayor of Derby Albert Green, it was a big step for anyone with the Bloomers' family background to contemplate anything outside industry. In fact 'success' for Stephen's father was measured by the fact that he himself had risen beyond the level of general labourer to the status of artisan worker with a company of Ley's standing, one rapidly asserting a national and local reputation for being progressive in a business sense but also looking after the welfare of its employees. While clerk, messenger boy or other white-collar work might just have been plausible for Stephen, to follow Caleb to the ironworks was quite a satisfactory ambition at a time of widespread national unemployment, but he first needed to acquire the basic skills to help take him there. Guided by his father in that direction, without even a passing nod on Caleb's part at the future possibilities of football, Stephen started work.

Apprentice smith and would-be 'saint'
Although some local Bloomer lore has recently suggested that he continued his schooling to the age of 14, going on to St James's Church School on Dairy House Road, no evidence exists to support this but there are a number of earlier accounts that intimate strongly that at 12 years of age he was apprenticed to a local blacksmith. Unless concrete evidence emerges, Stephen's early working history will always be the subject of conjecture but my own research supports the possibility that he first learnt his trade as a smith at the small home-based workshop run by his mother's brother and father. When Caleb and Merab moved to Derby, they both had their own family support with them; for Merab's part, her father and mother, Andrew and Roseannah Dunn, initially settled quite close to Yates Street at 4 Turner's Buildings in Depot Street, just off Normanton Road. Both only in their early 50s when they arrived around 1880, they carried on their trade as horse-nail makers helped by their teenage son

Jonathan, Stephen's uncle, just 11 years older than Stephen himself. His older uncle, Alfred, and teenage aunts, Lavinia and Ellen, completed the Dunn household. That Caleb and Merab should have arranged for Stephen, in exchange for a suitably modest wage, to be 'shown the ropes' by his grandfather and uncle from 1886 seems a reasonable conclusion to draw. Whether or not he truly did receive his smith's training from that quarter, he equipped himself over the next two years with the physical strength and skills which were later to enable him to join his father at Ley's foundry.

Muscle and technical know-how is one thing, though, and mental resilience is another. And something entirely unexpected had to be faced just two months before Stephen's 14th birthday, the first real trauma in his young life to date. The Bloomer family had grown to six children by 1887 with the birth of Florence May on 29 May. She was to be Merab's last child; just six months later, on 27 November, the family lost their mother to pleurisy, aged only 35. That was surely a hammer blow to the morale of the Bloomer clan far greater than any Caleb or Stephen had struck in the line of duty. Now, with only two earners in a surviving household of seven, and nine-year-old Alice as the oldest girl and Florence May still in the cradle, the everyday business of running the home and catering to the children's needs must have become difficult indeed.

Caleb's only consolation at this time was that he, too, had moved to Derby with other members of his family. His brother Farley, older by six years, then lived with his wife Eliza and children Caleb, Adelaide, Gemima, Mary Ann and Charles at 40 Graham Street, off Osmaston Road. The support he received from that quarter must have been a comfort. So, too, must the fact that Stephen and his brothers and sisters had aunties, uncles and cousins to call on when needed. Financially, too, a degree of retrenchment was called for; their former 'neighbour', Joseph Harlow, who had himself lost his wife since the Bloomers moved out of number 44, promptly joined them again over the road at 87. His contribution to rent helped balance the books and, as he was by then over 60 and confined to part-time gardening work, no doubt his presence in the household helped steady the ship while Caleb worked the long hours needed to keep everybody afloat. It was assuredly a case of having to grow up quickly for Caleb's oldest son. If he needed an escape valve, then his continued interest in one of the best there is was no bad thing…for despite having left school, Stephen had not forsaken football.

The 'Saints', first set up for the 1884-85 season, were one of many Derby church teams playing under that nickname. They were attached to St Chad's Church, just off St Chad's Road, and ran a senior and junior team, the latter playing their games as St Chad's Choir. As soon as he left school in 1886, Stephen joined the Saints juniors and played with them for two seasons between the age of 12 and 14, his first real team. It is possible he went to the Sunday School there, but equally likely that he fell in with them through a friend or perhaps even through the Bloomer's landlord, Thomas Coulthurst, Derby's Borough Surveyor and churchwarden of St Chad's at that time. Certainly the church teams enjoyed a degree of patronage which enabled them to turn out smartly attired in club colours and this professional approach gave Stephen his first taste outside school of the organisation and team spirit necessary to run a successful club.

Local inspiration from a higher level continued by way of Derby County's progress and, arguably, from an even 'higher' level again, the rector of St Chad's, the Reverend Llewellyn Henry Gwynne. Effectively Stephen's first 'manager', Welshman Gwynne epitomised the ethic of 'muscular Christianity', took to football with a religious zeal and made one appearance for Derby County in an FA Cup game at Crewe in 1887-88. What a colourful character he was. He later became Archdeacon of the Sudan, and Bishop in Egypt and the Sudan from 1920-1946, where he became known as the 'Flying Bishop' because of his frequent use of air travel in carrying out his duties. King Farouk once sent him a personal message expressing his horror after the cathedral and Gwynne's house were looted during riots. He was in his 90s when he died in Epping in 1957 and what tales he might have told about the young Bloomer… alas they remain unrecorded.

Inspired by such a man, St Chad's Juniors became one of the better sides in the local junior leagues and gave Stephen his first opportunities to shine in front of a Derby public taking their football seriously and turning out in increasing numbers to watch even the boys' games. Later in life, Bloomer well remembered those days:

"In my youth we used to play a knockout competition for the Derbyshire Boys' Shield, which it was a great honour to win. There were under-15 and under-17 tournaments and they were always played between November and April with the Finals on Easter Monday, a real big occasion in Derby football. I first got to the Final with St Chad's Choir in the under-15 section, but I was only 13 and got a lot of buffeting around in those days and some of the sides we played were just too strong. One such was St Luke's Choir, a side to be feared… they were our opponents in the 1887 Final and my junior side got beaten 14-0 that day."

That was Stephen's heaviest-ever defeat on a football field but it was important in several ways all the same. Played on the County Ground on the morning of 11 April 1887, there were 2,000 paying spectators present, the game being part of an all-day football festival culminating in an afternoon game between Derby County and Dumbarton Athletic, itself watched by a crowd which had swelled to 3,000. Not only did the Shield Final put Stephen on the same stage as the town's increasingly dominant club, in a match which some Rams' players and officials might well have watched, but it also gave him his first substantial press exposure. And even in defeat there was something about the young centre-forward's play that caught the eye of the *Derby Telegraph* reporter during the half-hour each way contest.

"St Luke's Choir had achieved some tall performances during the course of the competition and were generally expected to prove successful. They were in capital form and whenever they broke away their onslaught was inevitable. The whole team played together splendidly in winning 14 goals to none. St Chad's seldom broke away and they only caused the opposing goalkeeper to handle once. Bloomer played a good game in the centre for St Chad's but was badly supported."

Evidently Stephen showed promise of greater things to come. Another reporter commenting generally on the junior game at that time identified the matter of 'potential' in a particularly succinct way in saying: "Once in a while, amidst the general mass of lumbering bodies, one sees a clean built youth with speed and deftness stamped all over him."

Stephen Bloomer was just one such youth... it was time for him to step up. Both his football team and work place were soon to change.

Ley's striker and Derby Swift

Shortly after his 14th birthday in 1888, Stephen joined his father Caleb and uncle Farley at Ley's foundry, ultimately taking his place by the forge as a 'striker'. How curious that, long before that term was ever used in its now so familiar football context, it should be applied to one who was eventually to epitomise all that we understand it to mean; curious, too, that a description of that ubiquitous Victorian trade from an old practitioner should metaphorically mirror the arch goalscorer's craft;

"A striker knew his metal in those days. He would look at his hot iron and he would know, without the aid of a thermometer or any of that lot, he would know purely by instinct the precise moment to strike."

For a skinny youth with aspirations to make his way in football, wielding the hammer wasn't at all bad training and Stephen's physique developed not from an organised fitness regime but from sheer physical hard work. Although he was eventually to top out at a height of only 5ft 8in, the same as one Michael Owen, whose style is, I believe, very reminiscent of Bloomer's, his deceptively slight and frail appearance belied muscles of steel and his upper legs and arms, in particular, were all sinew. Not that life at Leys was all work and no play. It suited young Stephen down to the ground that company founder Francis Ley was himself an avid sports enthusiast and was enlightened enough to lay out a substantial sports ground adjacent the works for the use of his employees. Cricket and baseball, about more of which later, were both sports which Stephen took to during the summer months, which helped him to develop an all-round athletic ability and hone the physique which was essential if he was to play football on equal terms with the big boys.

If Stephen needed any further encouragement to move up the football ladder, 1888 was a truly inspirational year in Derby. At the start of the year, on 28 January, local side, Derby Junction, shocked the football world. Originally formed as Junction Street Sunday School by brickmaker Harry Bromage senior, patriarch of a famous Derby footballing family, they reached the quarter-final of the FA Cup and were drawn at home to the mighty Blackburn Rovers, winners of the trophy three times in a row in 1884, 1885 and 1886. No one gave

'The Juncs' a chance but they emerged 2-1 winners to reach the semi-final, where they lost to West Bromwich Albion.

That the astonishing conquest of Rovers should have been enacted on Stephen's own playground on the Arboretum Field in Rose Hill Street would certainly have brought home to the young teenager the potential glories that football promised. The 4,000 crowd went mad… "middle aged men hugged each other and some even flung themselves on the ground in a paroxysm of excitement."

Such early examples of Charlie Georgian behaviour from the ever-hedonistic Derby public, far from the strait-laced stereotypes of high Victorianism, were indicative of the town's enormous potential as a real hotbed of football, so when the Football League was formed later in 1888, finally pitting the leading clubs against each other on a regular and organised basis, the chance of a Derby club being voted in was more than a passing fancy. But it was increasingly powerful Derby County, not rivals Junction or Midland, who carried the town's honour into the League as one of the 12 founder members and in doing so shaped the entire history of first-class football in the town. As for the future of one Stephen Bloomer, that event brought his ambition of becoming a top level professional footballer that much closer, not least because he could now achieve it in his very own backyard.

As Bloomer himself relates, a club called Derby Swifts were next on the journey towards his goal, one he was becoming ever more determined to attain and for which he was prepared to practise earnestly while others of his age simply dabbled:

"With an ambition to become a first-class player, I suppose I became very keen and had that natural inclination towards the game, and an inbred desire to excel in it, which is so often the secret of real success. As a result, at the age of 14, I joined a junior team named Derby Swifts, who played in the Derbyshire Minor League, and from those early days I was literally boiling over with enthusiasm for football. Here was a good beginning, for my heart was in the game. Swifts was a side which helped me a great deal, for although we met worthy opponents they were never too strong for us and consequently I was enabled to practise certain methods which suggested themselves to me without being unduly bustled. Off the field, too, I practised… many was the time in my boyhood days I went out on my own into the fields near my home with a football. Never mind about company, getting the ball out whenever you feel like it is the thing to do. I used to drive sticks into the ground and dribble round them or shoot at just one from all angles, learning to keep the ball low, about knee high, the most difficult shot for any goalkeeper to save. It was not long before I learned the glorious art of kicking goals and I played with Derby Swifts, a real good side, during three seasons."

Such application in one so young, especially without the backing of a like-minded parent, suggests unusual personal qualities: self-motivation, single-mindedness, obsession. Call it what we may, it was that analytical approach and will to succeed, so often the province of the loner, which brought the young Bloomer to teenage prominence. Despite his rather quiet and introspective off-field demeanour, he was a great talker on it and the game became a vehicle through which he conquered his natural reserve. He was sufficiently gregarious in a team environment to become a popular member of a triumphant Swifts side and eventually their captain.

For the three seasons, from 1888-89 to 1890-91, Stephen turned out mainly at centre-forward or outside-left, first for the under-15s and then the under-17s, winning his first medal in the under-15 Shield Final of 7 April 1890. As a measure of the jump in standard he had taken, it was St Luke's Choir, perpetrators of his earlier 14-0 thrashing, who this time lost out 1-0. Although he was 16 at the time of the Final, he qualified to play because he was still 15 when the competition started and this gave him the chance to turn out in this game with his kid brother Phillip, who filled the right-half spot. Stephen trod in the steps of former local heroes that day, the match being played on Derby Junction's Arboretum Field in front of 2,000 paying spectators, and as he was so often to do in the future, he rose to the occasion like a true professional. Not for the last time did the press rather quaintly report that 'Bloomer did the needful', scoring the decisive goal after 15 minutes.

That was the start of a regular run of goals which began to suggest teenage prodigy status for Stephen and gave Derby Swifts a strong local following and the highest profile press coverage of all the junior teams. In his age group he became a minor celebrity and some of his goalscoring feats simply couldn't be ignored, although now and again there was trouble keeping count. The oft-told tale that Bloomer once scored 14 in one game, 'against Belper in the Shield which we won by twenty-something', emanated from his own reminiscences. In fact, the report of the game played on 20 December 1890 credits Bloomer with a mere seven in a 22-2 slaughter. Is that a case of selective memory on Bloomer's part or simply a case of the Swifts' secretary submitting a modified return in the interests of modesty or perhaps to conceal the true worth of his star man? We will never know.

But no matter… he was certainly knocking a few in. Later that season he notched a six and an eight, and on another occasion Normanton Athletic, failing dismally to live up to their name, walked off Swifts' Chester Green ground 15 minutes early when a Bloomer clutch left them trailing 12-0. Marvellous stuff for Swifts' followers, but some of the opposition, especially the Belperites, were sorely rankled by the propensity of this young whipper-snapper to 'shoot through' with such apparent ease. On the occasion of the League game against Belper later that same season, Stephen had good cause to remember being caught off guard by one such disgruntled, if unlikely, assailant:

"In 1891, having scored the winning goal of a hard and fast game at Belper Cow Hill, quite a famous Midlands team then, I was returning to the dressing-room in a public house close by when I heard a young lady in the crowd say, 'This is the fellow Bloomer who scored those goals against us,' and without more ado she fetched her umbrella down upon my head hard enough to smash her 'gamp', but fortunately not my head. However, I was young enough and terrified enough to take to my heels and flee and I came in for some merciless banter and chaff from my clubmates afterwards."

Undoubtedly Stephen and his young colleagues had great fun with the Swifts but the pain of defeat, far greater than that inflicted by any young lady's brolly, had to be learned too. While Phillip collected his winners' medal for playing in the under-15 side which won the Shield in 1890-91, Stephen had to be content with a losers', his team having gone down in the Senior Final against Chesterfield side Brampton Works after a replay necessitated only by a last-second and controversial Brampton equaliser. But even in defeat the press described him as 'the best young prospect we have ever seen'. That acclaim was scant consolation for an ardent 17-year-old, despite the achievement of scoring in both games, and it wasn't to be his last or greatest Cup tragedy, that's for sure.

Such occasional setbacks, though, were to be expected, and just before that Final, Steve had received an ideal antidote to any disappointment the Junior game might throw at him. His performances with Swifts had made him a target for bigger clubs at a time when a steady flow of quality youngsters was vital to keep pace with the expanding number of teams. Derby Midland invited Bloomer to try out with them in a number of reserve games while he was still playing with Swifts and he was given his first-team debut in March 1891. Although he was to have one last and triumphant fling with Swifts at the end of the following season, he left the permanent ranks of the junior side at the close of the 1890-91 campaign to try to make his mark in the adult game. Little did he know what a curious fate lay in store for his new club and what a fortuitous outcome it was to have for him.

Derby Midland to Derby County

Bloomer himself tells us, "I played for Midland for just part of one season," which might suggest his association with the club was an insignificant one. Nothing could be further from the truth because it was the means by which he first became officially associated with Derby County. When he made his debut for Midland in that end-of-season game on Friday, 27 March 1891, he surely hoped that a good performance might secure him a place for the next season, or even a part-time professional contract, as Midland had rather reluctantly embraced the new order like so many other clubs…if you didn't pay your best players they'd simply go elsewhere.

The match, away to Burton Swifts at the splendid Peel Croft ground, still little changed today and used by Burton RFC, ended in a 1-1 draw and Bloomer did well. Although he had only secured his place at inside-left due to a fixture pile-up and availability crisis, he took his opportunity well enough for the *Burton Evening Gazette* to report: "Bloomer made a most excellent show." Whether that was an attempted pun, considering the side that day also included Rose and Garden, we can only surmise. On the strength of that budding performance, in the company of such fine players as Harry and William Storer, Steve might well have anticipated a higher profile in the Midland set-up the next season, but in the event it was, I believe, the only full game he ever played for the railway team. The 1890-91 season duly closed and in the summer so, too, did Derby Midland. Had 'Bloomer' made one of his own?

The matter of sustaining several top sides in a town of Derby's size had proved difficult and inter-club rivalries, in the committee rooms and press more so than on the field, could be fierce. When Midland effectively killed off Derby Town, many supporters of that old club, the true forerunner to the Rams, had transferred their allegiance to Derby County, so County and Midland became natural rivals. Junction, too, were rivals of Midland, but of necessity also sided with them against County. As a result, competition for players and paying spectators was rife and sometimes the inducements offered exceeded the clubs' real ability to pay. In such circumstances financial disaster was always a possibility but Derby County, because of their League status, top opposition and resultant larger crowds, held an irritating edge.

Taking stock in summer 1891, the Midland's debts became all too apparent. Added to that, the chairman of the Midland Railway Company, Mr G. F. Paget, something of a puritan, let it be known that he was 'uncomfortable on ethical grounds about the involvement of a company of our status with a professional team'. The end of the line certainly loomed. Not that it was full steam ahead for Derby County, either, as mounting wages there had put a brake on the profits which the cricket club had been only too pleased to take in the early days. Their cause not helped by the systematic embezzlement of gate money by disgraced former secretary Samuel Richardson, the Cricket Club and Football Club split in summer 1891, Derbyshire allowing Derby County to continue to use their ground for a payment of £100 a year and to retain whatever profits 'might' be made. Richardson, incidentally, fled the town, changed his name and became court tailor to King Alfonso of Spain!

With just a hint of a possibility that Derby County, too, might throw in the towel, a radical decision was made to join forces with the erstwhile enemy and Derby Midland were absorbed lock stock and barrel by Derby County in June 1891. Midland resigned their place in the Midland League and Derby County announced that, funded by a £5 share guarantee system by which patrons effectively paid in advance to support the side, they were 'making a fresh start and would now play two elevens', effectively the start of the reserve side and squad system we know today. While all the nitty gritty of the legal and financial detail must have passed Steve by completely, it could not escape his notice that Derby County took on Midland's assets as well as debts...and the only true assets they had were the players. Most of those players, including Bloomer, became part of the package. The youngster already dubbed 'Steve' by the local press would start the 1891-92 season as a Derby County player.

Derby County amateur 1891-92
The importance to Bloomer's future career of this back-door entry to the Rams need hardly be stated and at the time he recognised this only too well, later saying:

"It was when the Midland became amalgamated with Derby County that I saw my first real chance of coming to the fore." Let it not be thought for a moment, though, that Steve's schoolboy reputation counted for anything. He joined Derby with Midland men far more experienced than himself and became part of a large squad of players that included some he regarded with awe, men of the calibre of ex-Kilmarnock, Great Lever and Preston forward John Goodall, a famous England international. What kind of impression could Steve make in the face of that sort of established company?

The initial signs were good. Aiming to make an impact from the start, he made sure to be there at the first training session with the serious contenders while others didn't take the trouble to turn up, and he made a good enough initial impression for the club to broach the question of a professional contract before the season started. Aged only 17 and with the achievement of his boyhood ambition apparently only a talk and a signature away, it is surprising that at that stage he opted not to pursue the opportunity, the local press reporting: "Bloomer has expressed his wish to remain an amateur, as he is desirous of helping out Derby Swifts in this year's Shield, but has promised to sign for the County for season 1892-93."

It surely seems probable that the restraining hand of Caleb played a significant part in making Stephen put his ambition on hold. Nevertheless, Derby County accepted Steve's motive and rewarded his on-field eagerness with a place at outside-right for the Possibles against the Probables in his first-ever public appearance in a Derby County shirt. At 6pm on Wednesday, 26 August 1891, the emergence of the new young hopeful on to the County Ground that evening prompted a famous observation from Harry Newbould, a spectator at the game and later Derby County's manager:

"He was just 17 when he first turned out for Derby, pale, thin, ghost-like, almost ill-looking, he caused the Derby crowd to laugh when they first saw him."

But no matter that some of the crowd found him amusing… he donned the same black and white stripes that day as fellow newcomers Jack Robinson, Jimmy Methven and 'Jonty' Staley, all of whom would make their first-team debuts just ten days later. Surely he was on the brink of achieving his ambition of playing in the Football League?

Alas, it was not yet to be. Perhaps his stature told against him in the company of bigger or stronger men – it was certainly a big step up from Swifts and one game for Midland in the last season, to Derby County the next. The harsh reality of making the elusive breakthrough was that Steve never got a chance in the first team that season. Even the treble-winning second team, who carried all before them that campaign in winning the Midland Alliance League and two cups, called on his services only a handful of times when stretched, and he spent most of the season very much in the cold, playing the majority of his games in the newly-formed third string. What confusion, incidentally, that caused the pressmen and public trying to follow the club's progress at various levels. At the start of the season Derby County officially proposed to call their three teams 'Derby County League', 'Derby County' and 'Derby County Reserve', but the local press pilloried this as a 'ludicrous state of affairs impossible to keep up'. In the event the club opted for plain 'Derby County' as the League side, 'Derby County Wanderers' as the second team, and stuck with 'Derby County Reserve' for the thirds, terminology which has led to a mistaken belief that Bloomer was a regular second-team player far earlier than he ever was.

By way of tidying up that little conundrum, the second team acceded to the newspaper's request for a degree of nostalgia by changing their name again at the end of the season to old favourites Derby Town. The thirds, meanwhile, who were essentially a representative side playing friendlies, and often included triallists in their depleted ranks, were regularly covered in the press simply as 'Derby County…a team'. That soon came to be known as the 'A' team, presumably a likely explanation of that curious term for the lowliest side in the club which is still in current usage to this day.

Etymology no doubt didn't concern Bloomer but his progress through the club's ranks surely did. Playing for the thirds against the likes of Derby Brewery Company, Breaston and Spondon deep in the winter of 1891 was a far cry from the glamour of the first team 'Leaguites'. It must have been clear to Stephen that where he had been a big fish in junior circles he was only one of the small fry among the elite of first-class football. What he ought to have told himself, and probably did, was to be patient and acknowledge that at only 17 years of age a place in the first team, and even the seconds, was a dream rather than an expectation. Nevertheless, when he reached his 18th birthday, on 20 January 1892, he might well have pondered what the future would hold. Although he had made football an important part of his life throughout his teenage years, the fact remained that, despite his promise to 'sign' for Derby County, he still did it only for fun and still worked at the foundry.

His father Caleb certainly continued to take a dim view of Stephen's aspirations at that time. Despite the fact that Phillip, too, had started at Ley's, and Alice, now almost 13, had her feet under someone else's table as a domestic servant, the household still needed money, and steady work was ever Caleb's watchword to his family. Bloomer later made it quite clear what his father thought:

"My father was always prejudiced against the game in my early youth and if he had had his way I would never have taken to the game as a professional. His chief prejudice against it was that it would mean a broken leg or other serious injury to myself at some time or other."

Caleb's concerns were understandable. Broken limbs were common enough and such accidents put men out of work and hardship was all too often the result. And, in days when medical care and the treatment of injury was less well understood, it could be worse. Deaths from infected cuts or severe chills were by no means unusual. And if Caleb had wanted to press home his point to advantage by introducing some local flavour, he need only to have referred back to the death from a ruptured bowel suffered by William Cropper in 1889. The Derbyshire cricketer and former Derby County player met his end playing centre-forward for Staveley at Grimsby after a reckless challenge by Daniel Doyle. Although the press had a happy knack of glorifying such things, reporting: "Later that day the great umpire 'death' called 'over' and William Cropper became numbered with the majority," that sort of rhetoric didn't wash with Caleb, not least because he couldn't read it. As far as he was concerned, his eldest son might well 'come a Cropper' too.

It was just as well that Steve was armed with sufficient defiance to continue pursuing his dream. Maybe he should have countered his father's cautionary tales by drawing on a subsequent yarn from cricket, a sport Caleb was known to like. The previous summer, with a sense of the macabre which the Victorians verily excelled at, the Midland Railway works had organised a game between One-Legged-Men and One-Armed-Men. No matter that the unipeds won the game, despite all being bowled out with ne'er an lbw or catch on the card – the point Steve might have made was that all the players were the victims of industrial accidents. Touché?

As season 1891-92 progressed into the new year, Steve got the first inklings of a reward for sticking at it. After scoring against Stretton's Brewery for the thirds in a 5-0 romp in February, the press described him as 'an especially promising young player' and when he followed this with all the goals in a 4-0 win over Darley Victoria in March, his reward was to be a game for the seconds, the all-conquering 'Wanderers'. April 1892 would be a month he could never forget.

Swift, Hawthorn, Wanderer and professional Ram
The fortnight from Easter Monday, 18 April 1892, to the end of the month, sealed Steve Bloomer's destiny and his involvement with Derby County to this day… but it was a saga that might well have been titled 'Carry On Football', which saw him play for three different clubs and sign professional for two all within 14 days!

First up were Steve's old friends Derby Swifts. Having reached the Shield Final again against old foe Brampton, who Swifts were convinced had conned them out of victory the year before, they were determined to wreak revenge. What better way than to recall a Derby County man who, again by dint of his convenient mid-tournament birthday, qualified to play for the 17 and unders? One can well imagine the young gang of conspirators plotting Brampton's downfall as Steve, true to his pre-season word, agreed to turn out. It worked a treat. He played his last-ever game for Swifts in one of their finest hours on 18 April at the Vulcan Ground, captaining the side at right-wing in a 6-0 drubbing. He lifted the trophy and, as the press reported, a special award besides:

"In addition to the usual medals, a splendid gold one, the gift of a generous Committee man, was offered for presentation to the captain of the winning seniors and thus Steve Bloomer became the proud possessor of the gift. As he received his award the crowd gathered round and enthusiastically cheered."

On the same day, Phillip's under-15 side won the Junior Shield, not a bad day's work for the Bloomer boys. Even to this day a reminder of the prestige attached to the Shield can be seen close to the site of the Vulcan Ground on a replica built into the brickwork of a house at 102, St Thomas's Road, placed there by the proud building contractor John Chapman, whose own team Wellingborough Villa once took the trophy. Steve's triumph that day was a wearing of the 'victor's crown' of sorts, which did more to raise his profile than anything before, but he still must have wondered whether that was the only level at which he would ever reign supreme.

His game with Derby County seconds in the Midland Alliance League was the next step on the ladder. Steve's inability to break into that side had largely been due to the sheer success of the regular second-team players. Scunthorpe had been beaten 20-0 that season and the forward line of Mills, Dunn, H. Rose, Ekins and Hardy had run riot in a side which scored 153 goals in 37 games. Who needed Bloomer with a record like that? On 23 April, though, the newly-crowned king of the Swifts was picked to play against the Sheffield Club at Mr Ley's Baseball Ground, by then an established venue for all manner of entertainments and a foretaste of things to come. In a 9-0 slaughter, Bloomer took the place of Charles H. Rose, better known as Herbert, who was given his debut in the first team just a few days previous. Playing inside-right, Steve notched a tidy brace and the press took due notice. But again Bloomer's satisfaction might well have been tempered with frustration, for Rose, who that season collected silverware galore with the Derby County Wanderers, was himself a mere youngster who had come to the club with Steve from Midland. To gain his place only on the back of Rose's elevation was a mite irritating for someone increasingly sure of his own true worth.

It wasn't not having a contract that bothered Steve. As ever for those who love to play, it was the lack of competitive football at the right level that really rankled. That frustration reached a head during the week after the Sheffield Club game. Saturday, 30 April was to be a vital day for the second team as a fixture pile-up had left them with two games to play on the same day, at home to Notts County seconds, 'The Rovers', and also at home to Grantham Town. The club needed to win both to clinch the championship and had no alternative but to pick two sides. In those circumstances Bloomer was quite naturally selected, but when he was told in advance that he would be required on the Saturday he was forced by other circumstance to respond in the negative – he'd already agreed to play for someone else on the same day!

That he should accept an offer to play for another side may seem bizarre, but the fact is that the third team that season had played only 15 official games and Steve had been left scratching around picking up whatever pieces he could get. As a free agent amateur, at least he could keep his options open to pick up the odd game outside the limiting confines of the Derby County fixture list and now his profile had been raised he was starting to get offers. As a result, anticipating not being involved in Derby Wanderers' final run in, he had already agreed to play for Tutbury Hawthorn that Saturday, 30 April, in their replayed Burton and District Challenge Cup Final against fierce rivals Gresley Rovers at the Crescent Brewery ground in Burton.

Of course it was a 'pot-hunting' expedition of sorts, but in pursuit of that handsome and most prized trophy, Tutbury were more than happy to stand Bloomer's train fare, and almost certainly a little extra on top, to get him in their team. For his part, Steve was pleased to be involved in a game that really mattered. While Hawthorn themselves were no mean side, although nothing like full League level, they came from a Staffordshire village well on the road to Aston Villa territory, and Burton itself, venue of the game, had two sides, Burton Swifts (later United) and Burton Wanderers, who would both soon be members of the newly-planned Football League Division Two. Were Derby County really prepared to let the rather vulnerable Bloomer stray into enemy territory for such a high profile game?

The answer came quickly. It is said that Derby County player John Goodall and local administrator and referee Arthur Kingscott, both of whom had recognised Bloomer's potential, brought the committee to their senses. Despite Bloomer's stated intention of signing for the next season, the club recognised and feared that he might be poached. Sometime between 21 and 25 April, almost certainly Thursday, 21st and definitely before his scheduled Tutbury date, professional forms were presented to Bloomer and he gave the most important autograph of his life. The signing was registered at the League on 26 April 1892...Steve Bloomer, 18 years and 97 days, was a professional footballer.

Bloomer later said he entered into the contract 'as meekly as a lamb' and it seems unlikely he had been deliberately manipulative in securing it. Derby County had always intended to offer him terms and he had always intended to sign. Although he did indeed become something of a football mercenary in the build-up to his signing, it was a combination of circumstance, naivety and a simple desire for meaningful games on Bloomer's part which led him down that track. At any rate it certainly forced the right decision from Derby County.

There is a rather farcical postscript to that week of defining activity. True to his word Bloomer still turned out for Hawthorn, despite being already 'signed' for Derby. And while Derby seconds were comfortably clinching their title with the two required victories, Steve created havoc over in Burton. In a real grudge match interrupted by fisticuffs on and off the pitch, he scored two in Hawthorn's 7-2 triumph. Carrier pigeons took the news from Burton back to Tutbury so when Bloomer and the team arrived back at the village it was already bedecked with bunting and the players' train was met by the Town and Sax-Tuba bands who led the triumphant 'Glassblowers' into the ancient village on a festooned wagonette. The celebration was described as one of the greatest days in Tutbury's history... that is saying something in a village where great mediaeval pageants and bull-baiting festivals once took place, Kings of England held court and Mary Queen of Scots was summarily imprisoned on several occasions.

But Steve and his team-mates were the latter day kings and remained so despite the inevitable objection from Gresley that 'Bloomer had signed professional for Derby County before the game'. Not surprisingly the footballing folk of Derbyshire and Staffordshire tore into each other in vehement arguments as to the exact date of Bloomer's League registration, and the Football Association itself had to be called in as an arbitrator. After an inquiry which dragged on several weeks, both sides were awarded 'winners' medals to keep but Tutbury were stripped of the winners' honour. Bloomer 'had' signed before the game. The locals cared not. The press said: "The past belongs to Hawthorn and we can never be robbed of the events of that day."

And as if all that hoo-ha wasn't enough, the anticipated after-match approach was made to Bloomer by ambitious Midland League side Burton Wanderers, themselves four times winners of the coveted Burton Challenge Cup in the 1880s and by 1894 to be a member of the Football League Second Division. When Mr Clarke, secretary of the Derby Turn Ground club, thrust a contract under his nose in a manner that was later to be reported by the press as 'persuasive', Steve held firm and, despite his youthful vulnerability, refused to sign anything. Clarke, though, had evidently set his mind on securing Bloomer for the influential brewery side and two days later, on Monday, 2 May, he came knocking at the door of Derby's committee.

Again he was given short shrift but, undeterred, tracked down his young target at a dance that same evening, where Steve lapsed into giving his precious autograph again, signing professional forms for Burton Wanderers! It was eventually to be the subject of an FA inquiry at which the committee were to rule: "The Wanderers' representative had acted in a most unseemly manner and used undue influence over Bloomer, whose extreme youth was some excuse for his conduct."

Maybe the poor lad was interrupted at his dance in mid chat-up or simply 'tired and emotional' after all the Tutbury revels. Of course, it was an illogical thing to do, although fairly characteristic of some of the rather quaint shenanigans and bungling which riddled football affairs of that era. While the episode was to be the cause of further objections the next season when a Sheffield Wednesday side beaten by Derby used it as the foundation for a protest, all Derby County fans should simply be thankful that the Rams got in first and that the League refused to register the Burton Wanderers' forms.

Doubtless somewhat embarrassed by the turbulence he'd unwittingly stirred up, Steve must have breathed a sigh of relief and looked forward to calm summer evenings of baseball and cricket, and his first campaign as a fully fledged 'pro'. His one season as an amateur with Derby County had been lower key than he might have hoped, his two high spots coming with Swifts and Hawthorns, but it had been a valuable learning experience and ultimately ended with the one valid contract that he surely coveted. Now he could ponder whether it might yet be wise to give up the steady day job at the foundry. After all, he'd still not played for the first team. Even worse than that, now he was a professional footballer he'd got some tough explaining to do to his dad!

COUNTY
GROUND KID
1892-1895

"Come rouse up supporters, for football is nigh,
Play Up! Derby County must soon be our cry,
Let us heartily welcome our old trusted band,
And rejoice that again autumn days are at hand.
We've bright prospects before us, our team's much the same,
As that which last season so heightened our fame,
Then Johnny's our captain, I need say no more,
For his play and grand leadership all know of yore."
Supporter's refrain Miss Theodora Wilson, September 1892

"WHEN I first put my signature to a League form for Derby County I was informed that my wages were to be seven and sixpence per week. Just fancy – 7s 6d – and I played in the First Division for that, but right proud of that wage I was at the time. When I first signed it was for three seasons, during which period I could not be transferred. That sort of thing ensures a certain income to players over a long period and, of course, such an inducement carries a lot of weight with players for they run the risk of injury and any nasty accident can be faced with greater calmness and more philosophically than if they are liable to be cast aside at the end of 12 months."

County Ground 'pro'
That recollection of Steve Bloomer's first wage packet as a professional footballer is surely tinged with the erstwhile wise words of Caleb. At any rate, perhaps influenced by the longer term nature of the commitment and his son's obvious desire to enter into it, Steve's father had no choice but to somewhat reluctantly accept the position. The wage was fixed at a level appropriate to a junior 'squad' member expected to step up into the second team and perhaps get a chance in the firsts should injuries strike…most of the regular first-teamers were on between £1 and £3 a week that season. It is difficult to translate seven and sixpence (37½ pence) into equivalent modern terms but it was a very modest sum, just £19.50 a year. The fact that it was the weekly equivalent of 15 football match admissions might suggest a reasonably healthy modern parallel of around £300 per week but current ticket prices are so much out of line with

what they were when pricing policy was truly geared to the working man that it is an inappropriate comparison.

Perhaps better is that one popular brand of football boots in 1892 cost exactly seven and sixpence a pair and the rent on modest terraced houses similar to the Bloomers' was seven and sixpence a week; a pint of milk was a mere half a 'new pence', cigarettes just 2p for 20 and a smart suit all of £1.40. With all that in mind, in modern terms I would put Steve's first pay packet at no more than £50 a week, just above the lowest level of current 'unemployment benefit' at which a man is expected to subsist. The headmaster at his old school earned 15 times as much as Steve did that first season, miners took home £1.50 a week and even some general labourers managed £1, so his starting wage was almost certainly below what he earned at the foundry. Big money it wasn't, but consider against this that Steve was a young, single man with no onerous financial commitments and still living at home…and the important thing, as always in football and life, was that 'the lad was over the moon'.

Thus armed with his first contract it is thought Steve left Leys either during the summer or early in the season as he was later described by one of his long-term playing colleagues, Jimmy Methven, as being 'one of the full-time pros in the County Ground days, who turned up regularly at training, unlike most of the old Midland men who generally kept at work and who we seldom met, except on Saturdays'. It is possible, though, that Steve may have stayed at work in that first season, waiting for his wage to rise before leaving. In the matter of training, although the club directors at that time recommended that 'all players not in regular employment should meet every morning at 10am and take such exercise and practice as the trainer directed', the regime under the first recognised trainer, Harry Daykin, generally settled into three days a week. It was the first time Derby County had put their training on such an organised basis and the schedules largely included sprints, long runs or walks into the countryside and some general game practice followed by a cold douche and vigorous rub down; a trip to the Turkish Baths in Friar Gate was a rare and much coveted treat. Certainly there was less tactical analysis and ball work than current players are used to. Fewer players too… although there were 36 on the books, only 20 turned up for the first evening practice on 17 August and daytime sessions often mustered far less, certainly not enough for full-scale practice matches. That was why the players favoured Wednesdays, the good old 'half-day', which generally included a game against a local mob which they dubbed 'Salmon Tin Rovers', sometimes as many as 30 or 40 turning up to pit their wits against the modest ranks of the pros in a general free-for-all which all but resembled hare and hounds!

Steve never forgot his time at the County Ground, although 'fond memories' might well be an overstatement:

"Every time I think of the conditions under which we did our training at the old headquarters on the County Ground I treat myself to a shiver and the vain wish that I had been born a few generations later. We didn't have a lot of high-falutin' gadgets in those days but we did have plenty of good fresh air and nice cold water and what many a club might have envied us in those years of infancy was the turf we played on."

Anyone who has sat watching Derbyshire there will know that even in the cricket season the winds can be chilling, and those who have played Sunday football on the pitches still known as the Racecourse will surely sympathise with Steve and his merry band of fellow pros. Whether it was that biting wind – or just a youngster's affectation to be different – which first started Bloomer's trademark habit of pulling his socks up right over his knees like a pair of ribbed tights remains unrecorded, but what the records do show is that the County Ground was the venue of one of the few first-class football matches to be abandoned because of high winds.

Although those sort of memories, mixed with a little imagination, present a fairly vivid evocation of what Steve must have encountered in his very early days at Nottingham Road, there is still much about the physical essence of his first HQ which has never been fully researched, not least the position of the playing pitch he hoped to grace as a first-teamer and the club colours he longed to don in doing so.

By way of a brief digression, in 1892 both the cricket arena and football pitch were within the inner ring of Derby Racecourse, that sadly long-defunct equine venue of 'straight-mile' fame which held its last meeting in August 1939. The cricket pitch was in a position newly-adopted in 1884, well left of where it is now, much nearer to the present Nottingham Road and Sir Frank Whittle Road. The football pitch, which had goals referred to as the 'Rifle Range' end and the 'Town' or 'Canal' end, was north of it. A pavilion erected by subscription in 1884, and aligned purely for cricket viewing, was especially relocated in 1886 nearer to the football field and had its blank rear face cleverly modified to provide a few privileged football patrons with a comfortable view of the winter game; it seems likely that step was a consequence partly of the ground's hosting of the 1886 FA Cup Final replay, but also of the general growing interest in Derby County. The hoi-polloi, by the way, had to stand on tiptoe and see what little they could from behind the ropes, placed well back from the playing surface in the interests of creating a half-decent sight-line in those largely pre-terrace days. The somewhat distant and splendidly ornate racing Grandstand meanwhile, so needlessly demolished in 1911, never afforded a realistic football vantage point. Sadly the double-sider, too, that characterful structure which was effectively Derby County's first 'main stand' and the sole on-site link with those early Bloomer days, was demolished much later, in 1955, when Derbyshire redeveloped the ground and again moved their pitch. Photographic evidence, both aerial and landscape, shows the pavilion stood at an angle within the current cricket boundary behind the far wicket, which would place the football pitch of 1892 on the area part-occupied by the existing scoreboard but mainly to this day an open grassed area of close-knit turf and only a stone's throw from the nearest Racecourse Park pitches on which sundry shambolic teams of the new

Millennium will again be assured a perennial 'brass monkey' welcome. Times may change, but football weather doesn't, no matter what the experts say!

As for club colours, it is well known that Derby first turned out in Harlequin-style shirts in the chocolate, amber and pale blue of the cricket club and they are believed to have worn these right into the 1891-92 season while the second string at that time generally favoured black and white stripes, colours which survived as a change strip right into the 1920s. Although photographs of the era show a variety of garbs, a supporter's ditty penned at the start of the 1892-93 season expresses the sentiment: 'What treasure t'will be to behold as of yore/The Red, White and Black on the war path once more.' That suggests a colour change had occurred sometime during the 1891-92 campaign and that is backed up by an early historical snippet on the history of the Rams which says they changed from chocolate, amber and blue shirts to 'cardinal and white' and only later to their famous black shorts and white shirts. If that is so, it seems likely that the strip which was the object of our young hopeful's affections was black hose and knickers with red and white halved shirts. Not that such rambling excursions into prehistory would have troubled Steve, whose first objective was to impress well enough in pre-season to make it into the second team, the newly-christened Derby Town. The first team was surely still a pipe dream.

Surprise debut 1892-93

As Derby County prepared to start only their fifth season in the Football League, the game had confounded all its critics. Some authoritative but ill-informed figures had suggested in the early 1890s that it was merely a passing fancy which would soon fade from the public's affections. Nothing could have been further from the truth. In Derby, despite the team having to apply, successfully, for re-election in their first League season after finishing tenth out of 12, interest had grown and subsequent mediocre finishes of seventh, 11th and tenth had not dampened the spirits. In the last season, supporters were simply delighted to precariously hang on to their place in a League which had by then grown to 14 clubs and with an ever-growing list of hopeful new applicants. As a result of that demand the League was to run two divisions for the first time in the 1892-93 season ahead, which introduced the potential new hazard of the dreaded relegation. Division One grew to 16 clubs with the introduction of Sheffield Wednesday, Newton Heath (later Manchester United) and Derby's keenest rivals Nottingham Forest, then, along with Notts County, popularly known to all Derbeians by the derogatory name of the Lambs. Just as it is so important now to preserve Premiership status, so it became vital for clubs' economic prosperity and, in some cases, very survival, to maintain a place in the First League. With that in mind, both supporters and the local press were more than happy to stick with the basis of last season's team to see them through the coming campaign.

When the line-up for the opening League fixture at Stoke was announced three days before the game, it had a familiar ring to it. The sole change from the last game of the previous season was the inclusion of Ernest Hickinbottom in place of the suspended Archie Goodall at centre-half and the only mild surprise was that Herbert Rose kept his place for only his second-ever start. That being said, the press picked out Rose and his brother Walter as the two likeliest of the second string to break through. Bloomer, although occasionally mentioned in dispatches, was effectively nowhere in the reckoning; quite understandable, as he had played in only three second-team fixtures the previous season and two of those were for the third team merely filling in due to fixture clashes. Only once, for the Sheffield Club game, had he appeared in the seconds' proper line-up. Steve would have been well pleased, therefore, when he was selected at inside-left to play for Derby Town in their opening game at home to Stoke Swifts. But he never did play that game as fate, something which Bloomer subsequently said he believed in strongly, took an astonishing turn…

New Derby County secretary William Parker got off to rather an unfortunate start in the discharge of his duties, registering three of the club's first-teamers with the League a day too late. Although Derby requested an emergency meeting of the Football League committee on Friday, 2 September, the day before the Stoke game, it was too little too late. Parker's boob meant that Hickinbottom, Sam Mills and Jimmy McLachlan were forced to stand down from the first team and emergency replacements had to be hastily rounded up. Bloomer was local so readily contactable; not only that, Derby captain John Goodall was a sufficient admirer of the lad's talent to suggest his name to the selection committee. Along with Ekins and Garden, 18-year-old Bloomer was called up; Ekins had already played for the firsts for much of the previous season, but for fellow ex-Midlanders Garden and Bloomer it was a debut from nowhere. They had less than 24 hours to compose themselves for a game which might well be a make or break opportunity; in the event, only one of them was to blossom. Bloomer always remembered that Football League debut:

"Johnny Goodall really put Derby County on the map and he was largely responsible for putting one Stephen Bloomer there too. Shall I ever forget the stomachful of excitement and nervous apprehension that was mine when I turned out, through Johnny's advocacy, at Stoke on 3 September 1892? Most emphatically 'No'. Nor can I forget what it meant to me when Goodall, in the course of the match, encouraged me with the advice, 'Go on yourself, lad, and shoot'. The very fact that one of his reputation and ability told me to do what I might have considered a bit too cheeky for a greenhorn gave me the confidence I badly needed. So I went on and shot and so materialised the first of my goals for Derby County, another one following the same afternoon."

Derby County won the game 3-1, a surprise win at the Victoria Ground for them and a dream debut for Bloomer watched by 1,000 travelling Derby supporters. The strangest fall-out from Bloomer's account is that the contemporary local newspapers, relying solely on the reports sent back by Stoke's own correspondent, gave both Bloomer's goals to Johnny McMillan. That is an understandable error as no one in Stoke would have known Bloomer; added to that, both goals came just three minutes into each half, the second in a torrential downpour that sent everybody scurrying for cover. It wouldn't be the first or last time a reporter got in place late and had an educated guess at the scorer or simply messed up his identification. Bloomer repeated the story of his two-goal debut on a number of occasions throughout his life and there seems little reason to doubt his memory or honesty on such a key incident, which gives him two more goals not accounted for. That is not an unusual state of affairs... records were not kept so rigorously before the turn of the century and were apt to be stated incorrectly or not at all by beleaguered pressmen not blessed with undercover positions or modern technology.

The *Derby Daily Telegraph* was quick to follow up by praising all the substitutes and observed that 'the fact that the team won has led some to believe that the registration error was a blessing in disguise.'

"Young Bloomer," it said, "ought to be heard of again in the first team and if he continues to improve as he has done hitherto he will make one of the finest forwards in Association Football."

Despite what ultimately proved to be remarkably insightful journalism, the possibility of a 'one-game wonder' can never be discounted in debut cases. Steve not only needed to be picked again but he had to produce the goods in front of his home crowd and press, potentially the two most powerful critics in football and quite able, in mutual praise or condemnation, to make or break careers.

His chances of selection a second time didn't look good as Derby played a testimonial, or 'guarantee match', at Loughborough on the following Wednesday, winning 4-1 with a full-strength team that excluded Bloomer. A day later Steve was selected for the Derby Town side with some unfinished business to attend to, beating Heanor at the County Ground in the Final of the Derbyshire Charity Cup held over from the end of the previous season. In a 4-2 win he 'notched the second amid much enthusiasm', just an early sign of the Bloomer mania beginning to ferment. It was only after that Thursday game that the team for the League match against mighty Preston North End was chosen, and on the strength of his outings thus far Steve was selected for his home debut, this time at inside-left, only after the committee had 'experienced difficulty deciding between Bloomer and Ekins'.

If the game at Stoke had him all a flutter, then Preston at home just seven days later was a potential nightmare. John Goodall's old club, with whom he had won the first-ever 'double' in 1888-89 when they won the League championship without losing a game and the FA Cup without conceding a goal, were known as the Old Invincibles and a huge draw for the crowds. A record League crowd of 10,000 for the County Ground, against figures as low as only 3,000 the season before, witnessed that match in beautiful weather and it must be regarded as a defining moment in Bloomer's life and career. Although Derby lost the game somewhat unluckily, 2-1 after an injury to John Goodall reduced them to ten men, Bloomer took his chance that day with an aplomb beyond the expectations that his pale countenance and wiry frame must surely have suggested. The application of a modern assessment to Bloomer's debut would show that he made excellent use of the ball, read the game well, was quick off the mark and over distance, was naturally right-footed but adept with the left, very quick to shoot, confident with his head, brave and not afraid to tackle but needing to build himself up physically. He seriously troubled the opposition on several occasions and his seven key touches were all good, including what the press described as a 'well-judged overhead kick', a 'little finessing', a 'splendid centre' and a 'clinking shot'.

It is on such assessments that careers turn. Ekins and Rose, Bloomer's rivals for the spare forward's place, went on to complete only 18 and five senior appearances for Derby while poor Garden, stand-in centre-half at Stoke, has only that one solitary appearance against his name; they all went on to other pastures, only Ekins making a go of his football career with Luton. Steve Bloomer, meanwhile, who had started on level terms with them all and fallen behind Rose and Ekins in the pecking order, went on to play 525 first-class games for Derby, 130 for Middlesbrough and 23 for England, scoring 422 goals in the process. Such is the way of things; while most of us inevitably join the Gardens of this world on a pleasant enough amble through life, it is talent and nerve, dedication and passion, and surely some unknown ingredient, which secures the few Bloomers of the football ether their place in history.

But that was all to come. With only two games under his belt Steve had much to learn and far to go, although he had delighted the crowds and impressed most of the press. One reporter said of him "…little Bloomer justified his trial although, despite his remarkable cleverness and capital shots and passes, we are inclined to think he is not yet big enough for a League club." I am inclined to think that that man didn't know his football; a rather better judge encapsulated the essence of Bloomer's debut thus:

"Of the forwards, Bloomer deserves most praise, not so much because he played best, as because he created such a good impression on the minds of those who saw him take part for the first time in an important fixture. On today's form alone he justified his inclusion in the team but then he has a great deal to learn, which with youth on his side he ought easily to do. He promises to become one of the finest players we have and is already fulfilling all we remember to have said of him when he played in the Boys' Shield competition."

For the rest of that first season he never looked back and became something of a novelty attraction on his travels to other grounds, his 'extreme youth setting everybody talking'. Still only 19 by the end of the season he was certainly the baby of a side which generally comprised men in their 20s and that probably worked in his favour with the crowd because he stood out as different; while nearly all the players wore moustaches, too, Steve always remained clean shaven, perhaps unable to cultivate the necessaries to compete in the luxuriancy stakes with the likes of John and Archie Goodall. It was important, of course, that the players took to him as well as the crowd and it is a testimony to his personality and demeanour that they did just that, John Goodall in particular going out of his way to take

Steve under his wing and coach him in the finer points. By his fourth game, at home to West Bromwich Albion, the youngster had gained the confidence of his colleagues to such a degree that he was handed the responsibility of taking a penalty, an innovation introduced only the season before... Steve duly kept his nerve and 'dispatched the leather' in the 1-1 draw. Growing in confidence as the season progressed, he became adept not only at scoring but at celebrating too:

"In my very early days as a player I must plead guilty to many displays of ecstatic joy. On the occasions when I scored a goal in my first season or two I invariably turned a cartwheel on my hands just as many a schoolboy does in the street, or took a great jump in the air and whooped aloud. Often I cartwheeled before the ball was in the net and word got around that I did this to put the goalkeeper off. Nothing of the sort was in my mind. It was simply that I knew intuitively that I had sent in a shot which the goalie would never save, and on impulse my cartwheel was turned out of delight before I realised I was playing on a crowded football field. I was always keen as mustard but as I grew older I took my successes and failures more philosophically."

And we thought Faustino Asprilla was the first!

Of course, the crowds loved it. Playing in every forward position in that first season, he finished with 11 League goals from 28 games, second only to John Goodall with 13. In a game at Repton, the famous Derbyshire public school, he even went in goal with Derby 6-0 up, letting two in as the Reptonians hung on to their dignity. As for the Cup, Derby went out to Sheffield Wednesday after a ludicrous protest and counter-protest affair which resulted in three games. Although Derby won the second, it was Bloomer's earlier Burton Wanderers 'signing' which saw him called before the FA as a witness to Wednesday's protest and the result duly annulled, the start of a Cup hoodoo for young Steve and the Rams which they never shook off until after his death

Johnny versus Caleb...1893-94

Bloomer tells us that his wage in this second season was raised to £1 a week, still a junior rate but a healthy increase reflecting his acceptance into the first team ranks. But that alone didn't mean he had made it for good. As the press had said, he still had much to learn, and he also still had a father who wasn't yet won over by this new-fangled and precarious profession. With Johnny Goodall and Caleb Bloomer advising him from completely opposite corners, Steve listened to both but only took heed of one.

It would not be fair to relate the Steve Bloomer story without at some point giving more than a passing mention to John Goodall as one of the prime influences on his career, and it was in the County Ground days, as Steve learnt his trade, that this influence was most marked. Goodall was born in London in 1863 but raised in Scotland, learning his football barefooted as a boy before becoming an iron-turner, joining Kilmarnock Athletic, and being lured into the English game for his handy debut with Great Lever against Derby County. Superbly adept at the Scottish-inspired 'combination game', he joined mighty

Preston in 1885, won the 'double' with them in 1888-89 and was credited with a staggering 16 goals in the club's record 26-0 Cup defeat of Hyde in 1887. Largely a centre-forward, capped 14 times by England, a club champion at bowls and curling, quite able to make regular 100 breaks at billiards, and a cricketer with Derbyshire and Hertfordshire, he was that rare bird... a gifted all-rounder but immensely modest to boot.

Described as kind and gentle off the field and a superb practitioner, strategist and leader on it, it was a real coup for Derby County when they signed him in May 1889 and as club captain he did so much to make the Rams a force in the land. Happily married to Sarah, for good measure in his spare time he kept The Plough, near The Spot, on London Road with rebel brother Archie, ran a sports shop on Babington Lane and once saved a man from drowning in the Derwent. If Steve needed a role model, Johnny All Good, as he was dubbed by the press, would surely do! Known to his team-mates simply as 'Goodally', he is said to have first seen Steve play with the Derby Swifts, and took such a shine to the young 'un, 11 years his junior, that he exerted an influence which Bloomer would later publicly acknowledge on several occasions:

"Johnny Goodall was a wonderful footballer, brilliant captain and Nature's gentleman, but little did I think when all the fuss was made over his arrival from Preston what an influence for good was being brought into my life. As my early mentor he talked to me and passed on his learnings... straight to the point he told you what to do and expected it to be done and I always maintain that no player has ever known so much about football and its methods and policies than this old friend of mine. The two fundamental virtues he passed on to me were complete ball control and an ability to think a moment ahead of the other fellow. Times without number he impressed that upon me, to think all the time the game was in progress, even when play was not actually near me. There is nothing better than being taken under the wing of an old player and I had the additional slice of luck of being endowed with a temperament which allowed me to enjoy my football lessons with relish. I'm sure I owe more to John Goodall than to anybody else for my ultimate success on the football field."

Goodall left Derby in 1899, playing for New Brighton Tower and Glossop before becoming player-manager and then manager at Watford until 1910, eventually bowing out of the game with a swan-song playing appearance for Welsh club Mardy against Swansea in his 50th year and passing away in Watford in 1942, aged 78.

Goodall's was a career which exemplified what a fine life football could provide and if only one Caleb Bloomer had been able to see what lay in Steve's long-term future he would surely have given blessing to his son's continuance in the game. As it was, he persisted in his opposition. It was not something which created a rift between father and son, but in this 1893-94 season Caleb's prophecies of doom came home to roost as Steve suffered his first and only broken bones.

As a regular scorer Bloomer was rapidly becoming a marked man. While the Premiership now demands the three C's from its most talented defenders –

Calm, Co-ordination and Class – the 1890s defender was all too often characterised by the three B's – Bold, Bad and Brutal. Having survived a constant and cynical battering from Newton Heath's Clements early in the season, it was a Cup game at Leicester Fosse on 10 February 1894 which put him out of action for seven League and cup games:

"Leicester had a half-back named 'Peggy' Lord, a Derby-born man and ex-St Luke's player, and on the journey there it became noised abroad that he intended to 'watch' me. During the game he got his shoulder into me, breaking my left collar-bone, and that accident caused my father to make one of his last big efforts to persuade me to give up the game. I was brought home from Derby station in a cab with my shoulder all heavily bandaged and my arm in a sling and my father's face was a study. I well remember him saying, 'What did I tell you? And what do you think of your football now? The next thing will be a broken leg I suppose.' He then proceeded to paint football in lurid colours. I was 20 years old at the time and of course had to listen to my father's counsels, but I was too enthusiastic and too young to think much of a broken collar-bone. When I was only half-recovered I was drafted back into the team at outside-left so I could have my damaged collar-bone turned to the outside of the field."

Thus it was that Steve survived his first major knock, rode out his father's opposition and continued to attend the Goodall school of excellence. Derby finished third that season, their highest position to date, and Steve topped the club's League scoring chart for the first time, with a prolific 19 goals from only 25 games, the pupil now outgunning the master.

Two seasons into his professional career, Steve's future looked decidedly rosy, although the club itself had to survive the sort of financial crisis that season which would become par for the course over the years to come. As a means of boosting the coffers they held a very successful bazaar at the Drill Hall in Becket Street in March 1894 and a couple of months earlier the players donned fancy dress in a comic match against the *Babes In The Wood* pantomime cast; Steve was due to play dressed as a convict but had to pull out because he was 'ill', although fit enough to score against Wolves three days later. We will give Steve the benefit of the doubt on this one, but he revealed on a number of future occasions a natural disinclination for those dressing up and acting daft routines which sometimes befall footballers in the line of duty. In personality terms there was certainly a hint of shyness and self-consciousness in Steve's make up which he only left behind on taking the field, and even much later in his first spell at Derby he was apt to avoid speaking at players' smoking concerts and the like, even when given encouragement to do so. It was just as well he didn't carry that reticence on to the field because in the final season of the County Ground era, Derby County were to hover on the very brink of their first relegation.

Ridiculous to the sublime... 1894-95

The season started with a ridiculous affair at Sunderland on the opening day, a match which became known as the 'game of three halves' which passed into folklore among the players. Quite simply the scheduled referee was late in arriving and the game started with a replacement. Derby were 3-0 down when the appointed referee finally arrived and they gratefully accepted the option of starting again before ending up with 11 goals against in one afternoon, promptly crashing 8-0 in the game proper. It was Steve's biggest ever first-class defeat. That didn't bode well for the rest of the season and it was something of a mystery why, with largely the same squad as the season before, they began to struggle so badly. Disrupted by injuries, a run of only two wins in the first 13 games spelt big trouble and with Bloomer again being shunted around every one of the forward positions, having not yet been given the inside-right berth to keep, his own form dipped below the standards he had set. With only ten goals in 29 League games it says much for the dire form of the team that Steve's total was sufficient to earn him top scorer spot again. But Bloomer's reputation was good enough by then to earn him the ultimate accolade, an England call-up.

On 9 March 1895 he played against Ireland on his own County Ground in his international debut. It was the start of a legendary England career which we shall cover in detail elsewhere. Suffice to say at this stage that Caleb went to watch his son for the first time ever that day and promptly cast off years of prejudice to become an avid convert; a proud day for Steve and dad and one which proves there is no defence against the virulent force of football.

Despite that England honour, won remarkably in only his third season, League matters still weighed heavily. When the fixtures proper came to an end, Derby lay 15th in a Division of 16 and had to enter into a play-off with a Second Division side to preserve their status. The games, known as Test Matches, were all or nothing; Derby would play Notts County, second in Division Two, while Liverpool, bottom of Division One, would take on Division Two champions Bury. The two winners would play in Division One next season...and the two losers wouldn't!

It was a poor system which was to be revised for future seasons but Derby were stuck with it. On 27 April 1895 the Rams travelled to Leicester Fosse's Walnut Street enclosure (later Filbert Street) to take on the 'Lambs' of Notts County. It was the sort of sudden death stuff guaranteed to cause palpitations among the travelling fans and Bloomer never forgot it:

"Talk about emotional matter! Notts were leading 1-0 with seven minutes to go but, in the time which remained, Johnny Goodall was a real inspiration and we snatched salvation from the bottom of the pan with goals from myself and Johnny McMillan. We won 2-1 and one of our directors' daughters fainted and another official broke his watch in his hand. Yes, it was as tense as that and I nearly fainted myself from sheer reaction when it was all over."

Bloomer's goal, the equaliser, came from a speculative long shot by full-back Jimmy Methven which hit McMillan on the back before dropping for Steve to stab home. Methven got an eye-full of mud standing on his head to celebrate and over 30 years later, canny Scot as ever, he was still claiming the goal as his despite the two deflections. Who can blame him? It would have been the only one he ever scored in a remarkable 511-game career with Derby! More of Methven later... in the meantime what did count was that McMillan's last-second winner preserved Derby's oh-so-precious First Division status.

It was a defining moment in Derby County's history, possibly ensuring its very survival, and it ushered in one of the most exciting eras in the club's and Bloomer's young life, the first of those rare but heady spells that supporters can live on for years. As the season closed, so too did the County Ground era. Derby County were never to play there again...the Baseball Ground beckoned. Although it is that uniquely-named football home which has come to be associated with the most enduring episodes from Bloomer's career, there is no denying that the really crucial formative years which preceded his long reign there belonged very much to the County Ground.

By the end of April 1895, only three years after collecting his special gold medal in his last Boys' Shield triumph with Swifts, Steve Bloomer was an established professional footballer, the darling of the crowd, the club's leading scorer, and an England international now on £3 a week, all achieved on the County Ground turf and all by the age of 21. What's more, his determination and eye-catching exploits had converted his father. What a pity his mother Merab never saw even the first fruits of his success... she, too, would have surely been very proud of her first son.

20 January 1874 might have been centuries away...it was a remarkable rise from obscurity to early success and the threshold of real fame. Slowly and surely the three pre-requisites of a young boy's footballing destiny had been fulfilled – close and constant exposure to the game, his capacity to enjoy it and, most important of all, his ability to take a chance when presented with it. That was the hat-trick that really mattered. The scrawny young lad had come of age, Stephen had become 'Steve' and the County Ground Kid was about to become King of the Baseball Ground.

BASEBALL GROUND HEYDAY 1895-1906

"A player one may truly call,
The best who's ever kicked a ball,
Respected, loved, admired by all...John Goodall.

The Prince of tacklers, strong as ox,
Artful and dodgy as a fox,
Heedless of kicks, trips, blows and knocks...Our Archie.

Who cooly checks the outside's dash,
Who settles oft the centre's hash,
And never does an action rash...Jim Methven.

Our Johnnie's pupil, Derby's pride,
The idol of the crowd beside,
Whose fame is spreading far and wide...Steve Bloomer."
Our Boys Miss Theodora and Arthur Wilson, 1895

"IT WAS hardly football weather when Derby County made their first appearance on their new ground, the sun shining brightly and the elements favouring spectators far more than players. It was a clever piece of work on behalf of the committee to have such a great attraction for the opening match, for Sunderland have such a reputation in Derby that a big attendance was a foregone conclusion. Sunderland have always been too good for Derby County in former years, for out of 11 matches they have previously played, the County have only won one."
Derby Daily Telegraph, 14 September 1895.

New home, new era
If there was a day for upsetting the form book, Saturday, 14 September 1895 was as good as any. Kicking-off at 3.30pm after the welcoming band had played 'a number of pleasing selections', Derby County beat the 'Team Of All The Talents',

champions for three of the last four seasons, by two goals to nil. It was the start of a new era which saw Derby's hardcore fan base grow well beyond that of the County Ground days, despite the club's initial concern that attendances might be adversely affected by a move. That was a needless worry because, the new home being situated in Litchurch at the very heart of Derby's industrial community, the likelihood of that sports-mad neighbourhood turning up in numbers was always good. Boosted by many coming in from the smaller Derbyshire towns, still a vital part of the Rams following today, 10,000 witnessed that victory over Sunderland and the fact that a local lad brought up right on the doorstep had scored both goals went down particularly well. Bloomer's second-half double christened the Baseball Ground's official opening and stamped his own indelible mark on the latter half of the 1890s and on into the new century.

Why the Baseball Ground? With apologies to those who already know the tale, that most American of sports enjoyed its brief halcyon days over here in the 1890s and in Derby in particular. Francis Ley, of Ley's foundry fame, had first taken to the game on a business trip to the States in 1889 and set about introducing it to England with an almost missionary zeal. He laid out a 12-acre sports ground for his employees with a baseball ground at its heart, a modest enough arena with its own miniature stands but still one described by a visiting American expert as 'the best baseball enclosure in all England'. Having established itself as a popular summer venue for Derby's prodigious baseball team as well as band concerts and athletic meetings, it was natural that Derby County should look to it when clashes with race meetings and the leaseholders of the County Ground made fixture-juggling there increasingly difficult. Two first-team games had already been held on Mr Ley's enclosure in March 1892 and November 1892, Steve playing in the latter game and already otherwise well-familiar with the turf from his days as a third-teamer and as a talented baseball player himself, of which more later; be that as it may, 1895 marked the date of Derby's permanent move and was the true start of the Baseball Ground's and Bloomer's heyday.

It might so easily have happened elsewhere in town because the committee seriously considered two viable alternatives, one on the Firs Estate at the end of Boyer Street and the other the Vulcan Ground on St Thomas's Road; in fact so serious was the Boyer Street suggestion, with a projected large 'kop' and an entrance from Burton Road, that the incorrigible Archie Goodall – he lived in nearby Wolfa Street – took a speculative option on the site and promptly caught a cold….probably well deserved! Imagine taking a large slice of Gazza's temperament, blending in a dollop of Del Boy, adding the grit and skill of a Dave Mackay and packaging it all into a 5ft 7in bundle of energy which might make Martin O'Neill seem calm and Gordon Strachan level-headed… that was Archie Goodall, just one of the characters which numbered among Steve's team-mates of the 'naughty nineties'.

Having got the casting vote as the new HQ for that lively bunch of players, the Baseball Ground was developed piecemeal to cater for the increased numbers nailing their colours to the Derby County mast, a term which one fan took all too literally; in the home FA Cup tie against Aston Villa in February 1895, an acrobatic ex-sailor entertained the crowd and players with his 'monkey on a pole' routine by watching the entire game in a variety of implausible postures from the club's flagpole on the newly-developed Railway Stand side, later the Popular Side. In front of a record 20,000 supporters, it was the first really big game at the ground and Derby won 4-2 with Bloomer again hijacking everybody's memory banks by bagging a timely brace. It was a game he later described as 'a red-letter one in my memory because I was so young at the time and the scenes at the Baseball Ground were very strongly imprinted on my mind'. While Steve's goals and undoubted charisma made a great impact on the crowds, it must never be forgotten that it was the 'team' of that era which really impressed… they finished second in the League in 1895-96 and were controversially beaten in their first-ever FA Cup semi-final after a Bloomer effort was dubiously disallowed to seal a 2-1 win for Wolves. Now established as a fixture in his favourite and long-term position of inside-right, he produced some of the best form of his career and always regarded that team of 1896 as one of the greatest he'd played in; indeed he remained convinced that the championship would have been theirs but for a disastrous tailing off in the last half-dozen games, five of which he missed through injury:

"Though I say it myself, the fact that I was out of action in the last five matches of that campaign probably had a considerable bearing on the circumstance that we finished second, four points behind Villa."

It was to be a familiar tale of so near and yet so far which dogged Derby and Bloomer for years. Third in 1896-97 and again reaching and losing the Cup semi-final, this time 3-2 to Everton, they followed this by going one better to reach the FA Cup Final in both 1898 and 1899, but again losing both. And so it went on…by the end of the 1905-06 season in which Bloomer was to sensationally leave his beloved Derby, the team could look back on a remarkable 11-season run which saw them reach three FA Cup Finals and play in seven semis without a single winners' medal to show for their efforts; and nothing in the Football League either. Was it the fabled curse of the gypsies, sworn to avenge themselves when they were turfed off the Baseball Ground site when it was first acquired by Ley?

We will cast an eye over the Cup Finals saga and one or two key League games later, but there seems little to be gained by a season-by-season analysis of Bloomer's career during these 11 roller-coaster campaigns. The approach thus far has been chronological only because the graph of Bloomer's life to 1895 was such a steeply progressive one; once he had made it as an established professional, even though he continued to develop his lifestyle and reputation, the annual rhythm of his existence took on a much more settled feel as seasons came and passed in the way all footballers must know. In simply confirming that Steve Bloomer became Derby County's top League and Cup scorer for every one of those Baseball Ground seasons, and finished top of the entire

Football League charts five times in the same period, all knowledgeable football followers will surely get the picture… Bloomer became a veritable phenomenon, the darling of the Derby crowds, a draw wherever he played and the very spirit of England itself on the international scene. When he left Derby as a much matured 32-year-old, he was a household name and a record breaker with the honour of both club and national 'benefits' accorded to him.

Less well documented, though, is the grey area which can capture what the essence of 'being' a professional footballer of that calibre really meant to Bloomer, what material or other benefits it gave him, what problems it caused him and what emotional support he was able to call on in his day-to-day home life. If Bloomer's life is to be better understood, such questions all need to be addressed, even if at the expense of many more ripping football yarns.

Home and family
As footballers understand better than their fans, there is a world outside the touchline comprising far more than the 90 minutes in which players come alive on a Saturday afternoon. Life for the Bloomers continued apace in a Litchurch progressively blessed with modern conveniences much earlier than some other areas, housing as it did some of the town's most influential administrators and entrepreneurs; trams trundled through busy streets lined with more shops and houses than ever before, electric street lighting was inaugurated in 1894, parks and places of entertainment were well established, and in town the library and other substantial facilities still in daily use today were newly open for the benefit of all.

Against such a backdrop the Bloomers moved on from Yates Street, possibly prompted by the death of their lodger Joseph Harlow or Steve's newly enhanced earnings. By the start of 1896 Caleb and family had moved into a more recently built terraced house at 41 St Thomas's Road, still there today and now an electrical shop. Close to Ley's works and the football ground, it suited Caleb and the two oldest Bloomer lads perfectly. At the start of the 1895-96 season, Phillip, too, had signed junior professional forms for Derby, playing in the reserves but being given a chance at left-back in place of the injured Joe Leiper for one first-team game against Sheffield Wednesday on 28 September 1895. Whether he might be able to give up his job as a 'moulder' at Leys only time would tell; in fact his last day's smithing did come at the end of May 1896, yet he only ever played that one game for Derby, albeit a victory which gives him a better record than his brother! On 5 June 1896, Phillip, a strong healthy sportsman quite possibly with a long Rams career ahead of him, died of peritonitis (infected appendix) after seven days of illness. It was Steve who informed the relevant authorities of his kid brother's passing.

That unexpected blow must surely have hit Steve hard and it is possible that it affected his emotional outlook at the time because just two months later he was to put a permanent seal on another partnership by getting married. Very little is known of Steve's early relationships with the fairer sex; surviving relatives of one Hannah Baines, born in Stockbrook Lane in 1876, say she and

Steve courted sometime in their teens. Hannah had entered into 'service' at 14 but soon left to work with Midland Railway in the express dining cars, quite possibly meeting Steve, an inveterate train user, through that channel. By all accounts Hannah was a rather feisty girl, a member of the patriotic and Conservative 'Primrose League' and something of an early feminist. Nothing enduring came of their liaison… perhaps she scared Steve off or maybe his prospects as a mere footballer were not good enough.

At any rate it was another Derby girl, Sarah Walker, who ultimately captured Steve's affections, and incidentally, lest anyone should think the name rings a bell, one of over 200 Sarah Walkers then living in Derbyshire. Born in 1875 to Herbert and Elizabeth Walker in a terraced home at 42 Litchurch Street, now demolished and enveloped within the site of the Royal Infirmary, Sarah lived there right up to her marriage. With two brothers she was well used to laddish ways and evidently saw something attractive in the young footballer-about-town. In the matter of desirability Steve's early rather undernourished look surely doesn't set the heart racing but he gradually thickened out and by the time of his marriage his boyish looks made him worth a second glance, so I'm told. Sarah's father employed several men in his boot-making business which had an outlet on Normanton Road in which Sarah was thought to assist…perhaps it was a football boot transaction that brought her and the rising star together. Steve's team-mate Jimmy Methven once made an interesting observation about Sarah's father, telling the entire readership of the *Derbyshire Football Express* that 'Bert Walker was a real snob of the old kind'. Lest anyone should be aghast at Methven's attitude to his fellow man, perhaps it should be explained that a 'snob' was the Victorian slang for a cobbler and that Bert was Derby County's first-ever paid boot-man in the 1890s. Incidentally it is the same term which was responsible for giving the later Rams' star Alf 'Snobby' Bentley his nickname, on account of him spending much of his boyhood playing in and around a cobbler's shop in Alfreton.

Stephen Bloomer and Sarah Walker were married on a Wednesday afternoon, 19 August 1896, at St Thomas's Church. Pretty and with thick dark hair, small and slim but strong-looking rather than frail, Sarah would be with Steve for nearly 40 years of marriage. The certificate is a conundrum of sorts… perhaps with a touch of devilish humour in mind, Steve, a full-time footballer already capped by England, stated his profession as 'blacksmith' while the father and father-in-law of the prolific scorer were appropriately 'striker' and 'boot-maker' respectively. In that hype-free haven of yesteryear, the local paper was matter of fact in its coverage of the event: "By the way, Steve Bloomer was married this Wednesday afternoon." Of course, there was no *Hello!* magazine in those days.

Just 22 and 21, Steve and Sarah set up home at 34 Cummings Street, off Normanton Road, a typical terraced sized house still standing trim and neat now, the only one in the street structurally detached, perhaps just a hint of one-upmanship which reflected Steve's earning power and Sarah's preference. It is a very old fashioned and rather distasteful thing to say that Steve married 'above himself', but it would probably be marginally true and in Victorian and later societies hidebound by excesses of class-consciousness it was the sort of thing that was said in closely scrutinising any marital pairing.

As is so often the case with newly-married footballers, Steve's form appeared to lack its usual vigour early in season 1896-97. When the season started with a Tuesday game only 13 days into his marriage, he drew a disconcerting blank on the scoresheet in the first three matches but any worries that the nuptials might have stolen his edge were cast aside in the fourth, a 4-3 home win over Wolves. By way of preserving his average Steve elected to score all four, following that with a hat-trick against Bury a week later and finishing the season with 31 goals in 33 League and Cup games, his biggest-ever haul and best career average…evidently married life suited him.

Their first child, Hetty Winifred, was born at Cummings Street 18 months into the marriage on 15 February 1898; with a second child later on the way the young family moved over the road in preparation, to number 81, a terraced house extending over the entry with an extra bedroom, and on 30 April 1900 another girl duly arrived. It seems that between the birth and christening, the British capture of the Boer capital on 5 June in the ongoing conflict in South Africa had inspired the patriotic Bloomers to bless their new arrival with an unusual second name; the latest little flower in the growing Bloomer bunch was christened Violet Pretoria. One imagines Steve might have harboured hopes of a boy but that didn't stop him kicking a ball around with the toddlers as they got older, anecdotes telling of him 'trying to teach his daughters football'; maybe they displayed touches of the tomboy…Steve used to take them into a local shop for sweets and was said to have nicknamed the two girls 'my little mucky-heads'.

On 27 May 1902 the 'sugar and spice' hat-trick was complete, Doris Alexandra being born at Cummings Street. That seems to have prompted a move up-market from the three-bedroom terrace to a four-bedroom house at 91 Dairy House Road, just a street away from the Baseball Ground and recently built on the fields where Steve might once have shot at sticks. Again the house was marginally one of the best in the road, an end-of-terrace this time with a small foregarden and adjacent the church. Solid but unpretentious, and well within Steve's maximum budget, it reflected his capabilities as the highest paid man on the club's books as well as an inborn caution and a desire never to get 'above himself'. With three children of five and under to look after, Sarah had her hands full but evidently coped admirably. *Athletic News* journalist James Catton was certainly smitten, and with the girls on their best behaviour he revealed Steve's nostalgic streak as a trophy hunter:

"I once paid a visit to the house of Steve Bloomer near to the Baseball Ground. His home was a palace, well furnished, everything so neat and clean and orderly that it was a pleasure to be there. His little girls were in white muslin frocks and looked like fairies, so tastefully were they dressed. On the walls of Bloomer's apartments were framed photographs of many teams in which he had played, and footballs, lettered in gilt setting forth the big occasions when they had been used, hung from the ceiling, more luscious to my eyes than Yorkshire hams in an old farmstead. The residence was a credit to his wife and I have never forgotten the half-hour I passed with 'Steve' and his family in their own surroundings... with such a helpmate, no wonder he played until he was turned 40 and later trained the young in the way they should go."

Alas, the memorabilia has long been dispersed but the house remains, now a centre for Derby's Vietnamese community... one wonders if the nail-holes in the ceiling might still be there under years of wallpaper. From all accounts Steve, Sarah and the three girls were a happy family and Bloomer valued the time he spent at home. He often expressed his dislike of the Christmas Day games and crowded festive fixture list for that very reason. That they were a close-knit family was much later born out by reminiscences from Doris. Perhaps most poignant were two items from her own scrapbook. On a photograph of Sarah she had written the simple note, "My darling Mama ...she was the best Mama in all the world." As for memories of Steve, unique among the items saved was a proud daughter's loving tribute to her very own football hero....from a large photograph she had cut out just the feet and placed the two pieces in an envelope where they remain to this day; again the short annotation said more than any lengthy tribute could ever hope to do: "These are my Dada's."

The Bloomer's lifestyle was comfortable for its time without being lavish, perhaps equivalent to living on a nice quality suburban residential estate now, and certainly after the turn of the century a lifestyle only sustained by the above average earnings of the head of the household.

Money matters
Bloomer tells us that he generally signed contracts for two and three years at Derby and that his wages gradually rose to 'a high water mark of £5 10s per week, but that for only two seasons', figures which are slightly more than the '£5 a week all year' which the Derby County minutes record for Bloomer for seasons 1899-1900 and 1900-01, but an insignificant discrepancy at that. What is significant is that it showed Bloomer had been freed of the summer wages reduction that some players were subject to and moreover that it confirmed him as easily the highest paid member of the team at that time, the next below him being £3 10s. Other clubs' figures show wages for the League professional generally ranging from £1 to £6 between 1895 and 1901 dependent, as today, on age, ability and negotiating skills. At a time of relatively limited inflation, many prices remained constant throughout the 1890s, increases where they did occur generally limited to 20 per cent or so in the entire decade, and the cycle of annual wage rises which is an expectation today simply did not exist. Consequently most Derby players remained at around the £3 mark year after year and Bloomer's more dramatic leaps reflected his very low starting base, his undoubted pulling power in terms of gate money, and his real negotiating clout. Basic wages could be supplemented by bonuses, usually £1 for an away win and ten shillings for a home and further discretionary awards were sometimes paid,

both Bloomer and Methven, for example, each receiving a match bonus of £2 10s in 1897-98 for 'standing out' in games against Liverpool and Wolves respectively. What all this meant for Bloomer was that from 1897-1901 his basic annual wage grew from around £150 to £260, but from 1901-02 he and others suffered the irritation of being subjected to a maximum wage of £4 a week, surely unfairly implemented by a Football Association concerned that money matters were getting out of hand. Commenting on the issue, *The Times* probably reflected Steve's own thoughts quite well:

"No doubt £4 a week is a handsome wage for the average well-tempered cog in the mechanism of a League, but players of superlative excellence such as Meredith, Bloomer and Crompton are worth much more, since they often win matches by the sheer force of their individual genius and the attraction of their personality brings additional thousands of paying visitors to the arena."

Even at that reduced £208 basic, though, Steve and the family did not go without… that at a time when the average business manager earned £250, the head of a village school £200, a miner £90 and a railway clerk £80. Again, precise modern translations are tricky but with a pair of trousers still only 40p, a decent overcoat at £2 and a two-bedroom terraced house at £300 to purchase, I would place Bloomer's best earnings at an equivalent of £25-35,000 today. That is peanuts against what a player of his status could enjoy now but it gave the Bloomer's Dairy House Road lifestyle an air well above the typical 'artisan' which could, if they wished it to do so, mirror the status of the 'middle class'.

Although Bloomer probably felt that he was lagging behind in the third quarter of the 1890s, I believe he appreciated his high water mark but was justifiably irritated, especially in retrospect, by the 'maximum' rule, which stayed in force right up to his retirement. That being said, I would suggest that the iron worker's son from Cradley always knew at heart which side his 'bread was buttered' as he knew only too well that in different circumstances it might not have been buttered at all. Years later, in 1930, Bloomer put it all in perspective:

"I often hear ignorant people declare that 'a player is not worth his high wages' but I would strongly emphasise that a man who is contented and has not to forego little luxuries for his wife and family is far more likely to do himself justice on the field than one whose wages are barely sufficient to keep body and soul together. My greatest football wish is that my career could have started about 1927 instead of 1892, now that the offside rule has changed and a player can progress to £9 or so a week and put something by for the proverbial rainy day. Don't think I'm jealous, it was just the misfortune of us old players that wages were not higher in our time. I say good luck to today's men, the game can stand it, and anyway the average footballer has not a great deal to look forward to when his career is finished. By the way, I must correct a correspondent who says I used to work in the pit. I have only once been down a mine and don't propose a repeat visit."

Better than being underground it certainly was, and Steve knew it, but what would he have thought of today's madness? He'd surely have taken the £30,000 a week or so that he would command now but one can't help feeling that he might have done so with more than a tinge of conscience, for as he once said: "Irrespective of the payment, football for me was ever a hobby."

Today's money men would have had a field day with Bloomer's marketability; he was not known to have had an agent, despite their services being offered and taken up by some players of the day, but he did what he could while he could to boost his basic pay and, without being greedy or over-ruthless, was known to be a canny player of the endorsement game. Jimmy Methven tells this perhaps slightly embellished yarn:

"I often think of the strange fads certain of my team-mates had, Steve Bloomer being a case in point. Most of the players had their own favourite boots and would wear them until they dropped off their feet. Steve was no exception but he was an expert at sampling different pairs and testifying that they were all the ideal boot. I should think he averaged a different pair every fortnight and he must have spent a small fortune in ink writing testimonials for the different firms, but in actual fact he had his one favourite pair and nothing would have persuaded him to forsake them."

That was undoubtedly delivered with a twinkle in the eye. As someone who played in or managed the team for all but 19 of Steve's games for Derby, and who probably even watched those 19 from the bench, Methven assuredly knew Bloomer and his little foibles better than anyone. Known as 'Logie' on account of arriving at Derby from Edinburgh St Bernard's, who played at Logie Park, Methven was a robust full-back who took great pride in 'looking after himself' on the field and was always a keen dressing-room prankster off it. Many a mischievous tale did he tell about those Baseball Ground days.

Steve and the Krazy Gang

Lest anyone should think that Steve was part of a 'golden age' of football characterised by a gentlemanly stroll on the greensward, politely applauding spectators, an after-match tea and an early night, they need only to read Jimmy Methven's memoirs, and many others, to put them right. The Victorian and Edwardian football scene did contain much of the true sporting spirit among both players and spectators, but it was also hard and raucous to a degree that the later eras of the 1920s and 1930s were not. Archie Goodall was up before the magistrates for 'landing one' on someone in the crowd long before Cantona launched himself on to the football scene, Walsall fans were merrily throwing bricks through the Derby team's train carriage window after nothing more vital than a Bass Vase defeat, players shoulder-charged each other with alarming gusto, unfortunate linesmen had their legs pelted by catapult missiles and an even more unfortunate referee in a minor game was attacked and killed by a player more than a century before Paul Alcock's delicate little pirouette at the hands of Paulo Di Canio.

And there is much more where that came from. Language could be excessively 'industrial' and certainly players needed to look after themselves and each other, which in turn helped to engender a strong team spirit. The rather cold and pokey dressing-room in the Ley's Institute behind the goal at the Osmaston End was no place for the fainthearted. Cold water soakings, mud fights and all manner of singular wagers are well documented – even the saintly Johnny Goodall had a penchant for firing pellets from his favourite air rifle at any player not on his guard. On their big match preparation trips to the health hydros at Ashover, Matlock or Ashby-de-la-Zouch, sometimes stays of a full week, the boredom was apt to be relieved by late-night card schools, schoolboy japes and sundry rumbustuous games.

On another occasion at the Baseball Ground, Welsh international full-back Charlie Morris walked into the dressing-room with a small donkey over his ample shoulders and on a 'training' trip to Blackpool the same player joined up with goalkeeper Harry Maskrey to win a wager from the rest of the lads… both of them walked along the sea-front dressed as women, loudly hooted and pelted with eggs by their team-mates as passers by stood agog. Wimbledon's Krazy Gang were just about 100 years behind the times, really there is very little new in dressing-room culture.

Despite being a popular member of that dressing-room scene in his own way, Steve seldom figures largely in these anecdotal yarns, and when he does it is more likely to be in the way of innocent victim or somewhat reluctant participant than ring-leader. Bloomer wasn't a goody-goody or prude, far from it, but his natural seriousness and modesty seems to have made him as much a background figure off the field as he was a leader on it, probably more comfortable in one-on-one social encounters than group situations. Even the hierarchy were known to comment on his reserve. FA secretary Sir Frederick Wall once said that he wondered 'whether Bloomer's uncommonly pale countenance is partly down to nerves, because he is often deadly serious'. On another occasion the Derby team, by virtue of Tommy Paton's father being the stationmaster, were allowed to walk over the Forth Bridge, surely the only football team ever to perform such a stunt… Jimmy Methven remembered that 'every time a train roared by, the players clung to the side, none more affectionately than Steve'. Fortunately that rather cautious 'belt and braces' side to Bloomer's character did not show on the field.

How curious it would be to spend a day or so in the company of that squad. One thing that might come as a surprise would be Bloomer's dressing-room nickname, which was 'Blood'. Its origin is unknown… perhaps an ironic reference to Steve's lack of colour or maybe from a word in common usage then, a 'blood' being a 'hot spark' or a term for 'any young member of a group who brings to it youthful freshness and vigour'. Bloomer certainly fitted that bill; 'superboy' or 'whizz-kid' might be a modern counterpart.

In such an atmosphere of high spirits it might be easy to forget that teams which win matches need training and discipline too; ever the individualist, Steve had his own views and a certain number of ups and downs in that department.

Training and discipline

Despite his 'ghostly' appearance, Bloomer was, in the words of one reporter, 'as sound as a bell' and, in spite of being a smoker, undoubtedly supremely fit. Nonetheless he gave the impression on a number of occasions that he sometimes found training without a ball something of a chore, even if he reluctantly recognised the need for it. By the mid-1890s Derby had an everyday regime in place under trainers Billy Leitch and Arthur Staley and their responsibilities to the committee were to deliver men who could do the business on Saturdays; players of old were no more immune to the potential monotony of training than today's finely tuned pros and Steve made his stance quite clear:

"I might as well admit that I have often obeyed 'orders' and trained in my early days when there was no real need for me to train at all. You see, when I was in my prime I was a lean man, ordained by nature to be thin, while others had a tendency to put on flesh. But it was pointed out to me quietly that, while I may not need to train, it was considered that I should not be an exception to the rule. Having always been a keen disciplinarian I accepted that, so there was no danger of my colleagues 'thinking things', but believe me there is no pleasure in stripping and going out training in all weathers."

Although Steve said that from a position of strength in 1922, it is almost certainly a veiled reference to an occasion in September 1898 when circumstances seem to have got the better of him and he ended up with a club ban. With seven-month-old baby Hetty at home, a degree of discontent over his wages and with only one goal in his first four games of the season, not one of them won, maybe the team's star was feeling the pressure. For almost the first time ever he suffered adverse press comment, one Derby paper stating after a dire 0-0 draw with Blackburn that 'Bloomer played in fits and starts' and another describing the forwards' shooting as 'feeble as could be imagined, the front line making a terrible hash of things and failing in the most unaccountable manner'. Amid such a crisis of confidence, Bloomer and inside-left Jimmy Stevenson were played in a reserve side for a friendly against Chesterfield Town on Monday, 19 September and despite Steve scoring twice in the 4-1 win there was every indication from the press that both players might be 'rested' for the coming Saturday's game at Sheffield Wednesday.

In the event the 'resting' wasn't necessary. Quite possibly uniting in a display of mutual disgruntlement after the indignity of the 'stiffs', Bloomer and Stevenson turned up for Tuesday training and were promptly reported for their 'attitude' and suspended by the committee 'sine die' for 'insubordination and inattention to training'. It was a turning point for Bloomer of sorts at a time when he might have become too big for his boots if left unchecked. Pilloried in the press for their 'prima donna' and 'sulky' behaviour and the 'recent trouble and anxiety caused by these two players', it was a testing time for their characters. John Goodall chipped in with his own admonishment in a timely article in the magazine *Sport and Play* while nationally the affair was well aired too, The *Sporting Chronicle* stating that 'times without number, Bloomer's little eccentricities have been overlooked'.

Stevenson's response was immediate – he disappeared back to Scotland without a word and never played for Derby again, eventually being signed by Newcastle United. Bloomer's response, too, was swift but more sensible. The papers said that Bloomer had 'felt his position most keenly' and, evidently filled with remorse, he sought a meeting with the committee at which the air was cleared and he apologised profusely. Having missed just one game Bloomer was said to have 'seen fit to make *l'amende honorable*' and his ban was lifted to enable him to play in the next game.

While this episode revealed something of an Achilles heel in his temperament, it was the sort of thing that happens all the time in football and the affair soon blew over. Rumours in a Sheffield paper stating he was on the transfer list were denied by Derby as 'utterly without foundation' and subsequent approaches for Bloomer's signature by Aston Villa, Sheffield United and later Southampton were completely stonewalled by a Derby committee keen as ever to hang on to him. While he was undoubtedly sometimes given the kid glove treatment by his Derby taskmasters, and occasionally stepped out of line again in the future, this all needs seeing in perspective. Bloomer attended thousands of training sessions in his career, the ups outweighing the downs overwhelmingly, and compared to the Robbie Fowlers of this world, his indiscretions were quite tame. Most important of all, though, was Bloomer's on-field response to his off-field hiccup; he finished his most 'difficult' season as the club's top scorer yet again with 30 goals in 33 games, his 24 in the League giving him top spot in the entire country. The period after his ban was the most prolific of his career – 29 goals in 29 League and Cup games included six in the 9-0 thrashing of Sheffield Wednesday, still the Derby County individual scoring record today. As the saying goes, you can't argue with that. If part of true 'greatness' is being able to deliver the goods in the face of personal adversity or weakness, then Bloomer's claim to lasting acclaim was strengthened by that season's ups and downs. The public and press knew it and so too, perhaps in a little more time, did his club and country.

On the field his disciplinary record was almost exemplary. He was known to be hard but fair, quite willing to remonstrate with referees when they disallowed his efforts but only ever sent off once, that for retaliation against Everton's Bert Sharp in the game at Goodison in December 1901. Again Bloomer was full of contrition after the referee almost apologetically told him: "You'd better go to the dressing-room." He was so convinced he'd been the victim of both an unfair battering and a particularly interfering linesman from Bolton, that he submitted a hand-written four-side appeal to the FA; alas to no avail… he took his fortnight's suspension and learnt another football lesson: "I took jolly good care after that to never retaliate again; I always think, take it with a smile, and many's the time I have said to myself… 'Remember Goodison.'"

Such trials and tribulations come with the territory. What the fans of that era cared about were not the occasional blots but the regular supply of Bloomer's special commodities… entertainment and goals.

League highs and Cup lows 1895-1906
Bloomer's six against Sheffield Wednesday took the biscuit but there were other feats in abundance. In the opening season at the Baseball Ground, hat tricks

against Nottingham Forest at home and away did no little harm in cementing his celebrity status and he reserved another triple for the Lambs in 1898. Nor did the art leave him as he got older... in the first 15 games of the 1900-01 season he netted 16 times and on an end-of-season tour to East Anglia in 1905 he helped himself to 16 in six games. Many were the battles against other characters of the day, none more keenly fought than those against Sheffield United's 'bogey' pair, giant custodian Willie 'Fatty' Foulke and Ernest 'Nudger' Needham, although Bloomer always contended his real bogeyman was Preston's left-half 'Ginger' Lyons. Yet for all the memorable tussles and net-bulging heroics, he never won a championship medal... that remained as elusive as that other desirable piece of metal, the FA Cup.

Both players and public, especially those from the North and Midlands, were equally ambitious to win their 'Dear little bootercup, sweet little footer cup', as *Punch Magazine* once parodied it, but Derby's lot, like a certain policeman's, was not a happy one. In Bloomer's first spell at the Baseball Ground they reached the Cup Final a creditable three times, Steve playing in two and missing one through injury... but not a winners' medal in sight.

1898, Derby County 1 Nottingham Forest 3 Having beaten their great rivals 5-0 at home just a week before the Final aided by one of those Bloomer hat-tricks, Derby entered this game as hot favourites, but Forest had a number of key men watching from the stands for the League game and started the Final much strengthened. Derby were probably over-confident ...Archie Goodall certainly was; as kick-off at the Crystal Palace neared and some spectators perched in trees to secure a precarious but unrestricted view, the compulsive speculator was still outside trying to offload his surplus tickets. Bloomer, evidently not amused, completes the tale:

"We never got into our stride that day and the only satisfaction I had was in scoring one of the finest goals I have ever headed... but to this day I honestly believe that Derby would have won the Cup but for that unnerving pre-match experience."

It wasn't all Goodall, of course. What Steve doesn't say is that he and others missed good openings that day; nevertheless a chance to put it right came only a year later.

1899, Derby County 1 Sheffield United 4 On paper Derby were again favourites against a team fourth from bottom of the League. In the first half they did everything their followers in the 73,833 crowd expected, going in 1-0 up; it could have been two as a further effort was disallowed and then after the interval Bloomer missed a glorious chance to give Derby command. Then as now, missed opportunities were invariably rued and after half-back Johnny May left the field injured, the Rams collapsed in the last half-hour. Again judiciously choosing not to recall his own miss, Steve was fair gutted:

"Jimmy Methven was our captain that day and was advised at that point to play the one-back game, at which he was adept, but instead he tried to hold on to the lead by moving MacDonald into the intermediate line. But Sheffield's astute general 'Nudger' Needham played on that weakness and all four of their goals came from that side of the field. When it was all over he linked his arm in mine and said: 'Steve, you have my sympathy, for I don't think we should have won if Johnny May had stayed on till the end.' If I missed my medal that year I had some consolation in knowing that a good friend and true sportsman had gained at my expense... I asked him if I might hold the Cup which, for a brief moment, I did."

It was the last chance Steve got; when Derby next reached the Final, in 1903, Bloomer was cruelly injured in a tackle by Peter McWilliam at Newcastle only eight days before the big event. Although he desperately wanted a medal, he tried out his ankle before the match and ruled himself out. Goalkeeper Jack Fryer, too, was extremely doubtful with a groin injury but insisted on playing. That was to be crucial in a game which still stands as the record FA Cup Final margin.

1903, Derby County 0 Bury 6 Again Derby were confident, in some cases too much so. Archie was at it again, this time the day before the game inviting some pressmen to 'come down and drink some champagne out of the cup with us tomorrow'. But it all went flat. Fryer broke down early on and both Methven and Morris had to fill in between the posts; Derby were simply overrun. Perhaps it was the colour clash that brought them bad luck...they played in red shirts that day.

The national press called it a farce and seemed to take some delight in Derby's embarrassing flop. Archie Goodall might have taken more care to think before opening his mouth to their scribes that the *Athletic News* was a Lancashire-biased newspaper; no wonder they set the office rhymster to work:

"Flip flip flippety flop, Derby's gone down and Bury's on top, Never t'would seem, Came such a gay team, Flippety, Flippety, Flop."

"Squeak, squeak, squickety squeak, Poor old Peak County (they're spelling it 'pique'), Their gloom can't be 'loomer', (Where were you, O Bloomer?), Squeak, squeak, squickety squeak."

Bloomer was later to say: "I have tasted deep of the bitters of defeat and the sadness of those tragic Finals took a long, long time to wear away. Derby is surely the most unlucky Cup fighting club in the country." We know the feeling, Steve, rest assured.

The press made much of Bloomer's failure to win an FA Cup medal, as they were later to do with Stanley Matthews before he eventually secured one, but in fact Steve always said he would have preferred a League championship honour, it being 'more indicative of true consistency and invariably won by the best team, unlike the Cup'.

Strangely enough, as trivia buffs are undoubtedly aware, Bloomer did win an 'English Cup' medal – but for baseball. He had played the game for Ley's in his teens ever since his first 'boss' introduced it to Derby and developed the game nationwide. Closely identifying themselves with Derby County, the Ley's team won the inaugural 'championship' in 1890 although Aston Villa lay a spurious claim to it. The English Cup came to Derby in 1895, 1897 and 1898 with victories over Fullers, Middlesbrough and Nottingham Forest, Bloomer being a key man playing at first or second base in each of those triumphs. Derby footballer Jack Robinson and Forest's Denny Alsopp also regularly donned Derby's smart American-style attire. For Steve it was an enjoyable summer diversion at which he happened to excel and he was described by an American aficionado, the comedian R. G. Knowles, as 'the best second baseman in England'. The story of Derby baseball, never fully related, is a fascinating one of triumph, skulduggery, intrigue and not a little humour. Most of the other Derby footballers wielded the bat for the club's own team from time to time and perchance the long-forgotten tale will be told another day. Cricket medals, too, fell into Bloomer's hands with relative ease, winning the Derby and District championship with Ley's in 1898 and playing with them for many seasons. By way of good measure he also took the prize for fastest man in the club at an athletics meeting in 1897 – in the 100 yard handicap Final he gave away up to four yards to some of his team-mates but romped home first in 11.5 seconds. Certainly he was an all-rounder… one has to wonder when Sarah ever caught up with him.

Despite not winning top football honours in Derby, Bloomer's legendary status at the club was secure and recognised by a testimonial. Seemingly somewhat unfairly, though, and almost certainly indicative of the club's mounting financial crisis rather than meanness or lack of appreciation, he had to share those fruits with another player. He and Ben Warren took around £100 each from the game against Everton on 9 December 1905, splitting the gate money between them. That was later boosted to a total of around £400 for Steve when a national subscription benefit was organised for him by the FA to mark his record-breaking 21st cap for England in April 1905, the first time a national tribute gesture had ever been sanctioned for any player. The organising committee included many of the real 'high-ups' in football administration and even Steve's amateur all-round counterpart C. B. Fry, known to be rather snootily disdainful towards the 'pros' and the 'prols' from time to time, threw in his lot. This said much about Bloomer's reputation, and of the many hundreds of words written by the press at the time, the following say as much as any:

"The representative character of the executive committee alone proves the estimation in which Bloomer is held both as a man and a player."

That was where Steve Bloomer stood as season 1905-06 started, and despite there being so many other tales of goals, games and incidents, it seems an appropriate point from which to move on. Bloomer, too, was to move on that season, as clubs continued to badger Derby County for his services. His parting would leave Derby supporters and Steve somewhat stunned, but in 14 seasons since his Derby debut 'Paleface' had become an irresistible target for the headhunters. Before following him to his new club, this is a timely juncture at which to assess just how hot a property he really was as allegedly the country's best inside-forward, England's leading international and football's first real 'superstar'.

FOR KING AND COUNTRY

"Bloomer is picked, and we shall watch some more,
His carving swoop adown the field,
Amid old enemies, who yield
Room for his fleeting passage, to the roar
Of multitudes enraptured, who acclaim
Their country's hero bearing down on goal,
Instant of foot, deliberate of soul…
All's well with England; 'Steve' is on his game."
Adapted from a poem by Alfred Ollivant

TWENTY-EIGHT goals for England in 23 games; it is that oft-quoted official record which was hugely instrumental in transforming Steve Bloomer's footballing reputation from local star to national hero. No matter what he achieved with Derby County or later Middlesbrough, it was his legendary performances for England which truly brought him national status. And the fact that so many of his better performances were reserved for Scotland was surely the icing on the cake, earning him lasting acclaim as the scourge of the old enemy and the nickname 'Hammer of the Scots'. He made his debut in 1895 and played his last England game in 1907. Six years later a stirring piece in the *Players' Union Magazine* summed up Bloomer's 12-year reign in simple but emotive terms: "He is the greatest inside-forward who has ever played for England and his name has for years been a household word wherever football has been played. Long into the future, in the winter evenings when icy blasts shriek through the streets, men will gather round the glowing fireside and recall the deeds of the great warriors of the game's past. One sharpshooter's name will always crop up and men will see again the deft pass, the quick dash and the catapult shot driving the ball home to the frenzied roar of the crowd… they will always talk of the 'Incomparable Steve'."

International days
Only 23 appearances for England? That is the question which all knowledgeable football lovers ought to be musing over now, despite the mistily reminiscent tone of that tribute. Billy Wright won a magnificent 105 caps following his 1946 debut and goalkeeper Peter Shilton later topped that with 125…so surely a measly total of 23 is nothing to get too excited about? The truth is, though, in the context of the era in which Bloomer played, his record was an unprecedented achievement and his goal ratio of 1.2 per game speaks for itself.

To fully understand the appearance record in its correct context it is necessary to appreciate the nature of the international set-up in the late 19th and early 20th centuries. Quite simply England played far fewer games during the period in which Steve turned out than we have become used to in more recent years. The World Cup and European championships, which now account directly or indirectly for so many of England's fixtures, held their first finals in 1930 and 1960 respectively; in the Bloomer era it was the Home International championship, now defunct since 1984, which was the annual ritual and centrepiece of the international calendar for England, Scotland, Wales and Ireland.

Although the first-ever 'international' match was played between England and Scotland on 19 November 1870 at the Kennington Oval in London, it has always been regarded in the record books as an unofficial affair because the Scottish side comprised only Scottish players resident in England and therefore deprived Scotland of their true strength in depth. For the record, unofficial though it may be, England won 1-0. Two further informal games were played, in November 1871 and February 1872, but it is the game played on 30 November 1872 at the West of Scotland Cricket Club, Partick, near Glasgow, which truly set the international ball rolling, a year and a half before Bloomer's birth, and troubled the official statisticians for the first time. A contemporary sketch of the game survives, showing what a quaint affair it was, long breeches and an unusual range of headgear being the order of the day. Nor were both sides' formations yet regarded as the norm; Scotland were somewhat advanced in the tactical department, playing a goalkeeper, two backs, three half-backs and five forwards, while England still played the antiquated eight forwards, one half-back and one back in front of the goalkeeper. Most of the players were from the upper strata of the social order and played out a rather gentle 0-0 draw from all accounts. Perhaps the only recognisable element from a modern point of view was the fact that England wore white shirts and Scotland blue, a tradition that, despite interim variations, has continued to this day. The contemporary journal *Bell's Life* summed up the game thus:

"Two o'clock in the afternoon had been fixed as the time for commencing play and both elevens were ready punctually to the hour, though a start was not made until about twenty minutes after two. There was a very large muster of spectators and the throng increased vastly as the game progressed. The weather was fine, as the faint attempt at a drizzle that appeared just before the outset had a praiseworthy regard for the rights of an international struggle, being only of momentary duration. The kick-off by the English gave the signal for warm work and finally the call of time arrived without the achievement of a goal by either side. Thus ended one of the jolliest, most spirited and most pleasant matches that have ever been played according to Association Rules and each member of the two sides was greeted by a volley of applause as he entered the pavilion."

While this sounds far removed from many of the later fierce battles, not least because both sides and the goalposts were kept fully intact and the crowd predominantly sober, it was an important occasion in the history of the game at national level. The 'large muster' of spectators was only 4,000 or so, but they had witnessed an officially recognised game described in the press as 'an international' and it was this that provided the humble platform from which the larger stage became set ready for one Stephen Bloomer to take on his leading role. As young Stephen entered the world in 1874, further fixtures were already being played and Wales and Ireland (not split until 1921) later entered the fray, playing England for the first time ever in 1879 and 1882 respectively. In season 1883-84 the fixtures between the home countries were sufficiently organised for the Home International championship to be officially inaugurated, and in 1885 James Forrest of Blackburn Rovers set the future trend by becoming the first recognised professional to play for England.

A year later, at a Football Association committee meeting held on 30 January 1886, a proposal to award English players 'international caps' was carried and by the time the Football League was formed in 1888 there were sufficient numbers of competent professionals coming through the ranks for the English teams to be an increasingly interesting amalgam of amateurs and professionals from both extremes of the social spectrum. So by the time Bloomer made his League debut for Derby County on 3 September 1892, all the essential elements of the structure under which he was to win his 23 caps were in place.

Because regular games against foreign opposition did not begin until late in Steve's career, and in many cases long after his retirement, the normal fixture list during the time he was available to be selected was a basic three international games per season and in this context the number of caps he won was an admirable total indeed. He made his international debut on 9 March 1895 against Ireland on his home territory at the County Ground, Derby, in only his third season in League football. For a 21-year-old lad from a non-privileged background to have sufficiently impressed the somewhat crusty FA selection committee to get his name on the England teamsheet is testimony to the obvious impact that his League form had on those of influence in the game. Thus began, late in Queen Victoria's reign, the national service which Steve was later to refer to with obvious pride as 'For King and Country'. There are many recent written studies of all the games in which Bloomer played but also sufficient reminiscences from Steve himself, and his contemporaries, to offer us the following on-the-spot account of his international career.

Season 1894-95 – debuts and goals

"Three years after becoming connected with the Derby County club, or to be exact on 9 March 1895, I took part in my first international match, and there is no doubt that the memory of this great event will last with me until the day of my death. It was against Ireland, the first of many I played against the 'Sons of Erin' and it was a great day for me. I was fortunate in two respects…first that the game was contested at Derby before a friendly crowd and second that the man to whom I owed most in my football career, John Goodall, was also one of the team. He more than anybody else was responsible for my ultimate success on the football field and, although I was always extremely keen to make headway, I often wonder if my ambition to possess an international cap would have been realised but for the tuition and assistance that I received from this truly wonderful player, who was probably the finest captain I ever played under.

"In that debut international, with Billy Bassett of West Bromwich as my outside partner and Goodall as centre, I felt fairly comfortable but, all the same, the ordeal was a most trying one. I am sure I was extremely nervous, as must be any player the first time he appears for his country. It has often been said that I was 'cool as a cucumber' in my playing days but that was just the way I appeared. I always tried to treat victory and defeat in the same way but in truth I seldom entered the field for big games without a fluttering somewhere inside me and if things went badly my 'sang-froid' turned to anxiety. As I look back on this game against Ireland I know I failed to do myself justice. I shall never forget my feelings as, just before the game, rain started to fall…I wanted to do so much and I knew that a slippery ball would be my undoing. That rain continued until half-time but we won 9-0."

This rather modest personal account of his debut perhaps underlines one of the most significant factors concerning this game, fully known to Bloomer and all other observers, that is that the Irish side were, as described by the *Derby Daily Telegraph*, 'woefully weak'. Nevertheless both Bloomer and Goodall scored two goals each and the importance of the game for Bloomer was that he had been given a chance on the international stage and had, as far as general observers were concerned, passed the test. Reporters described his right-flank partnership with Bassett as 'a beautiful thing to behold' and some years later Bassett himself recalled how frustrated the Irish defenders became: "At one point, having lost out yet again to Steve, I heard the Irish left-half remark: 'Oh well, let him have it,' and he walked off the pitch and stood outside the touchline for a minute. He soon resumed but just for an instant he was in a most abject state of despair."

It seems likely that Steve's selection for the game on his home ground was partly down to the desire of the committee to boost an anticipated meagre crowd, which in the event reached 10,000, and it is said that local influence in the shape of Goodall and Derby-based referee Arthur Kingscott, later a leading administrator, was brought to bear on the selection committee. No matter how it arose, it was evidently a proud moment for the 'Black Country Boy' to have risen to such heights and Steve later related the importance of the occasion as far as another member of his family was concerned:

"The game against Ireland at Derby was the very first game in which my father ever saw me play football. He was always prejudiced against the game in my early youth. However, I managed to persuade him to come and see this match and he was so delighted with it that he became an ardent follower of my and Derby County's fortunes."

That Caleb should have become a convert only at the age of 46 might appear strange but it illustrates that, for his generation, football had no sense of tradition behind it. He was never taken to games by his own father, Edward, in the 1850s simply because the organised game didn't exist at that time. He certainly wasn't the only Bloomer admirer that day; although Steve didn't play in the 1-1 draw with Wales at Queen's Club on 18 March, he had done enough to be selected for the showcase game against Scotland just a few weeks later, the traditional climax to the season, played, incidentally, on the same day as Derby's goalless draw at home to Blackburn. No fixture blank-outs in those days!

"I recall the first time I played against Scotland. It was 6 April 1895 at Goodison Park, Liverpool. Again Johnny Goodall came into things as it was a toss up between Johnny and myself for the inside-right position. He urged the selectors to give me the chance and they acted on that advice which I venture few people would have given in similar circumstances. In the event Goodall played centre-forward and I have vivid recollections of the manner in which Billy Bassett and I made life a misery for little Neil Gibson of Glasgow Rangers. The match was totally different from that with Ireland. Played before a crowd of some 30,000 people, there was more excitement and the shouts of the onlookers were quite uproarious as each clever movement was made.

"I scored a brace of goals and we won 3-0 but again I felt I didn't do myself full justice. Having said that, I was still feeling pretty pleased with myself as I walked off the field as I knew I had played an effective part in the championship decider and I was rather proud of the fact. But I have always remembered one incident which occurred that day far better than the game I played. In the dressing-room after the match my good friend Johnny Goodall shook hands with me and congratulated me on playing so well. 'But Steve,' he added, shaking his head wisely, 'don't let this get any bigger.' And he tapped my head! It was an excellent piece of advice from an old and experienced player to an almost raw recruit and I believe I took that advice to heart."

The official records, by the way, only credit Bloomer with one goal; the other that he 'claimed' was always put down as an own-goal by the harassed Gibson. Steve, like all members of the 'Strikers' Union', seems on occasions to have picked up more pieces than he was thought to be entitled to. Whether he really did get that vital final touch, only the man himself truly knows. Nonetheless, suitably chastised over his expanding cap-size by a wise old campaigner, and with his first Home International championship under his belt, Steve had apparently arrived in the England team to stay. That is not to say that his place in the side was always an automatic one as the selection committee needed to be reminded each season of any player's continuing ability. President of the Football League, J. J. Bentley, explained the procedure:

"In 1889 seven members of the FA Council were appointed 'as a sub-committee to select the international team', representing various districts so as to pretty well map out the whole country. Up to December each season not much notice need be taken of the players but, from that time forward, the selector worth his place will rarely miss a match somewhere or other and occasionally the whole of the committee arrange to visit one particular game, having special seats reserved. Views are exchanged and at the end of the game we generally have an idea as to which men have a chance of a cap. I know at least one club that used to be simply delighted when informed of the committee's visit, as one of their players always seemed to score more goals than usual. This was S. Bloomer of Derby County. One season, in January 1899 I believe, he had been quite out of it for a while, at least for a Bloomer, when we visited Derby. Their unfortunate opponents were Sheffield Wednesday, who were beaten 9-0 and Bloomer scored six. So after seeing as many players as possible to arrive at a general sort of idea, we fix up a trial match and the final selection is made."

It is this story which is generally responsible for the sometime related tale that 'Bloomer only tried when he wanted to and saved himself up for big games'. While it is true he often did do well in big games, a reasoned perusal of match reports and scoring records suggests that the 'not always trying' tag is an inaccurate one.

Once past the judgmental eyes of the all-powerful council of seven, an English international would find himself the subject of quite a strict regime but seemed on the whole to be treated rather well. J. J. Bentley again fills in the detail:

"When we play in England the players generally put in an appearance at lunch, never an elaborate one, just roast mutton and dry toast as a rule. Vegetables are barred and now very seldom asked for. There is no smoking after lunch, except possibly a small cigarette, then we get down to the ground and the trainer takes them in charge. After the game we come back to the hotel, the players make out their expenses and have the size of their craniums taken for caps before we depart homewards. If the match is in Scotland or Ireland, elaborate travelling arrangements are made. For Glasgow we all meet at a convenient station such as Hellifield (Midland Railway) or Preston (London and North Western Railway) and board a specially reserved first-class dining car where we enjoy a substantial dinner immediately on leaving. We always put up at a first-class hotel in Glasgow, having tea on arrival and then visiting a place of amusement. The interviewer always needs a lot of dodging before the game but all the same the 'interview' will appear; after the match we enjoy a good dinner then board the train, have a spot of supper, and get to our homes late and as best we can. For the Irish match the sea passage is taken on the Thursday to allow the time for ill-effects to wear off, for most good footballers are the worst sailors I've ever seen."

The players didn't have to content themselves simply with being well fed… during Steve's early England days they received an appearance fee of £1 per game, roughly a quarter of their entire weekly wage. This rose to £2, then £3 during Bloomer's time but only hit the dizzy heights of £4 in 1907, after Steve had played his last international game. With the material rewards came the wide acclaim of the watching world and all the atmosphere of 'celebrity' which gathered apace as the games took on increasing importance in the eyes of an ever-more football-mad public.

For Steve and any of his fellow professionals from similarly humble backgrounds such star treatment was certainly not what they would have been used to either at home or at their clubs and such was the rather dubious reputation of 'professionals' that in 1899, before the Scotland game, the English team's Birmingham hotel sought written assurances from the FA that no damage would be caused and fellow guests would not be disturbed…and this despite the fact that the England team contained the genteel likes of G. O. Smith and other amateurs of the reliable public school brigade, at a time when gentlemen knew how to behave like gentlemen.

This mixed social nature of the England set up no doubt made for some interesting inter-personal relationships, but we should note that the 'distinctions' between amateurs and professionals which prevailed in cricket right into the second half of the 20th century, were not nearly so marked in football. Separate changing rooms and travel arrangements were the order of the day for the summer game's practitioners and for a professional to refer to an amateur by any means of address other than 'Mr' was thought to be the height of disrespect. A contemporary football journal, in contrast, assured its readers that 'there is no distinction in the matter of rooms or travel' and further anecdotal evidence suggests that the matter of names was not regarded so crucially. Despite this there is some evidence that certain of the 'pros' did adhere to a degree of deference and Bloomer himself confirmed that amateurs such as Charles Wreford-Brown were reluctant to mix and not averse to bagging private dressing-rooms if there were any to be had.

Surely, though, the reason cricket and football should have developed differing degrees of apartheid in their ranks has everything to do with the nature of the games and the inherent character of the men who play them. Cricket, although a team game by name, largely comprises a series of individual and isolated performances from certain key team members…there is genuine room for the man who places himself on a pedestal in cricket, where one can perform miracles at the crease without the slightest assistance from any other team member. In contrast, teamwork is such a part of football that it seems to demand a level of democratic kinship quite different to that required in cricket. In any case it's difficult to remain aloof when you're covered in mud and getting kicked. All the evidence suggests that Bloomer nestled into this potentially unnerving set-up quite comfortably.

Without resorting to a complete match-by-match analysis, the following post-retirement reminiscences of that era present the flavour of the international scene in which Steve forged such a high reputation.

'Hammer of the Scots'

"Although those first two internationals I played will always stand out before me as the most trying in all my experience, as the years went on I played in many other battles so that such games became fairly common and held few terrors for me. The real red-letter day of the football season is when England and Scotland meet because the two finest teams which the two greatest football playing countries can place in the field are pitted against each other. After my

1895 baptism against the Scots at Goodison I missed the 1896 defeat in Glasgow but played at the Crystal Palace in 1897 when we again lost 2-1, although I had the satisfaction of scoring our goal. Scotland won the championship in both those years but we regained it in 1898 and well I remember the final game. Whenever I see my old friend and captain Wreford-Brown, the memories come surging back because he was captaining England for the first time that day.

"It was at Celtic Park, Glasgow, on 2 April 1898. The match was sheer science, football craft and skill at its very highest, and I believe the greatest international I have ever played in. I will always remember the game for one particular incident and, at the risk of shocking some of the highbrows, I can reveal one of football's inner secrets, a story I believe has never been told before. Wreford-Brown was keyed up to a big victory and told us he would be the proudest man alive that night if we won, but we had no inkling of what he had in store for the game. I ought to explain here that he wore good old-fashioned knickers which had side pockets in them and when Freddy Wheldon of Aston Villa put us a goal up, our captain fairly jumped with joy, dipped into his pocket and slipped a golden sovereign into Wheldon's hand. Freddy promptly asked the referee to look after it for him and it was not long after that I myself put England two up; sure enough Wreford-Brown slipped one of the gilt 'uns into my hand which I too handed to referee Tom Robinson for safe keeping. Ten minutes after the interval the Scottish defence stood appealing for offside when G. O. Smith slipped me a peach of a pass which I went on and crashed home. I was not offside by a long chalk and sure enough another sovereign came out of those mysterious pockets of our skipper.

"I remember Robinson saying to me: 'If you keep this up Steve, I shall have to go for my handbag!' We won the game 3-1, and the championship, and I might add I still have those two tokens of that great game, and nothing would make me part with them or break into them. After the match I have never seen a player so delighted as Wreford-Brown and before we had our baths we were invited to his rooms where he cracked champagne to celebrate the great victory."

Memorable equaliser

"Talking of G. O. Smith reminds me of the game against Scotland at the Crystal Palace in 1901. We were keen to win because, although we had taken the championship again in 1899 we lost it to Scotland in 1900 when I scored the goal in a 4-1 defeat at Glasgow. Probably no match gave me more personal joy than the 1901 game, even though England could only draw. It was 30 March and that afternoon was the Boat Race, which deeply excited 'G. O.' being an Oxford University man. Just as he was leading us on the field, a telegram boy handed him the familiar envelope and 'G. O.' put his hand up to us and said: 'Just a minute lads.' He opened it and with his face wreathed in smiles turned to us and remarked: 'Come on boys, Oxford has won; let's show Scotland how to row a winning oar at football.'

"Well, we tried our best to fill his cup of joy by winning, but Scotland were just as keen and in the end we had to cry quits. It ended two goals each and was the only international in which I ever felt tired and weary at the finish. The ground was ankle deep in mud and slush and the going was really terrible but many well-known followers of the game declare I scored the greatest goal of my career that day…and I believe they are correct, too. I received the ball just in my own half and dribbled right through, finishing with a shot which it was such an effort to make that I flopped down practically exhausted… it was the equaliser and it gave us the championship that year. That was the last game G. O. Smith played for England and I should say that he was worshipped by every professional player in those days. He was the finest type of amateur, one who would always shake hands with us professionals in a manner which said plainly that he was pleased to meet them. In those far off days professional footballers were looked upon with something bordering on contempt and many amateurs would not mix with us. But 'G. O.' was a true sportsman and brilliant centre-forward and he was beloved for it."

Triumph and tragedy

"The following year, 1902, I reached the height of my ambition when I was elected captain of the English side. And how can I ever forget that day when it was the occasion of the most appalling disaster so far known in the annals of the game? It is known to this day as 'The Ibrox Disaster' and what a catastrophic tragedy it was. One minute the game was proceeding calmly and being keenly followed by the vast concourse; the next moment there was a terrible crash like the many peals of thunder in a great storm joining together in unison. The players stood as though rooted to the spot and there before our eyes we saw part of a huge stand, packed with people, crashing to the ground. The memory of that awful picture is still with me, with people crashing through iron railings as if they were so much matchwood. The groans, cries of fear and the uproar which followed beggars description.

"Of course, the game was stopped while the killed and wounded were removed and attended to. The officials assembled inside our dressing-room and, though some asked for the game to be abandoned, the Football Association chairman Mr J. C. Clegg was firm in his advocacy that the game should be finished as most of the crowd did not realise the enormity of the disaster and he feared a panic if they were told. After a time we got on the field again but to do so we had to pass long rows of dead and terribly injured. I remember one of the reports of the game said: 'Bloomer captained the England team but was overweighted with responsibility, seeming inconsistent and irritable.' Well I'll tell you, it was the hardest moment of my life to continue playing after threading my way through those rows of dead and dying… maybe that's why I was inconsistent and irritable. I believe 26 people were killed and hundreds injured… and it was due to some unsound Russian timber on the wooden terrace being unable to withstand the strain… when it collapsed people just fell through the gaping hole. The game didn't count in the records and we later played a 2-2 draw at Birmingham and the Scots won the championship. With all my international successes it seems remarkable that such a disaster should have occurred on the one and only day I captained England against Scotland."

Memorable farewell

"Let me pass to pleasanter memories. I played against 'the old enemy' three more times after that without being on the losing side. I scored the winning goal in 1904 but saved what some describe as my greatest for my farewell international at Newcastle in 1907, when I was with Middlesbrough. I drove the ball home like a rocket from 25 yards and Colin Veitch of Newcastle, who gave me the pass, nearly hugged me to death. That goal is still talked about and the Scottish goalkeeper Peter McBride said to me: 'I had no more chance of catching that shot than a snowball in Hades.' Then our goalkeeper Sam Hardy chipped in: 'Aye, it wanted me alongside you Peter, then the two of us could have looked silly.' The game finished 1-1 so it wasn't a bad way to finish, even though Wales won the championship for the first time ever. All in all I played against Scotland ten times, scored nine goals and only finished on the losing side twice and nowadays the great international day can never come round without me thinking of those games against the men from across the border."

Despite the official records crediting Bloomer with a mere eight goals there is no doubt his performances against Scotland struck a chord in the nation's psyche, gave Steve a lot of personal satisfaction and were very instrumental in securing his status as a sporting icon of the age.

Wales…four, five or six?

Bloomer played against Wales on seven occasions between 1896 and 1907, scoring 12 goals and, despite a number of draws, never finishing on the losing side. Although the Welsh were certainly not a strong team during that period, they had a number of legendary players with sufficient ability to make life difficult for England on the right occasion. Foremost among these was right winger Billy Meredith and not far behind was Steve's Derby County team-mate, left-back Charlie Morris. Although the presence of such quality players ensured some good battles, there were also occasions when matters were all too easy for the English and it was in one such game, his first against the Welsh, that Bloomer made his lasting mark.

On 16 March 1896 at Cardiff, England romped to a 9-1 victory and Bloomer set a scoring record. There is some doubt over the extent of this, though; the official statistics credit Bloomer with five, giving him an equal share of the individual match scoring record set by Aston Villa's Vaughton in the 1880s, but some reports reduced his tally to four. Steve himself, writing in the *Derbyshire Football Express* in the 1920s, sought to put the record straight in a manner which was becoming by no means unfamiliar to his loyal readers. His elementary education had given him a reasonable head for figures and it seems that when adding up his international tally... 1-0-1-1-0-0-1 etc., Steve employed an advanced form of binary counting known only to the select few who scored goals for a living:

"I will always remember that game at Cardiff in 1896, for that day I set an England goalscoring record...I scored six!"

There is no suggestion that there was a deliberate attempt to mislead here, merely that it's not only fishermen whose memories can be enhanced by the euphoria of the occasion. Having said that, newspaper reports could be extremely unreliable and perhaps it was 'six of the best' that day. Interestingly enough, Billy Meredith, also writing in the 1920s, lent some weight to the theory, although studies of his own personally written goalscoring records have shown that he really was the master of enhancement. If he crossed for the centre-forward to bang home, Meredith thought nothing of notching it down to himself! Or maybe he was simply re-quoting Bloomer's own account? At any rate this is what he had to say:

"The first time I ever met Steve was in my second international match and never am I likely to forget the occasion. It was at Cardiff on 16 March 1896 and that day we lost 9-1 and Bloomer helped himself to no less than six goals, a record which still stands supreme in the records of international games. It was a wonderful triumph for the pale-looking Derby County player, who was only just 22 years of age. I verily believe that if the game had gone on for another 15 minutes Steve would have run his total into double figures. His one idea was goals and he always went after results and got them... and, because goals count for more than anything, when considering the respective merits of all the international inside-forwards, I would always give the palm to my old friend Steve."

Bloomer was never able to repeat this scoring feat in international games, although he again came close against the Welsh with a meagre four at Newcastle in 1901. Whether his 1896 haul was four, five or six, the Welsh certainly had every reason to remember Bloomer.

Irish adventures
Although he only played six times against the Irish, the limited opposition they offered presented the opportunity for Steve to add another eight goals to his total. With scorelines such as 13-2 at Sunderland in 1899 it's surprising it wasn't more. He managed only two in that game and committed an offence which he always insisted no professional should ever be guilty of, missing a penalty to deny himself a hat-trick. Although the pickings against Ireland were far too easy to be ranked alongside the Scotland performances, in terms of 'amusement' value Steve always reckoned the trips across the Irish Sea were well worth making:

"The records will show that I played in the land of the Shamrock on 21 occasions, club games, inter-league games and internationals all in, and I have nothing but the very kindest spirit towards the Irish even if some strange things happened there. Some of my happiest experiences were spent in the troubled island and some of my worst were spent in getting there. Have you ever crossed the Irish Channel? Of all the seas the stormy, turbulent Irish Sea is the wickedest of all; Billy Bassett was so ill on the 1896 trip that he would never have played on the Saturday if we'd had a reserve forward…as it was, all his strength was gone due to the sickness and after 20 minutes of the game he asked me not to pass it to him as he could hardly stand up let alone do anything useful. That same trip I shared a cabin with Billy Williams, the West Bromwich back, Jimmy Crabtree of the Villa and my Derby County team-mate George Kinsey…I remember clinging on to whatever we could and Billy being tossed clean off the upper bunk as the ship went into a dive. I honestly thought she was going to the bottom… how we escaped uninjured still remains a mystery to me.

"As for the games themselves, the 1904 game at the Cliftonville ground in Belfast was unforgettable. We had a strong team that day and it was something more than a sensation when the Irish Bhoys took the lead quite early on. Coming down the field for the restart I noticed two spectators jump over the rails and a few seconds later I nearly jumped out of the ground altogether when bang, bang, bang went revolver shots from behind me. There were the two excited spectators firing shots into the air, a revolver in each hand and a merry dance on either leg. I thought it best to get away a bit and did so until two burly policemen persuaded them to return to their places among the crowd. It was soon over and we went on to win 3-1, being cheered and praised all through and there were no signs of rough play. So what happened afterwards was a complete surprise…we had a four-in-hand and brake waiting to take us back to our hotel and there was a small crowd of youngsters waiting to see us off. When we clambered in a perfect storm of grass sods, bottles and stones was rained in on us and there we were, officials and players, ducking and diving out of the line of fire. It was a pretty hot fusillade while it lasted but the driver, encouraged by our yells, put on speed and soon left the laughing crowd behind. Fortunately only Alec Leake of Villa was injured, getting a nasty deep cut at the back of his head. I always like to think that it was just a little Irish exuberance but it wasn't the sort of send-off we appreciated at the time.

"Another reception we got was during the Boer War when we stayed at the Central Hotel in Belfast. We were invited to the Empire Music Hall the night before the game and, of course, attracted a good deal of attention. Everything in the garden was lovely until photographs of English and Boer Generals came on screen. That did it. All the British were booed and the Boers cheered as only the Irish know how. Then down came a lot of Irish 'confetti' from the 'gods' and a very high English official stopped an orange on his bald head, which was the signal for us to depart. Ever since then the England party has never stayed at the Central, they go to the Slieve Donard at Newcastle, County Down, a beautiful place overlooking a glorious golf course where peace and quiet may be sought and found.

"Having said all this, you might not believe it when I say that in general I have always found the Irish to be the most hospitable people I have ever come across and I have had some truly happy times there."

These sort of accounts, related in their rather quaint manner, not only give a good evocation of the atmosphere the Home International championship was able to generate but confirm again that incidents of crowd misbehaviour are by no means a new phenomenon in football – imagine being let back into the crowd now after firing off a few shots?

What about Woodward?

Steve's goalscoring and appearance records were inevitably beaten in the course of time. Blackburn full-back Bob Crompton took the England appearance record with 41 caps between 1896 and 1920, while Nat Lofthouse eventually topped Bloomer's 28 goals, but only in 1956. It is this last statement which some football historians might wish to challenge, although they seldom do. Vivian Woodward of Spurs and Chelsea, an unpaid amateur in the true spirit, made his England debut in 1903 and, like Bloomer, went on to play 23 times. While Bloomer scored 28, Woodward netted 29 – yet this 'record' has never been ratified. The reason lies in the fact that Woodward played three games against Austria, three against Hungary and one against Bohemia in the Continental tours of 1908 and 1909, when three of the games were played in the space of only four days.

Against terribly weak opposition the aggregate score in the seven games was England 48 Europe 7 and Woodward bagged 15. Although every goal has to be netted, the 'value' of these has always been discounted in the official England scoring records as the games have been regarded as 'unofficial'. This seems rather unfair on Woodward, who was an extremely talented player but, had Bloomer also played in these games, who knows what his own final tally might have been? As it was, Bloomer missed out, playing only once in recognised games against continental opposition, that against Germany in 1901 in a game when he is believed to have been captain and in which none of the goals were credited to the official records.

So it is that 28 in 23 is so often quoted in the history books as Bloomer's claim to fame. He was certainly the leading 'professional' scorer, at any rate. In truth it matters not either way. Both Bloomer and Woodward knew where the goals were and when Steve was 'retired' from the international scene there were many who felt he was left out too early. As it was the line remained drawn at 1907, although he nearly made a remarkable comeback against the Irish at Derby in February 1911, losing out in the selection ballot 6-5 to Swindon's Harold Fleming. By way of compensation he pulled on an 'England' shirt for the last time just a few weeks later, on 4 March 1911. It was in his old stamping ground, Glasgow, against the Scottish League for the English League, the 15th time he had been selected for the representative side.

Thus the curtain fell on Bloomer's eventful England career. His deeds while wearing the national side's shirt were so well known that the press would thereafter refer to him on many occasions simply as 'the Famous International'. But no more would the typesetters of the Glasgow papers grit their teeth as yet again they set the name (Bloomer) in the customary brackets. No doubt the Scots were glad to see the back of him.

BUT COULD THE LAD PLAY?

"If I could paint you, friend, as you stand there,
Aloof attacking force, lazy-eyed but yet aware,
Watching the tortured bladder slide and glide,
Pale of face and swiftly stirring as you spied
Your chance at goal
And promised victory for your side,
If I could catch you in that one brief moment as you score,
My sketch would have what Art can never give...and more,
Sinew, breath, body and joy; it would surely live."
Adapted from a sonnet by Edward Cracroft Lefroy

"THERE is only one Bloomer and his methods are his own; his style is unique. To watch him on the field in repose one could hardly imagine or guess at the gifts and graces of this man, but to see him in action is to see a figure full of fire and the brimming vitality that stamps personality on every action. He does nothing like anyone else; that dash for the goal-line is a Bloomer dash; that single-handed dribble a Bloomer dribble; that fierce rattling shot is a Bloomer shot; that superb forward pass is a Bloomer pass; that glorious bid for victory in the eleventh hour is the consummation of Bloomer's art. He has made himself the power he is and has been by reason of an irrepressible audacity, an irresistible desire to conquer, which intense vitality often brings with it; this triumph of the strong will, those ruling passions, have made Bloomer so great a footballer."

Golden goals or easy pickings?

On reading a tribute as stirring as that, it's all one can do to stifle the involuntary cry: "Steve for Prime Minister!" Such a splendidly readable description is everything which might be expected from Alfred Gibson and William Pickford in their beautifully produced four-volume survey of the game, *Association Football And The Men Who Made It* (1906). They go on to give a much longer and thoroughly entertaining eye-witness description of Steve's style, personality and abilities, a piece of eloquent prose which forms the basis for most of the more recent assessments of Bloomer by those who never had the pleasure of meeting him or seeing him play. Such pieces invariably conclude that he was the best inside-forward of his era and possibly of all time. There's nothing wrong with that at all – it's decent research in the absence of first-hand experience – but Gibson and Pickford were renowned for their 'enthusiasm' in describing many other players of the era, so it's tempting to try to strip away their glossy journalistic veneer to see if that glowing summation of the Bloomer art really did hold good.

There is no intention here to muddy the waters, merely a wish to seek wider evidence to support or deny Bloomer's ranking as the case may be. Surely a strong starting point would simply be to state his magnificent scoring record: 394 League and FA Cup goals in 655 games for Derby and Middlesbrough gives him an average of one goal for every 150 minutes of playing time. Knowing how difficult the act of scoring can be, and being aware of the prolonged barren spells that even prolific modern players like Alan Shearer or Michael Owen can suffer, that doesn't sound at all a bad testimony. In fact, Steve's League goals record of 352, set in 1914, wasn't beaten until Everton's William Ralph Dean knocked in his 353rd in the 1936-37 season, and 'Dixie' was a centre-forward, not an inside-right. And Bloomer's 28 in only 23 games for England was an astonishing strike rate, a haul which wasn't bettered in full internationals until the great Nat Lofthouse surpassed it in 1956.

Adding in all the goals Steve scored in friendlies and League representative games in his 22-year career, not to mention those he plundered in reserve outings early and late in his playing days, it's likely he found the net well over 600 times in 'competitive' combat. Surely there the case must rest?

It is not unreasonable to draw that conclusion but there are those in the football world who raise an eyebrow of doubt, stating the different time and prevailing conditions that Steve played in as a highly influential factor and concluding that 'he couldn't have done it nowadays'. Their general premise is that goals were simply easier to come by in the Bloomer era...is that true?

To answer that fundamental question we need to appreciate the tactical systems under which Steve played his football. By the time he turned professional in 1892, the strategic side of the game had evolved and settled into something of a regular pattern. Prior to that, in the very early days, scarce surviving field placement records show nine forwards and two 'behinds' and by 1865 that 'rushing' formation had given way to a goalkeeper, a goal cover, one back and 'only' eight forwards! All the accent was on dribbling the ball forward, probably quite reminiscent of the sort of game which very young schoolboys tend towards when left unsupervised. By 1870 the typical line-up was reduced to seven forwards playing in front of two half-backs, a full-back and a goalkeeper, a discernible move towards a more defensive approach. Between 1875 and the early 1880s the placement of a second full-back again further depleted the forward-line, this time to six players; and by the time Steve made his debut for Derby County, the basic formation in which he was to play all of his first-class football had been put into place: goalkeeper, two full-backs, three half-backs and five forwards.

Steve's own forward position, inside-right, was essentially akin to a very forward-looking midfield role, something we might now describe as 'playing just behind the front man'. The passing game, what the Victorians called 'combination', had become a much more prevalent art, leaving a place for both individualism and teamwork in the overall structure of play. The half-back line was the first line of defence, with much less emphasis on them to support the forwards than is the case with today's 'midfielders' – in effect they were a very deep-lying, defensive-minded, middle three. It was the left-half who was generally expected to take care of Bloomer, with the two full-backs mopping up behind.

With such an emphasis on the prevention of scoring, it would be wrong, therefore, to suggest that Steve had an easy time of it. And this is further backed up by a study of the total season's goals tally by individual teams during that period: in Steve's first season, Derby County scored 52 goals, an equivalent of 1.73 per game, and in his last the average was only 1.44. Admittedly that was a relegation side but it wasn't Derby's worst average during Steve's reign and even the champions of 1913-14, Blackburn, managed only 2.05 per outing. By modern standards, therefore, the scoring rates before World War One are not at all outrageous. Of course, there have been fluctuations throughout the last 100 years or so, periods when the game really tightened up, but Newcastle United's 1.95 per game in 1993-94, for example, was bettered only four times by Derby between 1892 and 1914. All the evidence suggests that if there was a relatively 'easier' time to score goals, this came in the late 1920s just after the modification of the offside rule when Steve, to his eternal chagrin, had finished playing!

Bloomer admirers in danger of 'over-gilding the lily' are apt to latch on to this, saying that the offside rule under which he played actually made goalscoring much more difficult, as it was far easier to get caught offside under that old regime. In Steve's day there had to be three men, not two, between a receiving attacker and the goal; as one was generally the goalkeeper, this made the two full-backs a potentially spoiling duo as it was only necessary for one to 'step up' in order to spring the offside trap against forwards seeking advanced territory beyond the defending half-backs. Many teams exploited this 'one back' tactic and as a result forwards were apt to get caught offside far more than they would have liked, arguably restricting their scoring opportunities and much to the annoyance of impatient crowds. Having said that, there is a counter argument to this – good forwards became aware enough to drop deep, looking to work the ball through the half-back line or simply playing 'on the margin' in an attempt to spring the trap; and, once the half-back line was breached, an onrushing forward was left only with the two backs to beat, gamely covering the whole width of the pitch between them. They were effectively 'twin sweepers' and if they played too far apart, a fast forward could break through before they could pincer him out; too close together and a forward had acres of room on the outside to go wide and shoot from a reasonable angle. Many of Bloomers goals were scored in one of these two ways. The offside argument, therefore, is really a two-way affair. It is true that when, in 1925, the rule was amended to 'two men', there was a glut of goals for a number of seasons, but this was only because defences were slow to adapt to the new system, not because it was easier to score *per se*. As soon as the likes of Arsenal manager Herbert Chapman implemented the 'three back' game, by dropping an advanced centre half to the much deeper 'stopper' between the full-backs, the forwards again had a lean time of it. Weighting these relevant offside and defensive ploys against one another, there is no reason to suggest that Steve had it any easier or any more difficult than he would have done in later periods.

There is only one area in which I personally feel he might well have picked up his share of soft goals, one which is very seldom mentioned. With apologies to any goalkeepers out there, I'm afraid we must look to the custodians and their techniques for the odd 'blooper'. From a study of very early film, match reports and literature comes the inescapable conclusion that goalkeeping techniques were simply not developed to their full potential in Steve's day. Narrowing of angles was naively approached, diving effectively at a forward's feet had not been perfected and the general fitness, technique and agility of the net-minders was well below later standards and an entire world away from the scientific approach to goalkeeping which has been adopted with such success only in the last ten years or so.

Because of that, Steve definitely scored some goals which later 'keepers would have routinely denied him. Once again, though, there are offsetting factors to restore a balance; it is not widely known that until 1912 a goalkeeper could, if he found himself in such territory, quite legitimately handle the ball outside his area. Quite frustrating for hungry forwards. And for free-kicks, always a potential hunting ground for Steve and his ilk, the defensive wall was only required to retreat a measly six yards until that was altered to ten in 1913. There are many other small rule and tactical nuances that could be thrown into the analysis regarding the true 'worth' of Steve's goalscoring achievements, but none that would add to the conclusion which I believe is a clear one. That is that the art of scoring goals and the rate at which they 'were' scored by competent forwards in Steve's day was every bit as difficult then as it has been ever since; so a goalscorer is a goalscorer is a goalscorer, irrespective of time. Steve Bloomer, if he were playing today and trained to the level of fitness current, would be a top-class striker scoring regularly. Quite simply, he'd be gold-dust.

A gallery of snapshots

Having substantiated Steve's claim to membership of the all-time great forwards' club, it remains to answer the question... how on earth did he do it? For those of us who never saw him play, the imagination must suffice in giving a reasoned response, but the authenticity of that necessarily subjective interpretation can be greatly enhanced by consulting the comments of those spectators and players who he performed for, with and against. Used in conjunction with a broad sample of relevant match reports it's possible to build up a picture of how Steve scored many of his goals, what his strengths and weaknesses were and which particular players of the modern era he might bear accurate comparison with. First place in the Bloomer appraisal dossier must go to those who saw him play:

James Catton, a leading football journalist, gained a number of exclusive interviews with Bloomer while editor of the renowned *Athletic News*. This early observation written as 'Tityrus' is from 1897, a number of years before Steve had truly established a sustained reputation. Catton always retained a soft-spot for Steve and his family:

"This youth showed such promise in 1892 that he was engaged by Derby with phenomenal success, needless to say rewarded most liberally by the committee. He is a clever dribbler at top speed, passes judiciously and scores with splendid shots from all angles. As inside-right he has, when fit and well, no superior, and in conjunction with John Goodall, or a man like Billy Bassett, Bloomer is an object lesson in what forward play should be."

And later, in his 1926 memoirs, Catton still felt the same way, including Bloomer as automatic choice in his all-time best England XI...

"Bloomer belied his ashen countenance... this man of the people, a type of the plebeian, staked his claim for inclusion in the gallery of famous footballers largely on his shooting; his patent oblique shots on the ground out of the reach of the goalkeeper, and his volleys, were tremendous."

R. E. 'Tip' Foster, an England and Corinthian footballer, Worcestershire and England Test cricketer, scorer of a record 287 against Australia in Sydney in 1903, made the following observation in 1902 when Steve was an established international of whom much, sometimes too much, was always expected:

"Steve Bloomer is in many ways the most brilliant forward of the day. He is very quick in his movements and has perfect control of the ball. He also excels in one very important direction, namely in his power of adapting himself to the various conditions of the ground; if the surface is at all greasy, Bloomer is at his best and he is always one of the most difficult players to tackle. His style of play somewhat resembles that of the amateur brigade as, when he likes, he can always play a short passing game. But the difficulty with him is that he is not consistently on the same level of excellence, with the inevitable result that the attack is much disorganised. It is a great pity that a player of such sterling ability should vary in energy and skill."

Ernest 'Nudger' Needham, was born in Whittington Moor, Derbyshire, in 1873, played for the famous Staveley team, then captained Sheffield United; he was also a left-handed batsman for Derbyshire. As a left-half he directly opposed Steve on many occasions and played with him for England. Working-class kindred spirit of few words:

"What I will say is that I never faced a more twisting tormentor or wonderful shot than Bloomer."

Alfred Gibson and William Pickford, those two erudite administrators and chroniclers of the game, continue their 1906 description of Steve somewhat more wordily than Derbyshire's 'Nudger':

"Picture to yourself a slight, pale-faced, indolent-looking lad, strolling on to the field in a casual manner. A more unlikely looking athlete one would scarce select as a great football player. Of physique in its general sense he has none, and is not the sort of man whose life any doctor would insure on sight, but if the truth were known he is as sound as a bell, possessed of a blacksmith's lungs and a four-cylinder heart warranted to work in any climate. Although slightly built [5ft 8ins and 11st 3lbs] he is full of wire and whipcord and hard as nails. He has no sense of fear and will dash up to the biggest back to brush him aside, hustle him off the ball or at least divert his kick.

"As a personality he is a strange compound of the philosopher and the stoic, giving the spectator the impression of being unnaturally calm…as he stands hand on hip one might imagine he had no interest in the game, but out of the corner of his eye he is watching and his brain is busy formulating a plan; when the supreme moment comes he pounces on the ball like a greyhound, darts past his opponent and swerves towards open ground. Before the defence know what has happened, the ball is in the net. He is a man of action, a living force, a strong, relentless, destroying angel."

Gilbert Oswald Smith, Charterhouse and Oxford educated, was described as the finest centre-forward of the 1890s. Known always as 'G. O.', football's equivalent of cricket's 'W. G.', he played against Steve for the Corinthians in challenge matches and with him for England to good effect if not always to G. O.'s cultured tastes:

"Bloomer was a most brilliant individualist and always worth his place as a magnificent shot, but he was not easy to play with and personally I would much sooner have played with other inside-rights. However, he was a match-winner if ever there was one. Whenever I shaped to pass to him, it was only necessary to say 'Steve,' and, before his name had died on my lips, the ball was in the net."

C. B. Fry, Repton and Oxford-educated scholar, was the most accomplished all-round sportsman of his day: Corinthians, Southampton and England full-back, England Test cricketer and many more skills besides. He played against but not with Bloomer. Not much given to praising the common man unless pressed, in his tribute to G. O. Smith, he lets slip a glowing back-handed compliment to Steve:

"G. O. was a genius in football and like all geniuses he rose on stepping stones of his real self by taking infinite pains in terms of his natural gifts. He swung a marvellously heavy foot in shooting, always along the turf and terrifically swift…in fact he was as straight and hard a shot as I have ever met… except perhaps only Steve Bloomer of Derby County, on one of Steve's special days."

James Crabtree, the celebrated Burnley and Aston Villa defender, faced Bloomer many times and played with him for England. In 1907 he credited Steve with displaying quick-footed skills now taken for granted but under-utilised prior to this date:

"The wonderful skill and dexterity with which men like Bloomer habitually slip the ball across to an unmarked comrade represents one of the greatest advances which has been made in football."

John Goodall, the Preston North End and Derby County legend, was a creative and steadying influence on Bloomer's early career development. He played many games with Steve for the Rams and England. Writing here in 1898, his modest understatement is typical of his character:

"I am uncertain whether the old-fashioned dribbling game was not more exhilarating than the new perfected combination, but of course the results from this primitive method would now lack success. Thankfully there still exists a class of clever dribblers, for even in modern football there are frequent opportunities for a single-handed dash downfield...in this game the name S. Bloomer suggests itself."

Billy Bassett, the speedy West Bromwich-born right winger, played outside Steve to great effect for England and against him for Albion. Genuine praise from a fellow Black Countryman in 1905:

"Steve Bloomer is the greatest partner I have had and the greatest living English forward. I have never seen anyone shoot so discriminately...he shoots to miss the goalkeeper, deliberately placing the ball into the net while so many forwards seem to shoot merely at the goal. And you never know what he is going to do...he will give you the most beautiful passes, five or six in succession, and the opposing half-back would instinctively turn towards my direction every time Bloomer got the ball... then unexpectedly Steve would cut in at great pace, run straight for goal and score with a powerful shot."

Billy Meredith, the legendary Manchester City and United winger, played against Bloomer in the League and at international level with Wales. Despite their rivalry as the two great superstars of the era, the 'Welsh Wizard' formed a lasting friendship with Steve and played with him in a number of benefit games:

"The international matches helped me to become known to some of the greatest players that have ever kicked a ball. My most vivid memory is of that greatest of all inside-rights, Steve Bloomer, the greatest sharpshooter the game has ever known. When in a certain mood – and he was so often in that mood – he was the biggest streak of lightning I have ever seen on a football field. He was unbeatable, simply unstoppable. He hit the ball so hard and so low that there wasn't a goalkeeper who could stop 'em...not even 'Fatty Foulke'. There'll never be another Steve."

Major L. Eardley-Simpson – 'the Major' was a stalwart Derby County supporter, veteran of many Bloomer games, here airing his reminiscences on behalf of the fans at the time of Bloomer's death in 1938:

"Bloomer was the man who raised Derby County to such a pitch of glory. In his early days he was very fast and always a great dribbler; the only objection ever made to his passing was that he was sometimes too quick for his partners, but that is a misfortune rather than a fault. I will always remember his shooting along the ground…in some extraordinary way the ball seemed to gather pace as it came on, until it entered the net at a blinding speed."

Charles Wreford-Brown, Charterhouse-educated, excelled at football and cricket and was credited with coining the usage of the word 'soccer' while a student at Oxford. He played half-back for Old Carthusians and the Corinthians, made his England debut in 1889 and played once for England with Bloomer. Interviewed in his old age in 1948, after being elected a life vice-president of the Football Association, he paid Steve the ultimate compliment:

"I saw all the great inside-forwards before World War One and Bloomer was the best of them all. Since then Stanley Mortensen, now playing so well with Blackpool, is the pick…only he, in nearly 35 years since Bloomer retired, comes close to 'Steve' and is the nearest approach in style too."

Bill McCracken, Newcastle United and Ireland full-back, king of the offside game, played against Bloomer many times. Interviewed at the age of 88, he remembered Steve both as friend and foe, but placed two other Derby County inside-forwards, from the 1930s and 1940s, ahead of him in some departments:

"We were great pals. He wasn't an artist like Jimmy Hagan or Raich Carter… they were the best inside-forwards I've ever seen. Steve was a simple ball player and a deadly finisher. I remember watching him play at Newcastle in his last ever international, against Scotland in 1907…he picked up the ball about ten yards inside the Scotland half and hit it from there… it shot into the net about three feet off the ground."

Jesse Pennington, West Bromwich Albion and England full-back, played against Steve and with him for England in 1907, Bloomer's last international and Pennington's first. Reminiscing as a 75-year-old in 1960, he tried to rank Steve against all the players he'd seen up to that comparatively recent time:

"When I was a schoolboy I saw Steve Bloomer play and later played against and with him. I know we have had some great forwards since then – David Jack (Bolton and Arsenal), Charles Buchan (Sunderland and Arsenal), Alex James (Arsenal), all wonderful players – but Steve Bloomer was the greatest of all time; he had splendid ball control, could use his head and, above all, was possessed of one of the strongest shots with both feet."

Sir Frederick Wall, leading administrator of the day, former secretary of the Football Association, recalled:

"The main reason for Bloomer's success was constant shooting. He tried to take every chance, every half-chance, from any angle that presented itself; there was no hesitation...seldom a desire to trap the ball or steady it. Bloomer wanted the ball near goal and lived to shoot, to pick up stray balls that rebounded off the back or were diverted to him accidentally. He was a great volleyer in front of goal, he placed his ground shots at a fast pace and goalkeepers used to say it was difficult to tell which foot he would use for a shot when he was bearing down on them.The greater the match, the better he played... this is the decisive test, the capacity to rise above normal form and give your best when the best was needed."

Ivan Sharpe, journalist and amateur international, won a gold medal with the Great Britain football team at the 1912 Olympics in Stockholm.He played outside-left with Steve at Derby for two seasons between 1911 and 1913, in the twilight of Bloomer's career:

"Bloomer's strong points were these: a gift for close combination; a wonderful eye for a quick, long pass flicked along the right wing or flung across field to outside-left; a sudden individual burst from midfield, ending in a sharp shot and, best of all, a knack of shooting without hesitation. Late in his career he became a most inspiring captain at Derby, a real driving wheel, his passion for the game and the love of his club combining to make him a forceful skipper. There have been few shots to equal Steve in strength... perhaps Joe Smith, who won the Cup with Bolton in 1923 and 1926, was one, and I think the most powerful was Bob Whittingham of Chelsea before World War One.

"How did Bloomer shoot? Well it came from nearer the toe than the instep, which enabled him to make the effort a moment quicker than other men who took a bigger backlift. He had few tricks...he was a magnet but not a magician. And our Stephen was a tyrant. He said what he thought and if things were going wrong, his partner had no pleasant Saturday afternoon. 'What d'ye call that? A pass? I haven't got an aeroplane!' This was a fair example of a Bloomer explosion and if you avoided his glare he would stand stock still, strike an attitude with his hands on his hips and toss up his head as if recording the beseeching angel to make a note of the blunder. Then he would stamp back to his position in a manner intended publicly to demonstrate his disapproval. Quite wrong, of course, and not good for the side, the alleged offender or the game, but those who knew Bloomer knew that he was really quite harmless,quite a peaceable person who meant well and got the best out of the players because of his inspiring example, his great unselfishness and his tremendous devotion to his team. So harmless, in fact, that within a week or so of joining the ranks of the great Bloomer's club, the budding juniors selected Bloomer for their dressing-room pranks."

In the mind's eye

The reason for quoting such a representative example of observations is not to attempt to deify Bloomer or stake a claim on his behalf as the best of all-time; it's simply to bring alive Steve's talents for those of us who could not have seen him perform at League or international level – anyone reading this book who 'did' is to be heartily congratulated as surely a telegram from Her Majesty is imminent. For those favoured few, the memory will suffice and the words may be superfluous, but for the rest of us they add some colour and real movement to the static monochrome world that Bloomer has perhaps inhabited in our mind's eye to date. No significant moving images or full colour representations of Bloomer at leisure or play are known to survive. Of course, we take the plaudits as we find them, as football people are apt to get carried away at times; but there is strength in numbers and the real veracity of his contemporaries' comments lies in the fact that they are all from characters with a good knowledge of the game and genuine first-hand experience of Bloomer's play.

Those memories which span the greatest number of years are particularly telling. Jesse Pennington, for example, watched football right into the Swinging Sixties. As for Ivan Sharpe's oft-quoted revelations of Steve's 'dodgy' on-field temperament, this needs viewing in perspective; only Sharpe and, to a lesser degree, G. O. Smith, have hinted at this critical side of Steve's nature and it may be significant that both these men came from the other end of the social scale to 'our Steve'. Perhaps they resented being criticised by a mere 'working-class hero', or maybe Sharpe had some genuine off days. Steve was his captain, after all, and surely had some rights to mete out criticism. There is no smoke without fire of course – it seems certain that Steve on occasions let his frustrations show, irritated that others were apparently unable to perform tasks which he found second nature. This type of impatient reaction is generally born from enthusiasm rather than malice and it would be incorrect to imagine that Bloomer made a life-long habit of it. Maybe poor old 'Sharpey' just bore the brunt and was a little thin-skinned.

What all of this leaves us with is our own perceived picture of Bloomer, coloured by the depth and timescales of our own football experience. It seems shades of Stanley Mortensen might occur to the older generation while youngsters may think of Owen and his like as displaying elements of the Bloomer game. Two-footed, fast over long distances, lightning over short, comfortable on the ball, possessed of instant control, superb vision, fine shooting skills, innate enthusiasm, quick feet and an even quicker football brain… there is nothing in this Bloomer armoury that we can't see every week in the Premiership in one form or another but when it comes all in one package it's the sort of gift-wrapped talent that today's managers dream about.

In truth, there has been no one individual Bloomer clone in the last half century; one thinks of the passing skills of Johnny Haynes, the quick feet of a Juninho or Beardsley, the close-in certainty and predatory instinct of Lineker or Rush in their prime, the one-on-one grace and assurance of Greaves or

Hector, the clinical finishing of Ian Wright, Alan Shearer or Andy Cole and the shooting style of Eusebio at his most venomous. Perhaps even some of the artistry of Pelé, the greatest inside-forward of them all. As for demeanour, the sly-witted languor of Leeds' Allan Clarke, always the prelude to regular cobra-like strikes, comes to mind and Derby fans might see in Bloomer's distant gaze, sallow face and boyish features, a hint of a less naturally blessed but still heroic Rams figure, Bobby Davison. As for the all-round game, Denis Law certainly suggests himself, as too does the superbly talented Dwight Yorke.

The more I read of Bloomer, though, and the more I see of Michael Owen – 5ft 8in, pale, short-cropped hair, frighteningly quick and aware…the more I equate the two, at least in the manner of goalscoring; many a run and goal of Owen's displays a distinct touch of Bloomer.

There are many more equally valid comparisons and we could also draw on Bloomer's own self-assessment if we wished. He wrote a number of articles along the lines of 'How I do it', but these tend to confirm what others have already said and it would be unfair to ask Steve to make a casting vote. Whatever conclusion one draws from the Bloomer profile offered here, it is to be hoped that our vision of him now is clearer than it was before and certain enough to validate his claim as one of football's finest ever forwards. The debate could progress indefinitely, as Latin scholar C. B. Fry so cryptically reminds us in his own discussion of the relative merits of 'G. O.', Bloomer and company: "Our old friend 'De Gustibus' always has the final say."

To you and me that means it's 'all a matter of taste'. Perhaps in an analysis which has thrust so many superlatives to the fore we should finish with just 11 simple words from someone else who had to contend with the Bloomer phenomenon on the field of play. With an understated but poetic lyricism typical of his nationality, Welsh full-back David 'Dai' Jones put it all so very simply:

"Such a beautiful player, it's a shame to go for him!"

'BORO GET THEIR MAN

1906-1910

"A County team that hails from Derby way
In days gone by a pretty game did play,
Their former glories gone, now have they sunk,
Perhaps they made a Bloomer...who can say?

Now 'Boro have the man who a score
Of times has played for his country's lore,
Though never overworked, a deadly shot,
Perhaps for England he will play no more."
Anon

"QUITE a sensation was caused in Derby football circles this morning when it transpired that Derby County had transferred Bloomer to Middlesbrough late the previous night. It will be remembered that at the end of last season the Teesside club were anxious to secure the transfer of Bloomer in order to strengthen their team so that they might keep their position in the League, but all efforts to tempt the County to part with him failed, as many previous attempts to lure Bloomer away had failed. Now, through a variety of circumstances, and bad play principally, Middlesbrough again find themselves in difficulties and during the past few days have been in negotiation with Derby for Bloomer's services and with other clubs for prominent players.

"Yesterday they secured the transfer of Brawn from Aston Villa and then their emissaries came on to Derby and succeeded in coming to terms for the immediate transfer of Bloomer and also Ratcliffe, the reserve full-back. Thus Stephen Bloomer's long connection with Derby County comes to an end and there is not the slightest doubt that the severance of the famous international from the team he has served so brilliantly for so many years will be greatly regretted."
Derby Daily Telegraph, Friday, 16 March 1906

A controversial prize catch
The tone of the Derby newspaper's announcement is not difficult to interpret, nor was their assertion of severe regret wide of the mark. Such was the

consternation among fans caused by the news of Bloomer's transfer, that huddles of men gathered on the street corners of Derby to bemoan what in their minds amounted to a betrayal...not by Bloomer, but by the directors of Derby County and the 'big bad barons' of 'Boro. Certainly the timing was bad from Derby's point of view as their position in the First Division was by no means secure; to sell a player who had been your side's leading League scorer for each of the past 13 seasons, and to a fellow relegation struggler at that, seemed a trifle unwise to say the least.

But it wasn't just that. The Derby public had come to idolise Bloomer and cherished him as their own...quite simply he 'belonged' to Derby and the hero worship that for years had confined itself to relatively local circles had not long since reached its national peak when Bloomer had broken both G. O. Smith's international goalscoring and appearance records in 1905. Those feats received tremendous press coverage and seemed to elevate 'Steve' to the status of national institution, being marked by the FA by a presentation to Bloomer of his portrait at the same time as his national testimonial fund. It was a source of great pride to Derby people that their team should be graced by the man who, at long last, they could justifiably call 'the most famous footballer in England' and, perhaps by direct implication then, the world. That he should now be let go in such an unforeseen fashion was tantamount to selling the family silver.

The shockwaves felt in Derby were echoed, too, in the North-East; make no mistake... this was a big signing and a hugely controversial one. To understand why, we need to look at what happened a full year before Bloomer's move.

As the newspapers suggested, the transfer approach wasn't made on impulse. Towards the end of the 1904-05 season, in early February, Middlesbrough had tried to get Bloomer and failed and by the time he broke Smith's England goalscoring record, in the 1-1 draw against Ireland on 25 February, a game played at Ayresome Park, 'Boro had switched horses and smashed the transfer record by paying the then staggering sum of £1,000 for England forward Alf Common from Sunderland. That sort of money was regarded by all and sundry as almost 'obscene' and definitely immoral, and it seems certain that the arguably unenviable tag of 'first four-figure transfer' would have befallen Bloomer had 'Boro won the day. As it was, Steve started the next season with Derby while the Common transfer brought widespread condemnation of the Middlesbrough club; cartoons lampooned the situation vehemently and the *Athletic News*, football's most august popular mouthpiece, made their own opinion quite clear:

"As a matter of commerce, might not ten young recruits at £100 a piece have paid better? And as a matter of sport, surely the Second Division would be more honourable than retention of place by purchase."

That sounds a naively high and mighty stance to take bearing in mind what goes on in today's game, but it fairly reflected the mood of the football authorities and public in 1905. 'Boro duly avoided relegation and the FA made it clear that they would take a dim view of any other high figure transfers and went so far as to set an upper transfer limit of only £350, the regulation 'implied' but officially delayed to take effect at the start of 1908.

It was against that sort of strong feeling that Middlesbrough made their renewed and successful move for Bloomer just over a year after the Common affair, which explains why the Middlesbrough supporters and the rest of the football world, at least outside the clubs, were so surprised; in the context of previous events it seemed a deliberately audacious and somewhat impertinent act guaranteed to create controversy, and so it did in no uncertain manner.

'Boro manager Alex Mackie already had a dubious reputation before he signed Bloomer. He had been at Ayresome Park only since June 1905 and came to the club from Sunderland with an illegal payments to players scandal hanging over him, so it was inevitable that when he signed Bloomer there should be an unusually strong public interest taken in the whole affair. Once the nature of the transfer and the figures involved entered the public domain, as they inevitably did quite quickly, it became crystal clear that Middlesbrough and Derby County had 'massaged' the figures. The agreed transfer fee was £750, well above the FA's interim 'guideline' limit, but by including Emor 'Jack' Ratcliffe in the Bloomer package both clubs were able, quite disingenuously, to suggest a reasonable split to be placed on each player's head...say £400 for Bloomer, prolific goalscorer and the country's leading international, and £350 for Ratcliffe, a reserve left-back who had made only 16 first-team appearances for Derby in four seasons! Little wonder that public and official opinion tended to swing away from 'Boro at that time, but that wasn't a view shared by all the other First Division clubs themselves. The feeling among some of the top division's hierarchy was that 'business is business' and anything goes. In fact there was a strong suggestion that there had been more than moral support given to 'Boro in what was coming to be known as the 'Bloomer affair'. The fact that Middlesbrough had made a record loss of £1,635 in season 1904-05 raised the very pertinent question of where on earth the Bloomer transfer money could have been dredged up from. The theory was soon put about that several leading clubs were keen to see a good 'gate' club of 'Boro's status survive and would be quite equally keen to see relegation candidates Bury go down instead – quite simply some of the money, so it was said, had been 'loaned' to 'Boro by their fellow clubs.

An FA inquiry was inevitable and in May 1906, just two months after Bloomer's arrival, a commission met in Manchester to examine Middlesbrough's books, revealing a 'can of worms' amounting to all manner of irregularities. Manager Mackie resigned in June 1906, before he could be banned, and opted for the simpler life of landlord, running the Star and Garter Hotel in Marton Street, Middlesbrough. Thereafter the FA resolved to examine the club's books regularly and keep a close eye on all internal affairs. Much later, in the course of one of their 'visits', it was discovered that Bloomer had been paid £10 to sign-on again for the 1906-07 season and he himself received a two-match ban. Bearing in mind manager Mackie's track record it seems very likely

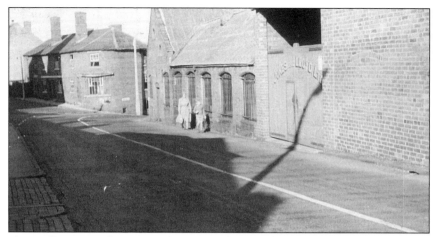

The Cradley street where Steve Bloomer was born. Bridge Street is the road bending down to the right. The house on the corner bears a nameplate and this is where Bloomer is said to have been born, although there is no proof of this. There was a row of terraced houses below it and he could have lived in any of them.

The earliest surviving photograph of Steve Bloomer in his Rams days. He was 19 and this was taken not long after his League debut in September 1892.

this will be investigated

Sawley Park Rangers: A. Baker, goal; W. Brookes and T. Smith, backs; W. Rice, E. Smith, and G. Butler, half-backs; S. Clegg and T. Meads, right wing; W. Hall, centre; T. Beresford and T. Bosworth, left wing.

Long Eaton Wanderers: J. Roe, goal; J. Fairbrother and T. Nelson, backs; W. Mellors, G. Lewis, and J. Stafford, half-backs; S. Osborne and R. Thorpe, right wing; A. Sheldon and J. Thorpe, left wing; Austen, centre.

Umpires: Messrs. J. Duesbury and Geo. Leech.
Referee: Major Bemrose.

THE JUNIOR COMPETITION: ST. LUKE'S CHOIR v. ST. CHAD'S JUNIORS.—This match, in which the competitors were necessarily less than 15 years of age, turned out a one-sided affair. St. Luke's Choir had achieved some tall performances during the course of the competition, and they were generally expected to prove successful. They had the wind in their favour in the first half, and they gave their opponents little chance from the outset. During the first half St. Luke's scored six goals, and in the second half against the wind they added eight more, thus winning by 14 goals to none. St. Chad's seldom broke away, and they only caused the opposing goalkeeper to handle once. Bloomer played a good game in the centre for St. Chad's, but was badly supported. St. Luke's were in capital form, and whenever they broke away their onslaught was inevitable. The play of Hearne and Eley on the left wing was a treat to witness, and these players ought certainly to be heard of again. Lester, Riley, Armitage, and Rose also played well, though the whole team played together splendidly. The following were the players:—

St. Luke's Choir: Wheeldon, goal; L. Broughall and A. Hooley, backs; Trueman, Lester, and Riley, half-backs; B. Gutch and Armitage, right wing; Hearne and Eley, left wing; Rose, centre.

St. Chad's Juniors: Mason, goal; Spendlove and Chadwick, backs; Fletcher, Bagnall, and Ellis, half-backs; Briggs and Swan, right wing; Cooper and Walters, left wing; Bloomer, centre.

Umpires: Messrs. Ellis and Wigley.
Referee: Mr. S. Richardson.

The shields and medals were afterwards presented to the winners by the Hon. Mrs. W. M. Jarvis.

The first mention in a newspaper of the Bloomer football genius, a match report of the game between St Luke's Choir and St Chad's Juniors in April 1887.

The house at 34 Cummings Street, Derby, looking much the same today as it did in 1896 when the newly-wed Steve and Sarah Bloomer set up home together. They later moved across the road and also lived in Dairy House Road and Portland Street.

Derby County's first team players in 1895 with Steve now fully established. Back row (left to right): J. Methven, A. Staley (trainer), J. Leiper. Middle row: W. D. Clark (secretary), J. Cox, A. Goodall, J. Robinson, G. Kinsey, J. Staley. Seated: J. Goodall, J. Paul, J. Miller, J. Stevenson, H. McQueen. On ground: Bloomer and J. McMillan.

Steve looks thoughtful in this 1898 Rams photograph. Back row (left to right): J. Methven, J. Fryer, A.Latham (trainer), J. Leiper, J. Reilly (director). Middle row: J. H. Richardson (secretary), J. Cox, A. Goodall, J. Turner, H. Newbould (manager). Front row: J. Goodall, S. Bloomer, J. Boag, J. Stevenson, H. McQueen.

Steve Bloomer (extreme right, striped shirt), in action at the Normanton End. This photograph was taken during a 3-2 win over Bury in October 1904. The original caption states that it is a Bloomer goal, although Edwardian caption writers used some licence when it came to sports pictures and there do seem to be a lot of bodies in the way.

Oil painting of Steve Bloomer in England's colours, striking a suitably heroic pose.

Bloomer pictured with fellow Rams and England star Ben Warren, who met a sad end after suffering a mental illness.

Ten of the England team which met Scotland at the Crystal Palace in 1905. Back row (left to right): Ruddlesdin, Bridgett, Smith, Sharp, Roberts, Linacre. Front row: Spencer, Bache, Bloomer and Leake. It was Steve's record cap.

Scene of the tragic accident at Ibrox in 1902 when 26 people perished. England skipper Bloomer had to lead his team back on to the field past rows of dead bodies.

The Bloomer countenance was well-known all over Britain, even in those days before television and mass-circulation picture papers. The reason? His image was used to advertise a host of products.

THE BOOT THAT NEVER FAILS TO SCORE

The above is a facsimile reproduction of a medallion which is printed on both sides alike on stout gold bevelled card and attached to every pair of our

STEVE BLOOMER
LUCKY GOAL SCORERS

by means of coloured cord.

The effect is very pleasing and is calculated to attract the prospective buyer of football boots.

READ WHAT THE
GREAT INTERNATIONAL
STEVE BLOOMER
SAYS ABOUT OUR
"PERFEGRIPPE"
FOOTBALL BOOTS

Here Steve, 'the Great International', extols the virtues of Perfegrippe football boots.

Rams players and officials in 1903-04. Back row (left to right): A. Latham (trainer), J. Methven, B. Hall, W. Sargent (assistant secretary), H. Maskrey, C. Morris, J. May, H. Newbould (manager). Middle row: B. Warren, J. Mercer, S. Bloomer (captain), G. Davis. Front row: C. Leckie, J. Hodgkinson, G. Richards, J. Warrington. The official holds on to Steve – but not for much longer.

A DERBY FOOTBALL SENSATION.

BLOOMER TRANSFERRED.

Quite a sensation was caused in Derby football circles this morning when it transpired that Derby County had transferred Bloomer to Middlesbrough late the previous night. It will be remembered that at the end of last season the Teesside club were anxious to secure the transfer of Bloomer in order to strengthen their team, so that they might keep their position in the League, but all efforts to tempt the County to part with him failed—as many previous attempts to lure Bloomer away had failed—and Middlesbrough gave a thousand pounds for Common. That being so it is fair to assume they would have offered quite that amount for Bloomer. Through a variety of circumstances, and bad play principally, Middlesbrough again find themselves in difficulties, and during the past few days they have been in negotiation with Derby for Bloomer's services, and with other clubs for prominent players. Yesterday afternoon they secured the transfer of Brown from Aston Villa, and then their emissaries came on to Derby and succeeded in coming to terms for the immediate transfer of Bloomer and also Ratcliffe, the reserve full back. The sum which Middlesbrough have paid for Bloomer has not transpired, but we are officially informed that it is a very hand-

How the *Derby Daily Telegraph* broke the shock news of Bloomer's transfer to Middlesbrough in March 1906.

Middlesbrough, 1907-08 with Steve Bloomer fourth from the left of the middle row. Alf Common, whose transfer for £1,000 had earlier prompted a control on fees, is fourth from the right of the middle row.

Steve is back! A local newspaper cartoon celebrates the great event.

Bloomer pictured in 'Boro's colours shortly after his transfer.

Rule 14.—Each Club must send the results of League Matches, together with the names of the Players competing therein, and Officials to the League Secretary, within 4 days of each match. In case of default, a fine of 10/- to be imposed.

THE FOOTBALL LEAGUE, Ltd.

SEASON 1910-11.

SECOND DIVISION.

Date of Match...Oct 1st...191...

Home Club...Derby County...... Visiting Club...Lincoln City...

Results :—Home Club...5...Goals, Visiting Club...0...Goals.

Total No. of Matches Played...6...

Won...2......Lost...2......Drawn...2...

Total Goals for...11......Against...9......Points...6...

Signed...W.S. Moore......Secretary of...Derby County...Club.

TEAM.

NOTE.—The Surname, with Full Initials, must be given.

Goal	E. Scattergood
Backs (Right)	J. Barbour
,, (Left)	J. Atkin
Half-Backs (Right)	E. Garry
,, (Centre)	B. Hall
,, (Left)	Bagshaw
Forwards (Outside Right)	W.T. Grimes
,, (Inside Right)	S. Bloomer
,, (Centre)	Bauchop
,, (Inside Left)	+ Barnes
,, (Outside Left)	D. Donald

Referee...JH Smith...

Linesmen...W Archer...
R.S. Bradshaw...

,, ...

Remarks

The Rams team sheet for the Lincoln game which shows Steve Bloomer back in the line-up.

Rams group for 1913 with Steve Bloomer effectively moved to the backroom staff. Back row (left to right): Bloomer, Aitken, Scattergood, Barbour, Betts. Middle row: Methven (manager), Hardman, Bagshaw, Buckley, Richards, Waugh, Latham (trainer). Front row: Grimes, Walker, Leonard, Barnes, Neve. John Hardman would be killed in action in France in 1917.

The cover of the Ruhleben Camp magazine.

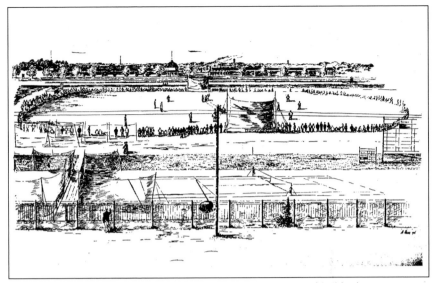

An internee's sketch of the cricket ground at Ruhleben, situated inside the racecourse. Bloomer scored a few centuries here as he waited for the war to end.

Teams for the Ruhleben 'farewell' match in 1918. Steve is eighth from the left of the back row.

The Derby Daily Express

SATURDAY, NOVEMBER 23, 1918.

DERBY BOROUGH POLICE.

A DANGEROUS PRACTICE.

BLOOMER BACK HOME.

After Four Years' Captivity as Prisoner.

WHAT SPORT DID.

FOOTBALLERS' FAMILIES.

BLOOMER TO ASSIST IN DERBY CHARITY MATCH:

TO AWAIT ESCORT.

SUCCESSFUL DERBY CONCERT.

THE 'FLU EPIDEMIC.

DERBY'S CINEMA PRECAUTIONS.

The *Derby Daily Express* reports that Derby's most famous footballing son is back home in England after four years of wartime captivity.

Derby War Memorial Fund.

FOOTBALL MATCH.

Baseball Ground, Derby, 18th April, 1923.

SOUVENIR PROGRAMME

Edited by W. LESLIE UNSWORTH
in collaboration with
W. RUTHERFORD, Hon. Asst. Sec. War Memorial Fund.

Steve Bloomer's "Old International" Team.

DERBY COUNTY

The programme for Steve's last 'serious' game.

And his team that day. At the age of 49 he bowed out with a penalty. Back row (left to right); Tommy Barbour, Alec Leake, Harry Maskrey, Bob Crompton, Albert Lloyd, Charlie Morris. Front row: Billy Meredith, Steve Bloomer, James Cantrell, Harry Leonard, George Wall.

SEPTEMBER 1, 1928.

NUMBERING OF PLAYERS.

Steve Bloomer on Unwanted Stunt—Londoners Ignorant of Play and Players—Destroying Personal Touch.

BLOOMER AS COACH.

Derby Boys Beat Birmingham Boys—A Good Even Game—A Severe Penalty—Home Lads' Stubborn Defence.

Bloomer the newspaper columnist. He had strong opinions about all aspects of the game and also proved a popular coach and reporter of local matches.

The *Derby Daily Express* announces Steve's very last appearance on a football field, as a 57-year-old in a charity game at Belper.

As a 'general assistant' at the Baseball Ground, Steve, still a revered figure, holds court with (from left to right): Sid Wileman, Sammy Crooks, Dally Duncan, Jack Nicholas, Jack Barker and Jack Bowers.

Steve Bloomer (centre) pictured with officials from the New Zealand FA during his recuperative trip to Australasia.

In 1910 the *Derby Telegraph* had announced Steve's return from Middlesbrough. Some 28 years later they reported another return, this time from the holiday designed to cure his health problems.

Just over three weeks later the *Telegraph* used the same photograph to announce the death of the most famous footballer in Derby County's history.

The *Telegraph* reports Steve Bloomer's funeral which drew tens of thousands of people who lined the route of the cortege.

The memorial plaque which was originally on the outside of the directors' entrance at the Baseball Ground and which is now on display at Pride Park.

Something grander...the Steve Bloomer memorial situated in Derby's Lock Up Yard.

What would they be worth today? Some of the greatest stars – and goalscorers – in the game's history attended the unveiling of the Bloomer memorial. Left to right are Johnny Morris, Arthur Rowley, Nat Lofthouse, Sir Tom Finney and Wilf Mannion.

that Steve also received a 'gesture' of the Manilla envelope variety at the time of his initial signing, although nothing was ever proven to that effect.

So there are the shenanigans of football, as riddled with intrigue as ever it has been before or since, a simple transfer beset with apparent skulduggery at every turn. Bloomer's involvement in the whole affair seems relatively innocent – offered what amounted to two and a half weeks' wages to commit himself to the club for 1906-07, his first full season, he wouldn't think twice; in fact he probably didn't think at all, at least not about the legality of taking the money. What he might have reflected on instead was whether the move to Middlesbrough was a good one for him and his family and where it would all lead. As for the club themselves, all their actions were vindicated as far as results went; on the last day of the 1905-06 season they were left needing a point at Blackburn to avoid relegation. In a 1-1 draw Bloomer got the goal, his sixth in just nine games since his transfer. Middlesbrough stayed up and so did Bury and Derby County. Accompanying the already doomed Wolverhampton Wanderers into the Second Division were a team that Steve's erstwhile Derby followers might just have thanked him for putting there... Nottingham Forest. All's fair in love, war, and football.

A good career move?
Amid all the ill-feeling caused by Bloomer's transfer in Derby and the wider football community, it is all too easy to forget the player and his family. Middlesbrough and their fans were certainly delighted with their famous catch, but what of Steve himself? Since the age of five he had lived nowhere else but Derby; his wife Sarah was a Derby girl and his three children, all at or coming up to school, were all born within earshot of the Baseball Ground roar. If Steve had been a somewhat nervous prodigy in his teenage years and a rising local hero in his 20s, at the relatively mature age of 32 at the time of his transfer he was established as one of the country's leading sports personalities enjoying a comfortable enough lifestyle in a pleasant home close to his place of work in an environment with which he was both familiar and happy. There was no reason for him to move and there is no indication that he ever wanted to in an active sense. Years later in the 1920s, Bloomer was to reflect in one of his newspaper columns on the financial rewards available to footballers and made it quite clear that, although he had some retrospective regrets, he had no real dissatisfactions at the time.

"When I see what some of today's players earn and how by moving around they can work the system, I sometimes regret that I didn't leave Derby County early in my career and play for several different clubs. Maybe I'd have done better financially but I can honestly say that it never really occurred to me then. I always enjoyed playing for Derby and I never felt that I wanted to leave them. And after I went to Middlesbrough and returned with that club to play against Derby County, all I wished to do was my best, to show the Derby people that I was still a power and that I might be playing football still with my old club had they kept me."

From that we may fairly assume that Bloomer himself took no active part in lobbying for a move…indeed, there is a suggestion that he felt quite hurt that the powers that be within the Derby set-up felt able to dispense with his services. Manager Harry Newbould was always a Bloomer admirer and there is every suggestion that he, too, was firmly against the move. That being the case it seems certain that it was the Derby board, seeking to bolster the club's ever-teetering financial position, who ordered the transfer to take place. It was a huge risk for Derby; Bloomer had already scored 12 goals in 23 games before his transfer, including two hat-tricks, and they still needed points to ensure their continued survival at the top level, having never been relegated in their history. In the event they did survive despite only two wins in the last ten games after Steve's departure, including shameful 6-0 and 7-0 defeats at Aston Villa and Wolves. But survival was a short-term measure as the next season, without Bloomer, they slumped to their first-ever relegation and spent the next four seasons in the wilderness of the Second Division. From that point of view it might be argued that Bloomer's move to Middlesbrough secured him continued top flight football, as 'Boro stayed in Division One throughout his stay, but it is all pure conjecture as Derby supporters were convinced that it was Bloomer's departure itself that sealed their relegation fate.

The more tangible facts are that Steve Bloomer left 91 Dairyhouse Road, Derby and moved to 34 Parliament Street, Middlesbrough to play for Middlesbrough Football Club. They were not regarded as such a famous club as Derby County, being relative newcomers who first entered the League as a Division Two side in season 1899-1900, but they were hugely ambitious to make up for lost time. They gained promotion to Division One for the 1902-03 season and moved from their Linthorpe Road ground to the impressive new Ayresome Park for the start of the 1903-04 season. Their first League game there, against fierce local rivals Sunderland, attracted an attendance of 30,000. Although that was exceptional, the crowds Bloomer was to play in front of at Middlesbrough were much larger than he had been used to at Derby; 5,000-10,000 was the norm at the Baseball Ground but at Ayresome Park it was generally 15,000-20,000 and sometimes much higher. In that sense there is no doubt that Bloomer had moved to a 'big' club with ambition from a club with a rich history whose better days seemed to be behind them. For a 32-year-old that had to be a good move, as many players of that age were thinking of retirement rather than high profile transfer. So what sort of mark did Steve make at Middlesbrough? A season-by-season résumé presents the case.

Season 1905-06…Avoiding the drop

Bloomer was signed to score goals. Those goals would keep Middlesbrough up…that was the simple aim. Record signing Alf Common had weighed in with 13 in 39 games between his own arrival and the signing of Bloomer, not a bad return but not as high a rate as Bloomer was used to and one which the 'Boro board certainly felt could be bettered. If Steve was in any doubt about 'Boro's plight when he arrived, it was quickly brought home to him in his debut at Liverpool on 17 March 1906 as 'Boro were thrashed 6-1, and further reinforced by a 1-0 home debut defeat at the hands of Sheffield United. At that point 'Boro had won only three of their previous 24 games and one imagines that the spectre of relegation loomed large in Bloomer's thoughts at that moment. But Steve was made of stern stuff and, whatever the situation, had proved himself in a crisis many times before. He scored his first goal in his third game, a 1-1 draw at Notts County, and followed it up with five more in the remaining six games.

What's more, Common also started to hit the net regularly. Playing centre-forward alongside Steve's usual inside-right he plundered eight goals in the last six fixtures. It was a remarkable turn around in form which saw 'Boro win four and lose only once in the last seven games of that season. Manchester City were thrashed 6-1, Stoke brushed aside 5-0, Woolwich Arsenal beaten 2-0 and Sunderland overcome 2-1 with a goal apiece from Bloomer and Common. As we know, Steve scored the goal which kept the club up only on the slenderest of goal-averages and as an escape act it must rate as one of the greatest of all time. They scored 18 goals in the last seven games and it was only that, irrespective of the points they won, which ultimately saved them and sent a stunned Forest hurtling through the gaping relegation trapdoor in their place. Whether it was Bloomer's arrival that turned the tide it is impossible to prove categorically. Certainly the signing of Brawn at right-wing was a factor too, but the evidence is mighty powerful in suggesting that Bloomer's signing saved the club from the dreaded drop in those final ten games of the season.

Season 1906-07...Leading scorer

Twenty goals for Bloomer in 36 League and Cup appearances, despite his two-game ban, easily secured him the position of leading goalscorer this season ahead of Common with 13 from 31. Steve's haul included his only hat-trick for 'Boro, a stunning four in the 5-3 home win over Woolwich Arsenal on 5 January, and that being his seventh game in 15 days over the festive period. Steve made it clear he never liked the cramped Christmas schedule but it didn't seem to affect his form. What would the likes of Alex Ferguson say about that fixture programme one wonders?

Steve's record compared well with most of his seasons as a younger man, indeed back in his first-ever campaign as a teenager in 1892-93 he had managed only 11 in 28 games and in his last full season with Derby his return was just 13 from 30. So not only was he maintaining his scoring rate – even at the age of 33 by the end of this season – but the move also seemed to recharge his batteries to the extent that he actually improved on his most recent returns at Derby. Any thoughts of flagging powers were quickly dispelled. He played twice against his old club this season, which were to be the only two such meetings as the Rams suffered their first-ever relegation to Division Two. 'Boro lost 1-0 at Derby and won 4-1 at home, Steve notching one of the goals. The game at

Derby on 6 October was something of an occasion for his old mate Jimmy Methven, who played his last-ever home League game that day for the Rams. Methven had replaced secretary-manager Harry Newbould in August to become the club's first recognised full-time 'manager', in the modern sense, blessedly relieved of the onerous secretarial duties. Just short of his 38th birthday Methven continued to play the odd game but evidently knew the 'Boro match was his League farewell to the Baseball Ground – ever the wag, he appeared wearing his Scottish representative cap.

'Boro, too, had a new player-manager very well-known to Steve. Scottish international defender Andy Aitken, younger than Bloomer at just 30, joined from Newcastle just after the start of the season. He and Bloomer had played against each other on many occasions and there seems every reason to believe that the relationship was a good one, although Aitken said there was always one person at the club he 'never got on with'. He never revealed who this was but it seems unlikely it was Bloomer. With Common later being deprived of the club's captaincy in 1907 and being fined £10 for 'drunkenness and violent behaviour' it seems more plausible that Alf was the man but we may never know. At any rate this season ended successfully with Middlesbrough finishing a creditable 11th, a full nine points ahead of Derby County. Bloomer's return to form was noted by the England selectors; having been left out of the Home International games at the end of the 1905-06 season he played against Scotland and Wales, his last-ever appearances, in March and April 1907.

Season 1907-08… 'Steve' a real tonic
Bloomer had a much leaner time of it in his second full season but still finished as joint top scorer with Sammy Cail, managing a relatively disappointing 12 goals in 35 appearances while Cail scored his own 12 in a remarkable 16 games, having won his place only in mid-season. As an out-and-out centre-forward the form of Cail caused some reshuffling as Common was moved to inside-right and Steve put out on the right-wing. Goal-hungry as he was, this may not have pleased Steve but he battled on as ever and 'Boro finished sixth, their highest-ever position in the top flight. As for financial rewards for such success, Bloomer and the other leading players were still hamstrung by the maximum wage regulations limiting them to £4 a week, but Steve was able to capitalise on his fame by product endorsement deals which probably made him 'Boro's top earner at that time. Although players had done deals at the latter end of the 19th century, the climate had changed as the 20th century progressed and by 1907 players were becoming 'public property' as they had never been before. Reporting styles were becoming less stodgy and magazines such as *Football Chat* ran interviews and features on players which revealed more about their private lives, personal habits and tastes than ever before. With that, of course, came commercial opportunity. Despite occasional minor aberrations in the past, Steve had a sufficiently clean-cut image to be a prime target for the agents and marketing men and he took the opportunity to endorse a tonic called

'Phosferine', appearing in their newspaper advertisements under the banner of supreme athlete promoting 'The Remedy of Kings'.

"To tower head and shoulders above every other player in England is an achievement of which Steve Bloomer, the famous international, may well be proud, for the man who excels in so brilliant a fashion undoubtedly possesses remarkable physical qualities. But this is no use unless those qualities are properly developed and the whole secret of Bloomer's superiority is contained in the intelligent manner he has built up and safeguarded his bodily powers. In a more than usually interesting letter written from Middlesbro' Football Club, Bloomer says that his pre-eminence and capacity for endurance are based upon the fact that he invariably repulses the effects of overtraining and muscular lassitude with a course of Phosferine."

What Phosferine could do that a decent pint of Bass couldn't will inevitably remain a mystery, but Steve was in good company here. The other leading sportsman used to advertise the product was cricketer-footballer and supreme all-rounder C. B. Fry, while fellow users of the wonder product included the Emperor of China, the Empress of Russia, The Royal Family and the 'principal Royalty and Aristocracy throughout the World'. Not a bad deal then for a lad from Cradley. True or false though the claims may be, it's heartening to know that Steve was able to boost an arguably unfairly 'capped' income with a bit of judicious business sense, and such evidence suggests that he knew what he was doing off the pitch as well as on it.

Bloomer and his fellow 'Boro team-mates also benefited from the 'perks' of overseas tours at this time. Unlike in later years when most such tours were pre-season affairs, in Bloomer's day they were regarded as a reward for a job well done after a successful season. The club had already toured Denmark at the end of the previous season and went back again at the end of 1907-08, coupling up with a visit to Czechoslovakia for a game in Prague. Steve scored two in a 5-2 romp against a Danish XI and later recounted how he always enjoyed such tours 'although they were very much in the way of pure pleasure jaunts rather than serious footballing affairs'.

Season 1908-09...A goal every other game

Fourteen goals in 28 out of a possible 38 League appearances was not sufficient to secure leading scorer slot for Steve, the first time for 15 seasons that he had failed to achieve that honour. It was the end of a remarkable run but at an average of one goal for every two games his return earned him runner-up and was still an excellent one, far better than the previous season and in fact his best average since 1903-04. His season wasn't helped by missing a run of nine games through illness in December and January, his longest-ever lay-off to date, and the mantle of leading scorer was taken by John Hall, a new signing from Brighton with a prolific 18 in 30 games. Steve's illness was in fact a serious affair; a bad cold caught on his way home from a meeting developed into a severe chill, and quite probably pneumonia, which had his medical adviser, Dr A. Bryans, describing his condition as 'critical' at one point and the press telling its readers that 'the famous international has had a very narrow escape'. At a time when deaths from ailments we would now take in our stride were still quite commonplace, Steve's full recovery prevented a tragic premature end to his life and career.

By the end of the season it was over three years since he had left Derby and there is every indication that Steve had settled well in the North-East and among the players was making some friends who he would keep for a lifetime. Fred Pentland, who won a fairly regular place this season playing outside Steve on the right, was one of his best acquaintances from that time. Pentland being Wolverhampton-born, the two of them shared Black Country origins and were later to share both bad times and good together in Germany and Spain after they'd finished playing. As for the family, all the girls were by now settled at school but one suspects Steve's wife Sarah felt the most displaced of the family group. She doesn't generally figure in Steve's reminiscences but, as later events were to suggest, there is a strong possibility that she was suffering a degree of loneliness known to footballer's wives the world over. There is no indication that this was a major problem, merely a hint that Sarah missed her native Derby and would not say no to a return were it ever offered. Meanwhile, Middlesbrough it was, and a finish of ninth was again creditable. Derby County finished fifth, but unfortunately still in Division Two, and Baseball Ground regulars continued to chunter and harp on about Bloomer's departure while the Derby press regularly reported the doings of 'Steve', adding their justification on one occasion: "Even though he is now with the Middlesbrough club we make no excuse for reporting his deeds as we still regard him as one of our own." Prophetic stuff perhaps?

Season 1909-10...End of a memorable career?

The record books show that again Bloomer finished as second top scorer with ten in League and Cup against John Hall's 12, relatively paltry totals which presaged 'Boro's finish in a disappointing 17th position, only two points clear of relegation and suffering 18 defeats, their most in a 38-game season. Aston Villa scored 84 goals in winning the championship while 'Boro could manage only 56. Obviously the lack of firepower became a concern to the management as the season progressed and there was a degree of chopping and changing...Bloomer started as a regular and scored in each of his first four games but injuries and competition for places in the Middlesbrough camp again brought an unsettled feel to the side. Cail, Hall, Common and Bloomer all wanted a piece of the action up front but could seldom be accommodated together. Indeed, Common played the first six games at centre-half before eventually claiming the inside-right slot while Bloomer was either left out or moved to both centre-forward and right-wing.

As his 36th birthday arrived he had only managed three goals in his last nine appearances and from the New Year onwards Bloomer played less and less and, like all professional footballers who thrive on a regular first-team place, he found this a frustration. He hadn't suddenly lost his ability but it was certainly a bad patch. With his England years behind him and the loss of the guaranteed selection he had been used to, it seemed possible that the long career might fizzle to an ungainly end. Eye-witness accounts of his later games for Middlesbrough suggest a lack of sharpness, and photographs show a distinctly fuller face and figure than hitherto. Steve always admitted to a dislike for rigorous physical training regimes but he had generally done the work and seemed to keep a naturally trim figure in his younger days. But as many of us have found, there comes a day when the usual notch of the belt seems uncommonly difficult to locate and the extra pounds show a marked reluctance in shifting. Maybe the Phosferine supplies were running low, but Steve seemed to be struggling more with fitness than at any time in his career.

A particularly telling observation comes from one of the most respected football journalists who ever wrote about the game, Don Davies of the *Manchester Guardian*, who lost his life in the Manchester United Munich Air Disaster in 1958. He was only a 17-year-old schoolboy when he saw Bloomer play in what turned out to be Steve's third from last appearance in a 'Boro shirt and the occasion of his very last goal for the club. It was on 5 February 1910, a 1-1 draw, and years later Davies was to recall his impressions:

"Burnden Park, the home of Bolton Wanderers Football Club, was a focal point of my boyhood and those football match assemblies drew me into a strange fascination from the very first. It was in those schoolboy years that I first caught sight of Steve Bloomer at the time he played for Middlesbrough and I paid sixpence for the privilege. Looking back I recall with amazement that it seemed at the time sixpence grievously wasted. Schoolboy-like I had expected to see a forward fastening greedily on the ball and running round hosts of opponents somewhat in the manner of Swindon's Harold Fleming but what actually occurred astonished me. Here was a portly individual with close-cropped hair and a great white moon of a face apparently bored to death by the proceedings. Only years later was I to learn how emphatically that seeming indifference was the essential Bloomer. There was no skilful ball manipulation and everything he did to the ball that day seemed so natural, so inevitable, as to escape a schoolboy's perception altogether.

"Towards the end he kicked disdainfully at a ball rolling towards him and through turning his back immediately was the only player on the field who apparently did not know he had scored. There were 'Ohs' and 'Ahs' of admiration and prolonged headshakings of the elders in the crowd, yet to me it all seemed grossly overdone. But the records show that his supreme gift lay in his lightning perception of a chance and on its instantaneous acceptance and Bloomer in his prime walked to his place in an English soccer side as uncontestably as Don Bradman walked into Australia's cricket teams."

That is a curious little reminiscence, part hero-worship partutter disenchantment, a first-hand but distant sketchy memory filled out by reference to other descriptions of Bloomer read by the author at a later date, but somewhere in those schoolboy observations lies a germ of obvious disquiet…was it the end for Bloomer?

Reading between all the lines it seems likely that Steve was not only adapting his style of play to suit his advancing years but also rather going through the motions in the closing stages of his 'Boro career, struggling with fitness and somewhat disenchanted with his sporadic appearances in the first team. Probably the best thing for him at that time would have been a move, but the question remained as to whether any top flight club would come in for him. Maybe a drop into the Second Division, where his great experience might still count for much, would be the best bet. In the event he played his last game for 'Boro on 25 March 1910 in a 4-2 defeat at Aston Villa. He didn't score, nor were other clubs queuing up to sign him. He stayed with 'Boro for the rest of the season and was still in the town at the start of the 1910-11 campaign, but had not been re-signed by the club. For the first time in his career, Steve was out in the cold and the prospects looked bleak.

'Boro sunset and a new dawn

Inevitably Steve was to leave Middlesbrough and his time there passed into memory and columns of statistics. While he has gained a place in folklore at Derby, though, his treatment in the 'Boro history books is much lower key. In a recent publication, 'Boro's Best, a panel of fans and officials were asked to vote for the club's overall greats. The top five forwards of all time were Wilf Mannion, Brian Clough, Bernie Slaven, John Hickton and the 'White Feather,' Fabrizio Ravanelli. Nor was Steve included in the pre-war top five. While some of those selections may be surprising, it is understandable, if not justifiable, that Bloomer was excluded. It was a long time ago and he appeared for 'Boro in only five seasons, not really long enough for his deeds to have been related from generation to generation.

But more important, whereas in Derby County's history he tops the all-time scoring chart by a mile, at Middlesbrough he has been eclipsed by some truly prolific marksmen. Bloomer scored 62 goals in 130 matches for 'Boro, compared to George Camsell's 345 in 453 games between 1925-39. And following directly on from Bloomer between 1909-25 was George Elliott, with a 'mere' 213 from 365. A certain Brian Clough, too, had a half-decent strike-rate which made even Steve's look patchy – 204 goals in 222 games is legendary stuff. Then there are Wilf Mannion, Alan Peacock, Alf Common and at least a dozen others above Bloomer. Nevertheless it is surprising that the Middlesbrough heritage lobby has not made more of him. For a short time they had football's biggest star which surely even now deserves to shine more brightly over the Riverside Stadium than it seems to. One must suppose that it's because it's all in the past and to a certain type of armchair football fan the past is far less important than the next live satellite game.

Middlesbrough football was in Bloomer's own past, too, from October 1910. There is no evidence that he ever regretted the move there and on the few occasions he did reminisce he always praised the way the crowd treated him, remembered the quality of the turf, 'the finest in England', and recalled jolly away trip japes involving mistaken identity and club trainers indulging in bouts of fisticuffs with hotel waiters...all the usual football fare! But at the end he did need rescuing. He was never one for being very proactive in his life-plan, preferring to respond to the call of others rather than decide on a definite course of action for himself. In that sense the Bloomers were wandering in the wilderness as the 1910-11 season got under way, in dire need of a passing shepherd to round them up and point them towards greener pastures.

Bloomer might never have guessed that his saviour would be an old acquaintance with a Scotsman's dry wit, a nip of the national water in his flask, and a penchant for taking to the field in caps. One day in September 1910, Jimmy Methven came calling to ask Steve to rejoin the flock...there were some fine young Rams back in the Midlands in search of a wily old leader. On Saturday 24 September the chuntering in the factories and pubs of Derby turned to raucous cheering and incredulous exclamations.

"Ay up, 'ave y'eard? Bloomer's back."

The 'Incomparable Steve' had re-signed for Derby County.

THE 'SECOND BLOOMER' 1910-1914

"But sometimes during the dullest play,
Something comes back from an earlier day,
A fleeting moment, a hint of grace,
Brings back a feeling, a time, a place."
Gordon Jeffery

"STEVE BLOOMER, the famous inside-right, holder of the record in the matter of the number of international caps gained for England, has been re-signed by his old club Derby County! No more sensational news than this will have been anticipated by any supporter of the Rams and we doubt not that it will be received with gratification by many who remember the brilliance of this most famous of players.

"Each season since relegation to Division 2 it has been the Rams' lot to be among the strugglers for promotion, but it has yet to be, and now the veteran forward has returned to his old home to help regain the position the club held during his association with it. The idea that he would one day return to Derby has been dreamt of by some but never been regarded with much seriousness and it has come as a great surprise which we do not doubt for a moment will be welcomed by all and sundry. Always the idol of the crowd at Derby, one can well imagine what an ovation he will have when he steps on to the Baseball Ground wearing the Rams' colours once again."
Derbyshire Football Express Saturday, 24 September 1910

Old partners in a new era
What a contrast in tone between the press reports of Bloomer's return and those of his departure four and a half years previous; but one has to wonder if a 36-year-old, however committed, would be up to the job. The expectations were such that there was distinct pressure on Steve to make something happen because the years after his departure had been lean ones indeed for his old club. Derby's first-ever relegation befell them in the very season after Bloomer left, winning only nine of 38 games and suffering the joint lowest goals tally in the division. The lack of quality delivered during that dismal campaign had a subtle effect on the patterns of supportership at that time. Football fans, ever as fickle

then as they are now, are great ones for 'eras', and some who had watched the side right from the birth of the club in 1884 decided that Bloomer's departure signalled the end of the 'good old days'.

That 1906-07 relegation season saw average crowds at the Baseball Ground dip to below 7,000 for the very first time since the Rams had moved there in 1895; and although the fans rallied round for 1907-08, the first season in Division Two, perhaps buoyed by the curiosity of visiting away fans and the prospects of seeing different teams for the first-ever time, the average was again down to below 7,000 for 1908-09. All this had a negative effect on finances and in December 1908 the press reported that the club were £2,000 in debt and losing £50 a week. The club's own books suggest that might have been an exaggeration but such was the crisis that Derby County very nearly went to the wall and were saved only by a new share issue taken up by the club president and local business figures.

Such an unsettled atmosphere in turn made the job of manager Jimmy Methven extremely difficult indeed and, although they finished a creditable sixth, fifth and fourth in the Second Division before Bloomer's return, that little extra needed to regain the top flight seemed to elude them. Methven had worked long and hard in completely rebuilding the team now that all the old guard of the 1890s sides had retired or moved on and it was he who first mooted the idea that Steve's return might rekindle some of the passions of that lofty era and get the Rams back where they surely belonged. Methven and Bloomer knew each other inside out as they'd played in the same Derby team together throughout Steve's time there, and were well aware of the recipe for success. As their later written reminiscences were to reveal, while they may not have been 'best buddies' there was a healthy bond of common experience and both a mutual admiration and affectionate degree of chaff between these two interesting but different personalities.

Methven: "One of the best teams Derby County ever had was that of 1895-96, and Bloomer, our Steve, was a member of that side. Shall I 'introduce' you or shall I shan't, as Algernon might say? Steve was Steve and there's no need for me to tell anybody that he could play a bit. If only the England selectors could inoculate him with some monkey gland and get him for just one day for the 1928 international with Scotland, in his old match-winning form. What a treat it would be for soccer enthusiasts of today, with Hughie Gallacher on duty for Scotland and Steve at his best for England. I venture to suggest that there would be no enclosure on this or the other side of the Tweed big enough to house the crowd. Anyhow, if I had the opportunity, I should chance the weather and take the receipts for my 'benefit'…there goes that Scottish blood again."

Bloomer: "The company one keeps can compensate for nearly everything else and in my career as a first-class footballer I made many rare friends, grand fellows whom I am proud to have known and played with, the best of all the stars of England, Ireland, Scotland and Wales and always the true pals in the ranks of Derby County and Middlesbrough. I have often been asked which of my Derby County colleagues would make up the finest-ever team and it is a question I have usually 'shelved' as hypothetical, but this much I will say. The Rams have never had a superior defence to Jack Robinson in goal with Jimmy Methven and Joe Leiper at full-backs, the trio that helped us to the Cup semi-final in 1896 and a rearguard rarely bettered in the whole history of the game. Jimmy Methven later became my manager when I returned to Derby from the 'Boro and I well remember during his playing days what a champion leg-puller he was…he and Archie Goodall had ample scope for their genius at finding ways and means of having a game at the expense of their clubmates, but, methinks, they did not have matters their own way all the time."

It's tempting to suggest that had the imminent new footballing partnership floundered in any way there might always be a career in music hall waiting for 'Methven and Bloomer' – 'Logie' as the wee Scots droll and 'Stoneface' as his ever-suffering stooge – but fortunately, in September 1910, both men had their sights firmly set on sustained and improved football futures. Jimmy Methven recalls both the frustration he felt in managing the club at that time and the great satisfaction he gained from persuading the directors, despite a continuing dire financial climate, to allow him to pursue his target:

"When I accepted the offer made by Derby County to become manager of the club, little did I dream of the trouble I was running into. The idea installed in my mind was that it was an easy job, with money for nothing, but I can honestly assure you it is not. During the season a manager is never finished and even most Sundays his time is pretty fully occupied on club business of one sort or another, and after doing his level best he seldom gets any thanks for it. If the results are satisfactory the players get the credit, likewise the bunce accruing from the gain of points, and if the results are not pleasing then the manager's share is 'the other stuff'.

"But life has many compensations, and in the course of numerous visits to different parts of the British Isles one certainly comes across some real fine sports and makes many good friends. I have any amount of stories to tell about different players I have signed on for Derby County, but first and foremost the bringing back of Steve Bloomer from Middlesbrough in season 1910-11 will always remain in my memory as a pleasant job I did for the club. During the summer vacation Steve had recommended a player to me, the Middlesbrough half-back Tommy Wilson, so when he received my wire asking him to meet me on Middlesbrough railway platform Steve naturally thought I was after the player he had mentioned. When I popped the question, 'How would you like to come back to Derby?', I could see by his face that he was under the impression I was pulling his leg. Then it dawned on him that I really meant business and I never saw such a happy countenance in my life. When Mrs. Bloomer was informed that Steve had re- signed for Derby County, a similar expression crossed her face. After all, Derby, with all its slow motions, is worth coming back to. The transfer fee we paid for Steve was £100 and that sum was nearly realised by the enhanced gate at his very first match. It was a grand stroke of business when the directors decided to go for Steve's return."

That Bloomer was pleased to come back to Derby seems without question. The *Derby Daily Express* put it in a nutshell when they said: "Through all Steve's time away from the club he has never lost his many Derby friends and he never really settled in the North-East… his heart was always with Derby."

That is not to say that he was 'unhappy' at Middlesbrough, indeed Bloomer never said as much, but, like many people who leave their home town, he found he was more content in Derby than out of it and chose not to cut the strings when he left. The news of his transfer broke in the town on Saturday, 24 September 1910, and he arrived at Derby Midland Station on Monday the 26th; his name went straight on to the teamsheet, as captain, for the home game against Lincoln City on 1 October. The two home games already played thus far had brought a return of only two goals and no victories and in the days leading up to the Lincoln game the press milked the opportunity for a big build-up. Much rested on Bloomer's shoulders and perhaps his mind might have cast itself back to his first home debut in 1892. As a hungry 18-year-old he had grasped that opportunity…now he was double that age, could he again make the most of his chance?

A hero's welcome

While the press and supporters speculated on the season's prospects ahead, Steve was engaged in more practical matters. He moved into 35 Portland Street, quite a substantial end-terrace house with a small foregarden right on his home patch, no more than a short walk from all his previous boyhood and marital homes and just a five-minute stroll from the Baseball Ground. His girls were now 12, ten and eight and this was a suitable family house which Steve was destined to remain in, between his further travels, right until 1936, by far his longest association with any property in Derby. As far as the records indicate, he always rented and never became a private resident. This wasn't lack of ambition, rather just the prevailing convention of the time for a 'working man', and despite his renown in the football world Steve was just that.

Footballers then may have been elite in their achievements on the field but had nothing like the financial status of today's players. The Bloomers might have afforded something a little grander perhaps, but the house was in a pleasant and respectable area and Steve was never one for the high life or undue pretensions. Number 35 still stands much as it did, although the character of the locality is much changed. Next time it comes for sale, one wonders which of Derby's ever-thrusting band of estate agents, most of whom support the Rams, will be favoured with the opportunity of citing 'Bloomer' in their sales particulars?

Such mundane matters as Steve's home-hunting, and sorting out schools for the girls, were well beyond the average supporter. All that interested them was the game ahead and very high hopes were raised in the 'What they say!' column of the local paper; and what they did say was 'that the unerring goalgetter, despite his years, ought to be a power for good in the Rams' front rank,' and 'that his ripe experience will stand the team in good stead and keep the van up to the mark'. Other correspondents were not quite so sure that Bloomer's future was spelled out so clearly, hence a letter from a realist: "I have not heard whether it is the club's intention to play him regularly in the first team, but he should be invaluable to them as a coach to some of the younger players."

Whether this particular correspondent had a shrewd insight or would be later castigated in the guise of 'Doubting Thomas', only time would tell.

Crowds began to build early for the Lincoln game and by kick-off there were over 12,000 inside the Baseball Ground, double the previous home attendance against Blackpool. The sun shone and as the band thumped out *See The Conquering Hero Comes*, all eyes turned to the Osmaston End – at that time the players still changed in the Ley's Institute building and emerged from behind the goal. Supporters who were at that game have described the roar which greeted Steve's appearance as the loudest and longest they have ever known. As he trotted on to the field with the ball on the palm of his hand, he punted it skywards à la Dave Mackay to make his entrance in the fashion that many would come to remember as his trademark.

Even those who had watched Derby since the very early days were astonished by the welcome, the press later exclaiming: "Whatever leather lungs the Rams supporters possess, we were not well aware of their utmost power till Saturday, when hundreds who had never seen Steve Bloomer in their lives were carried away in an exhilarating wave of emotion." It was evident that the people of Derby had an unusually warm affection for Bloomer, one that has been preserved to this day, and Steve himself, who was never known for outward displays of emotion, later recalled that 'on that day the welcome I received from the Derby crowd brought tears to my eyes'. Beneath his impassive exterior, the poker-faced 'Napoleon of Football' was a sentimental soul at heart.

As for the game itself, it was fairytale stuff. The crowd 'cheered with renewed lustiness when Bloomer showed his paces in the opening passages of the game' and when, after 20 minutes, he opened the scoring with 'a driven shot which was not to be saved' this 'raised the spectators to extraordinary enthusiasm'. The mass delirium continued as Bloomer added his second with a penalty 20 minutes into the second half and two goals from Scotsman Jimmy Bauchoup plus one from Horace Barnes saw Derby cruise through to a 5-0 victory.

Those who had doubted that Bloomer could still 'cut the mustard' were forced to admit that he had exerted a definite 'influence' on the side, while those who were already converts were quick to press their point home. Again the local press reports convey the mood:

"The thousands that passed through the turnstiles with merely a desire to see the famed football warhorse witnessed a still virile and dangerous looking Bloomer infuse a deal of the proper spirit into the team, and his presence should have a good effect in achieving the much desired promotion at the end of the season."

Whatever the longer term outcome, the deeds during this period preceding World War One of what the press were to dub the 'Second Bloomer' have, in retrospect, had a marked effect not so much on the club's long-term history as on the way the Bloomer legend itself has evolved in Derby since that time. Had Bloomer remained at Middlesbrough and settled there in his retirement, he would surely have garnered an enhanced long-term status in the North-East while memories of his time at Derby would have forever been confined to the era pre-1906. The combined result of that might well have been a dilution of the overall Bloomer phenomenon because in Derby it is the 'Second Bloomer', and the subsequent 28 years he spent among the townsfolk, that is the true foundation for most of the memories handed down to today's generation.

The Lincoln game not only saw many of the older supporters renewing their waning allegiance to the Rams but, more important still, it fired the enthusiasm of a new generation of young and impressionable supporters to attend their first-ever games. Some of those supporters, still alive now and approaching or beyond the mystical centenarian status, can talk lucidly about 'the Second Bloomer' as a player even as the new Millennium is upon us. It seems a long time ago but it is largely their memories, passed in turn to their own children and grandchildren, then overlain on to the earlier memories of the long-departed supporters of the Victorian age, which has been responsible for developing and sustaining the 'mini-industry' which we might now call Bloomer folklore. Responsible, too, for the sometimes related tales that Bloomer was 'slow' and 'never a dribbler'...Bloomer Mark 1 and 2 were distinctly different animals. All that analysis, of course, was to come only in hindsight. As Sunday, 2 October 1910 dawned the fact remained that Bloomer had played only one game. True, it was a memorable one, but whether the momentum could be maintained, only a full season or more could reveal.

Season 1910-11...Down to earth

After the euphoria of the Lincoln game the season settled into more of a reasoned rhythm and Derby performed well enough to establish a place among the front runners. By the end of February 1911, following a run of five straight wins since the New Year, they were extremely well placed and the predictions of promotion seemed ever more likely to be correct. The signs on the goalscoring front looked especially promising as Bloomer, Alf 'Snobby' Bentley, Jimmy Bauchoup and Horace Barnes regularly found the back of the net. Useless fact though it may be, it 'is' a fact that, out of 82 League and Cup goals scored by Derby this season, 72 were scored by players with the initial 'B', only Wright, Halligan, Hall, Garry and Donald preventing the clean sweep. Never slow to latch on to such matters, 'County Onlooker' and his fellow football buffs at the *Derby Express* quickly labelled Bloomer and his forward partners the 'Busy Bees' and cartoons of hapless opponents being unmercifully stung by a stripey-bodied 'Steve' and chums were the order of the day on more than one occasion.

As points accumulated, dreams of another FA Cup Final appearance mounted, too, as the Rams stormed into the quarter finals with a 5-0 rout of Everton at the end of February in front of 22,892 at the Baseball Ground, an attendance record which lasted ten years. Perhaps it was the strain of the Cup run, but League form dipped alarmingly from that date and when the quarter-final was lost 4-0 at Newcastle, the sense of proportion that all football fans know and hate took a firm gut-wrenching grip. Derby finished sixth, lower than the previous season, and a full nine points off the promotion spot. There was very little carping, though, and all seemed agreed that it had been a truly memorable season. As for the man of the moment, Bloomer made 32 League and Cup appearances and topped the scoring chart with 24, his best aggregate since the start of the century.

Such was his form that he very nearly added another England cap to his collection. For the game against Ireland in February 1911 he was in the hat for selection but just lost out to Swindon's Harold Fleming. What a sentimental England farewell that might have been, for the side that day was under the charge of former Derby manager Harry Newbould and the game, a 2-1 win for England, was at the Baseball Ground. No matter, having proved himself as prolific a marksman as ever, if not in the top flight at least in the Second Division, the season was a personal triumph for Bloomer. He had regained the fitness and zest that had left him in his later days at 'Boro, ensured his place for another campaign and preserved the opportunity to finish the job he had been hired to do.

Season 1911-12...One to savour

Whatever Jimmy Methven contemplated during the close-season, he seems to have recognised that Derby's ultimate failure in the previous season lay not in a lack of goals but firmly in the goals-against column. A total of 52 League goals conceded was far worse than any of the teams finishing above them and only three less than Gainsborough Trinity who narrowly escaped relegation in 18th position. Like all good managers, Methven acted on this knowledge and promptly signed a defender in the close season, followed by another early in the campaign. Although Methven's actions seemed perfectly controlled and rational at this stage, those of a superstitious nature might well speculate whether the pressure of it all had got to him.

Indeed, the sort of people who refuse to leave the house on Friday 13th might fairly assert that the Derby manager had become alphabetically challenged, developing a paranoid fixation around the letter 'B' which only permitted him to deal in the transfer market with certain players and clubs. Betts, a back, was signed to join new arrival Buckley, from Birmingham, to bolster the existing 'Busy Bees' brigade of Barbour, Bagshaw, Bloomer, Bauchoup and Barnes, and in the other direction it was bye-bye Bentley, who went to Bolton. It certainly gave the headline writers ample scope for the sort of corny mirth-making which increasingly characterised much of the reporting.

Rest assured, though, Methven's sanity was never more intact and his shrewd transfer dealings paid early dividends. Frank Buckley, who had fought in the Boer War and was to play a leading role as a major in the Footballer's Battalion in World War One, was a truly influential signing at centre-half. Starting a run against Glossop North End in October and finishing it with a 5-1 win against Clapton Orient, both unfamiliar names now, the Rams put together a three-month unbeaten spell. Such was Buckley's social stature and authoritative demeanour that Bloomer later readily acknowledged that he thought Buckley should have been given leadership of the side:

"Sages among Rams supporters will remember that I was skipper of the side for four seasons, leading Derby County on to the field at a good quick trot with a hefty kick of the ball into the air, precisely the same way as Bob Crompton, the Blackburn and England full-back. But there is more to good captaincy than that and I never rated myself as a leader in the capacity of someone like Sheffield United's 'Nudger' Needham... as a matter of fact I contended that Frank Buckley, who was with us for three of those seasons, should have held it, for, as men such as Johnny Goodall and others have proved in their periods of skipperdom, the captaincy should not be merely a courtesy office."

If Bloomer was suggesting that his leadership of the side was all down to sentimentality he was wrong. It may have started at that but he would quickly have been stripped of the honour if the board had felt he wasn't the right man. Indeed, supporters and players from that era have particularly remarked on the influence he exerted. Even Ivan Sharpe, the famous amateur international left-winger in that side, signed from Glossop, conceded that much, despite his well-known and previously-quoted assertion that Steve's tolerance of his team-mates' perceived deficiencies was not all it might be. Much has sometimes been made of that apparent irritability which descended like a dark cloud on Bloomer when matters on the pitch didn't go to plan, and it is true that he never suffered fools gladly. He was, one concludes, cursed with an affliction that befalls many people of natural ability, namely that he found it difficult to understand why some of his colleagues were unable to do to the ball what he himself accomplished with complete assurance. In fairness, though, his tut-tutting, such as it was, was always confined to the pitch, spontaneous, never vindictive, born entirely of frustration and an insatiable desire to win, and by no means a regular feature of his game.

That said, it was a weakness but perhaps, perversely, one that benefited the side, as some footballers seem only to be motivated when their deficiencies are highlighted. One thing is certain...while Bloomer may have 'criticised' others, the standards he demanded from his colleagues were matched or redoubled by those he expected of himself. Ivan Sharpe, described by manager Methven, and not disparagingly, as 'a toff on and off the field', put Bloomer's wider contribution at this time into perspective in describing him as 'the driving wheel of the side, an inspiring example to his players and tremendously devoted to his team. A curious personality, too, but then genius runs that way.'

For Bloomer's part, he never resented Sharpe's psychoanalytic tendencies and was an admirer of the winger's own undoubted abilities: "Ivan was as fast as a greyhound in that team, a magnificent sprinter and superbly clever in ball control."

Whatever the methods that season, they worked. Derby County won the Second Division championship to regain their place in the top flight. For Bloomer and the lads it was 'mission accomplished' and, when the top spot was clinched with a 2-0 win at Cup Finalists Barnsley in the very last game, a reported 20,000 fans stretching right down Midland Road turned up at Derby Midland Station to greet the returning champions. Methven and Bloomer were carried shoulder high as the team were ushered into waiting cabs and taken in triumphant procession to the Royal Hotel on the corner of Victoria Street and the Cornmarket where balcony appearances preceded a night of celebration. The *Titanic* might have sunk barely a week before, but Derby County's buoyancy that night was undisputed; it was Bloomer's finest day with the Rams, and Methven's too. It was all very satisfying for everyone connected with the club and, curiously, it was the only championship medal Bloomer ever won in the first-class game.

Of all the sides he played in, he had fond memories of that particular bunch of lads and the team spirit engendered among them. Several of the boys had common interests off the field… fishing, for which he won a number of angling club trophies, was one of Steve's favourite relaxations and his love of cricket was shared by almost the whole side, including manager Methven who had captained Derby Nomads for years until they disbanded in 1908. Bloomer still played regularly for Ley's Institute with fellow Rams Jimmy Bagshaw and Horace Barnes, quite a celebrity line-up, and such was the love of the summer game that an annual challenge match was played by Derby County against some of the leading cricketing names in the country at Longford Hall, home of Lady Coke, former lady-in-waiting to Queen Victoria, where, according to manager Methven, 'the lads were treated like lords'. Methven himself, who died in 1953, deserves much credit for the assembly of the 1912 championship side and the relaxed atmosphere he created within the dressing-room. As Bloomer recalls, it suited him to a tee:

"For a team to be successful they must be friendly…that was what won us the Second Division championship in 1912; no better lot of lads ever played on a football field… we were all pals both off and on."

Those carefree and peaceful times in that immediate post-Edwardian era, balmy days soon to be so ingloriously engulfed by the chilling darkness of war, were some of the happiest of Bloomer's career. He well knew that he was approaching the stage, at 38, where every game was a bonus, every goal another notch on a tally that must soon be full, but he made the most of his 'second chance' and embraced the game with all the passion he could muster. With the benefit of hindsight it might have been an apt moment for the victorious captain to hang up his boots while the going was good; but with 18 goals he had again finished as the club's top League scorer, his 15th time in succession for Derby County, and the lure of just one last crack at the First Division was more than he could resist. Perhaps, as a fisherman, he might have thought twice before taking the bait.

Season 1912-13…A final flourish

Had Bloomer called it a day after the promotion season it would have brought his career to a nicely rounded close, but at least by having another shot at the First Division he established a claim to having finished where he started, 'at the top', something which has always been held dear to a certain breed of footballer, and invariably the good ones. So in 1912-13, back came the big names in Bloomer's fixture list. Second Division clubs such as Leicester Fosse, Stockport County, Leeds City and Glossop had all provided stiff opposition but they could not match the draw of Blackburn Rovers, Sunderland, Aston Villa, Sheffield Wednesday and their ilk, clubs against which Steve had fought some of his finest battles. Back on the big stage Bloomer missed only one game in the first half of the season and in truth he justified his decision to play on and the faith of the selection committee and manager in continuing to pick him.

Two games in particular might well be given 'swan song' status: on 26 October 1912, in the 4-2 home win over Liverpool, he scored a first-half hat-trick which the *Football Express* described under the headline banner 'Bloomer Makes Merry' as 'a splendid achievement, a reminder of the old days'. In the very next home game, two weeks later, he bagged another hat-trick in the 5-1 trouncing of Sheffield United, a feat which nowadays would surely tempt the tagline 'Bloomer's away as United caught with pants down'. This was the final high…although he managed two in the 5-0 home defeat of Tottenham in January 1913, just two days before his 39th birthday, those were his last goals this season. In the remaining nine games he played in that campaign, the blank which he drew in each one constituted his worst-ever run without a goal and increasingly Horace Barnes or Harry Walker were given the inside-right berth while Bloomer was left out.

He finished the season with 14 goals in 30 League and Cup appearances, by no means a bad return and certainly not his worst. In fact it was both a better total and aggregate than that he had achieved in his very first season in 1892-93, and highly laudable for that, but in a club context it represented the first time in 16 consecutive seasons for Derby, either side of his 'Boro spell, that he failed to claim top scorer spot. That honour went to Harry leonard and Derby finished a creditable seventh.

Bloomer's reappearance in the First Division placed him firmly back in the public eye but he was being viewed increasingly just as a revered 'national treasure' rather than a player with any future. Invitations to benefit matches rather than international call-ups were the order of the day – he appeared for Billy Meredith in 1912 at Wrexham – and that is always a clue that the better days are gone, that as the ability to latch on to a through pass recedes, the entitlement to a tram-pass draws ever closer. Now it really should have been retirement time, but Steve signed on for another season. Who can blame him? It's always nice to be wanted. In the event, though, it proved a season too far.

Season 1913-14... 'Anno Domini' the victor

Bloomer played only six first-team games in this, his last-ever season in the first-class game as a player. He scored two goals, a brace in the second game of the season in a 5-3 home defeat at the hands of Sheffield United on 6 September 1913. If Bloomer could no longer do it, neither, regrettably, could the team as a collective unit. Despite 24 League goals from the increasingly sought-after Barnes, shortly to move to Manchester City – for a £2,500 fee which equalled the British (and probably the world) record at the time – Derby were relegated whence they came. Bloomer played only a fringe part, acting largely as understudy to whoever was injured; if there had been a subs' bench in those days he'd have been on it, but in the event he played a number of times for the Reserves in the Central Alliance, effectively taking on the role of manager-coach to that side.

He certainly didn't lie down without a fight; his first Reserves outing this season came against Shirebrook at the Baseball Ground in front of 300 hardy fans, and Bloomer scored four in a 6-1 win. Against the Notts County second string in early January he notched another hat-trick which helped to justify his final call-up to the first team. His last League appearance for Derby was in the 0-0 draw at Bradford City on 24 January 1914, four days after his 40th birthday, at centre-forward. The local press for once had no need for superlatives:

"For the game at Valley Parade, Derby made the experiment of introducing Bloomer as leader of the attack in place of the injured Leonard. He was given the captaincy but failed to name the coin, though he was far from being a failure at centre-forward. True, he is slow, but he distributed the ball with judgement and skill."

The use of the word 'failed', even in such a routine matter as the toss, was not typical in connection with Bloomer. A week later, 31 January 1914, he played his last-ever game in the fourth round FA Cup tie at Burnley, again as captain. The Rams went down 3-2 and the headlines screamed "Goodbye to the Cup". Derby would renew their acquaintance with that coveted trophy on other occasions but for Bloomer the finality of that headline was clear. In the ball-by-ball account of the game he was mentioned only once: "Bloomer lost the toss and Derby had to face the wind for the first 45 minutes." As if that didn't say it all, the summing up declared: "Bloomer was not fast enough for the centre-forward position although he did some good work."

And there the report, and Bloomer's first-class playing career, abruptly ended. No one knew it for sure at the time, nor was Derby's relegation a certainty at that stage, but the writing for Bloomer and Derby was on the wall. The supporters were disenchanted and some, especially the armchair brigade, found the position all too difficult to swallow. This letter from an exiled young

Derbeian in America has 'clutching at straws' written all over it… for someone who hadn't seen a game all season he seems to know an awful lot:

"Here in America I receive the *Derbyshire Football Express* by mail every week. I am sorry to see that Derby County are in such a bad position but I suppose that now Bloomer's days are over they will go down into the Second Division… that is where they landed when Steve left before and they could not return until the management got him back. It was through Bloomer that the County won their way back into the upper League but now the old timer's days are about over, let me see what will become of Derby County. I think as long as Bloomer can hold up on two feet he should be included as his generalship amounts to a great deal, and besides, I would rather see an old 'has been' with a head any time before I would want to see a young player who had to stop and think twice what to do when he had the ball at his toe in front of an open goal. Put Bloomer in such a position and in spite of his 40 years I bet he would make the net buzz!"
21 March 1914

Although that letter carries elements of the truth, it is fraught with misplaced emotion. Bloomer himself, reflecting on his retirement some years later, displayed a much better balanced view of the situation:

"Beware of the player who is having it forced home to him that his best days are done and who does not like it. I have heard of a few old stagers not at all happily reconciled to the inevitable and liable as a result to turn nasty on the field. It is a sure sign of faltering powers in a player when he starts trying to save his legs by sweeping those of his opponents from under them and those who yield to that temptation are the quickest to slide down the scale to oblivion. I know all about that funny feeling which comes with the first notice from Anno Domini and that it is getting nearly time to quit. It is galling to find that you cannot make that little extra effort you used to be able to pull out, but we all get it in some form or another and it is no use kicking against it. The only thing to do is to face the fact that the human system is fallible, then make up your mind to think more and run about less as a means of compensating to the best of your ability for deficiencies of bellows and vitamins. Keep a clear head and a check on your temper but, when you feel the pension stage is upon you, an old hand should take a firm resolve to go quickly if go he must."

Although Steve hung on longer than his self-advocacy seems to recommend, the sentiment is sensible enough and suggests he was able to take a philosophical view of his retirement and handle the final parting with dignity.

The boy who had arrived in Derby as a five-year-old and made his debut for Derby County as a 'wee bit laddie' had come a long way in his 40 years. A total of 394 goals in 655 League and Cup games for Derby and Middlesbrough was quite a record. Some 22 years as a professional footballer and a place as England's leading international at a time when the game had made such great strides had truly made Bloomer a legend in his own lifetime…a fairly auspicious journey for the son of a humble Cradley puddler born into poverty.

If anyone should doubt that, it is only necessary to look at the press for the duration of his career and there is evidence in mounting abundance of the status he had gradually attained in the eyes first of football followers and then of a nation. One has to think in terms of cricket's W. G. Grace or football's Sir Bobby Charlton and Sir Stanley Matthews as comparables. Even those who didn't share the prevailing passion for football came to know Bloomer, even if they didn't admire him, and he simply became known in the press as 'Steve'. That doesn't happen to many people – 'Martina' managed it in the tennis world and both 'Frank' and 'our 'Enery' in boxing – but it occurs more in the shallow world of television now, where 'Des', 'Delia' and their glossy like have reached the peak in their chosen careers and are icons of sorts. 'Steve' was more raw and accessible than that but he was a 'household name' in that age before television, popular radio and big-time cinema, when only footballers and music hall artists were as near to soap stars as you could get, and he attained that superstar status above all others in football. Only Welshman Billy Meredith came close.

Supportive evidence of their place in the country's psyche sometimes emerges from unusual sources. The great English comic writer P. G. Wodehouse might not be an immediate candidate but his inclusion of the two football characters in his short story, *The Goal-keeper and Plutocrat*, first published in the January 1912 edition of *Strand Magazine*, shows how well-known both men were at that time:

"Daniel Rackstraw was a millionaire but at heart he was a spectator of football and his football museum had but one equal, that of Mr Jacob Dodson. Between them at enormous expense they had cornered the curio market of the game…it was Rackstraw who had secured the authentic pair of boots in which Bloomer had first played for England but it was Dodson who possessed the india-rubber ball used by Meredith when a boy. Even so, Dodson would frequently pay a visit to Rackstraw's house to spend hours gazing wistfully at the Bloomer boots."

The yarn proceeds with Rackstraw wagering the boots against Dodson's ball in a football challenge match and in victory he succeeds in achieving a life's ambition, the ownership of both. All very tongue-in-cheek of course, and not really a 'Plum' effort in the splendid Wodehouseian tradition, but a sound indication that Bloomer's name had entered everyday usage in the English language, even among the relatively erudite readers of the splendid P.G.

Away from the airy-fairy world of literature, which was certainly not the province of the working class, others gave voice in more vehement terms in support of Bloomer's status in the game. Close to his retirement we might choose to quote any one of numerous newspaper tributes but perhaps the last word should go to the organ of the players themselves, the *Football Players' Magazine*. When Bloomer was not invited to the FA Jubilee banquet held at the Holborn Restaurant in London in November 1913 they had this to say:

"He is the greatest inside-forward who has ever played for England and his name has for years been a household word wherever football is played. He has done as much for the game as any man who ever kicked a ball…and he is not going to the FA Jubilee banquet. He was the best marksman of his day, a great genius, a sportsman of splendid nerve, yet some of the people who will be there have never kicked a football in a match of importance in their lives."

Steve no doubt appreciated being 'looked out for' in this way but there was no malice in his exclusion and it is difficult to imagine that he lost any sleep over missing a night out with the 'stuffed shirts' of the football world. In any case, in time, he had far more important matters to concern himself with. Like what to do with the rest of his life. In the early summer of 1914, while supporters and players looked forward to the 1914-15 campaign, he considered his options. Bloomer didn't know what his own destiny held and neither was anyone else the remotest bit aware that a campaign of an altogether different sort, on foreign fields, was about to shatter so many lives.

OH WHAT A LOVELY WAR?
1914-1918

"On through the hail of slaughter,
Where gallant comrades fall,
Where blood is poured like water,
They drive the trickling ball.
The fear of death before them,
Is but an empty name,
True to the land that bore them,
The Surreys play the game."
'Touchstone'

"**A**T THE AGM of the Derby County Football Club last week it was noticed that Steve Bloomer's name did not appear in the list of players signed on again for next season, nor was it mentioned amongst those who had been transferred. Speculation as to the future of the famous international has been rife but all rumours can now be put at rest by his departure this week for Germany where he has accepted a position as coach to a Berlin club."
Derby Daily Telegraph, 9 July 1914

Pastures new

That short paragraph was how the people of Derby were effectively informed that Steve Bloomer had played his last game at first-class level for Derby County, or indeed for any other club. After 22 full seasons as a player, the future that lay ahead of Steve must have seemed an uncertain one, as every footballer who has ever 'hung up his boots' before or since must surely confirm. Although former players at that time did enter management, as evidenced in Derby County's own case by the ongoing occupation of the hotseat by old stalwart Methven, there were simply not enough positions to go round. Not only that...there was a certain degree of social selectivity applied by football club directors in appointing their key personnel, so that a high proportion of club managers tended to come from the better educated or business backgrounds rather than the solidly working-class origins shared by Bloomer and many of his fellow professionals. Because of that discernible pattern, hugely respected though Bloomer was in the annals of the game, his chances of walking straight into a club management role were relatively limited and he faced the very real prospect of having to look outside the game for ongoing employment.

To someone who had a love of football coursing through his veins as strongly as Steve did, the idea of a life beyond the boundaries of the only one he really knew undoubtedly held little appeal and any opportunity which enabled him to continue an involvement in football in some capacity would have to be seriously considered. It was against this background of some anxiety that he was offered and accepted the position of 'coach and instructor' at the Berlin Britannia Football Club, an opportunity he was alerted to by his much-travelled Derby County playing colleague Ivan Sharpe. The England amateur international left-winger had toured the Continent a great deal and was socially adept enough to make many influential contacts, one of which occurred after a match at Karlsruhe during a tour of Germany with a team called 'The Pirates' in 1908. Summoned to the pavilion for an audience with Prince Max of Baden, later to become German Chancellor in 1918, Sharpe was asked a very direct question by the 'handsome figure in uniform and Prussian helmet': "Our country is taking a great interest in football and I feel sure it will go ahead by leaps and bounds, but can you offer any advice as to how the game should be developed in popularity and standard of play?"

Sharpe's immediate reply, very much in Captain Mainwaring vein, was that 'professional coaches from Britain will soon teach Germany the proper methods' and that advice was taken to heart, with several English or Scottish professionals being appointed to key positions at German clubs in the larger cities. Steve Bloomer's name and reputation was certainly known abroad at that time and indeed he had scored against the touring German national XI in an unofficial international against the 'Professionals of England' at Manchester City's then Hyde Road ground in the autumn of 1901. The gulf in quality was embarrassingly obvious as England ran out 10-0 winners with Steve captaining the side from inside-right. Reports suggest it could have been many more as the German goalkeeper Luedecker was generally hailed as 'man of the match'.

So it was that when Sharpe was able to recommend Bloomer as a possible coach to the British-founded Berlin club, they were only too delighted to offer their English target a definite contract. The final decision, of course, lay with Steve himself, and he opted to take this opportunity to move to pastures new. Travelling without his wife Sarah, as was then the norm for many overseas contracts in all sorts of professions, he left Derby and 35 Portland Street behind and arrived in Berlin on 14 July 1914. Three weeks later, Britain declared war on Germany, and from November onwards Bloomer was interned in a civilian prison camp for almost the entire duration of what became known as the Great War. When he next saw Sarah and crossed the threshhold of his Derby home, the date was 22 November 1918 and almost one million British Empire servicemen had died in conflict.

Midnight capture

In retrospect it seems inconceivable that Bloomer should have chosen to go to Germany only three weeks before such a cataclysm. One imagines he and everybody else must have seen the storm clouds gathering but the truth is that Britain's involvement in the war came as a complete surprise to all but the most alarmist civilians and a handful of acutely perceptive or in the know 'top brass'. The assassination of the Austrian Crown Prince, Archduke Franz-Ferdinand, by 19-year-old Serbian student Gavrilo Princip, had already occurred in Sarajevo on Sunday 28 June, but reminiscences of many British citizens abroad at that time confirm that they felt the whole thing would blow over or, if a war was provoked, it would be a localised affair which they could keep well out of, and Britain could not possibly be involved. Despite Austria using the incident as a pretext for declaring war on Serbia on 28 July, there was no panic – indeed, a sizeable party of British tourists, including several honeymoon couples, arrived in Germany to begin their holidays on Friday 31 July. But, as the larger powers inevitably stuck their noses in, the happy holidaymakers got even more excitement than the brochures promised. Germany mobilised the next day and declared war against Russia and then France; on Tuesday, 4 August the incredible blow fell as 'the lamps went out all over Europe' and Britain declared war on Germany. All British subjects in Germany became 'enemy aliens' – businessmen, musicians, teachers, students, golfers, jockeys, music-hall artists and sundry other occupations were all treated alike and there was no special dispensation for holidaymakers, even if you were on your honeymoon, or footballers, even if your name was Steve Bloomer. Years later Steve was to recall his feelings just before that fateful day:

"It doesn't seem so long ago that I was one of the happy throng of Britishers assembled on the boulevards of Berlin at the start of August 1914. I remember one night we went home, aliens in a strange land, and there was rumour of war in the air. Ah well, what did that matter? It hadn't been declared and there was plenty of time to do something about it when it was an accomplished fact. So we went home perfectly happy and not a bit worried!"

There was certainly a degree of rather poignant naivety and not a little British superiority in such an attitude, yet despite some early arrests and a degree of police supervision, most of the 'aliens' passed August to October in relative freedom. Steve himself communicated his position by a letter to his wife sent through the American consul at the start of October, saying simply: "I am quite all right and at present engaged at coaching the young fellows in Berlin. I cannot say a great deal about their ability on what I have seen of them so far, except in regard to their anxiety to achieve a high standard."

But by the end of October the sacking of a mere handful of Germans from their jobs in England and their retention in improvised camps had inflamed opinion in Germany. An ultimatum for their release was given and ignored and an ominous decree, massively disproportionate as a retaliatory measure, was issued by the German authorities:

"All male British subjects except clergymen, doctors, lunatics and bed-ridden invalids, between the ages of 17 and 55, and all British officers of whatever age, should be arrested on 6 November 1914 and taken to an internment camp selected for them."

The third on the list of exceptions might well have embraced goalkeepers but certainly not well-balanced inside-rights. The Germans wasted not a minute's time in implementing their threat; on the very stroke of midnight on 5 November, a knock on the door of Bloomer's lodgings sealed his fate for the next four years. Up to 5,000 others were simultaneously arrested throughout Germany and taken immediately to the nearest local jail before being transferred the next day to their camp. Some went to Sennelager, others to Celle, but the majority, especially the civilians, were destined for Ruhleben. Bloomer was among 600 or so rounded up that night in Berlin and became part of a camp society extending to over 4,000 men at its full capacity. The suburb of Ruhleben lay two miles west of Berlin's 1914 boundaries, its name, cruelly ironic, meaning 'peaceful life'.

Stiff upper lips

Although Steve himself was always rather reluctant to be drawn into any detailed accounts and analysis of this period of his life, there is a rich seam of source material available to scholars of Ruhleben camp. The holdings of the Imperial War Museum and Harvard University include books of reminiscences, diaries, letters, camp magazines and all manner of ephemeral material which paint a vivid and sometimes uncomfortably frank picture of day-to-day camp life, how the men developed both a structured society and a fully operative 'town' out of a situation which, at the outset, was nothing but grim, cold, disorganised and completely dysfunctional. The detail is staggering and Bloomer is mentioned many times in the archives, for 'everybody knew Steve'. Indeed, an entire book on 'Bloomer's War', perhaps even a period film, would make an entertaining and moving account, but within the narrative of his entire life story a reasoned summary must suffice.

Having spent his earliest professional footballing years being bitten by the chill winds cutting relentlessly across Derby Racecourse, Steve might have been forgiven for a wry smile as he was ushered unceremoniously to his new home, for Ruhleben camp was itself a racecourse, and in the winter of 1914 a cold, damp and swampy one at that. There were three grandstands, a restaurant called the 'tea house', a club house known as the 'casino', limited staff residential quarters and offices and 11 two-storey stables, simply stalls with hay-lofts over them. Racing had stopped as soon as the German army mobilised and the whole compound had been ringed with high barbed-wire fences. It didn't take the newly-arriving internees too long to realise which part of the course their new quarters lay in – and cosy 'B & B' it certainly wasn't, as graphically described by one of Steve's fellow inmates, the stables were the only option:

"At five o' clock in the evening of 6 November, the first long column of men entered through the gates, their harmless civilian appearance making the bristling demeanour of their police escort seem slightly ludicrous as they were marched between the waiting rows of spiked-helmeted armed guards. Each column is herded into a long dimly-lit stable corridor and a German sergeant thrusts open the sliding door of a horse-box, barking the order 'first six in here'. When the lower boxes are all filled, the remaining men are turned into the haylofts above. The floors are cold concrete strewn with a thin layer of straw and some of the boxes are covered in manure. At first the men stand or lie huddled on the floor but at intervals are given a straw sack or a plank bed and a horse-blanket. The lucky ones get a military iron bunk. The early arrivals are given a tin bowl of muddy cocoa or a kind of watery 'skilly' and a piece of repugnant blood sausage. The late arrivals that night are given nothing.

"Into each box measuring 11ft x 11ft, six men or more are placed... stable ten was designed for 27 horses and originally housed 365 men! There was no heat, very poor light, two taps and 15 earthenware bowls to be shared by all of these; the toilets and latrines were completely open and communal, 35 or 40 in a row; each man was given a coarse cloth like a dishcloth, a tin bowl to hold his food, but no knife, fork, spoon, cup or soap. Some men gamely tried to make a joke of it all but most were quiet and apprehensive and a few close to tears. All seemed tired, hungry and dazed by their sudden arrest and the next day we all learnt the routine of parading, washing and dressing by 6.30 each morning as the guards tramped through the stables bellowing 'Aufstehen!' and bewildered men opened their eyes on the strange world in which they were to spend the next four years."

Of course, the duration of their stay was entirely an unknown factor to all concerned in those dark early days and surely most of the men were initially sustained by the thought that this was a temporary state of affairs...at least until the grim realisation set in that an early release was nothing but a vain hope. Despite the shock of all the initial hardship, most men coped well in the first few weeks and Steve himself, housed firstly in Barrack 1, later summed up the mood:

"When that happy crowd of us gathered in the Berlin boulevards, little did I know that shortly afterwards I would be one of the same throng herded together in that hell which became known as Ruhleben Camp. For the first few days in captivity, though, nay weeks, none of the English were worried. What did a few weeks mean? Nothing! Kitchener would swipe the Jerries and Jellicoe would smash their fleet and it would all be over by Christmas. Then we could go back on the boulevards and tell the Germans what fools they had been to try and fight Johnny Bull. Then came realisation. The war wasn't going to be over in a few weeks. What happened? I'll not mention the names of other nationalities but I saw much of other nations stamping around and cursing everybody. But the Britishers didn't. We set to make the most of a bad job and though there may have been times when some of us actually cried ourselves to sleep or held the bitterest of thoughts, there was a stiff upper lip to be seen in public and many a smile and a laugh. Then when the 'up against it' British spirit had shown an example, the hell of Ruhleben became as near a heaven as a German internment camp could ever be."

Bloomer was certainly fiercely patriotic and at times boldly jingoistic in his 'British Bulldog' enthusiasm, but he spoke as he found and in fact this short but touchingly rousing little battle cry effectively encapsulates the story of Ruhleben and helps to explain many of the truths, myths and conundrums which have surrounded its history.

Deckchairs or dysentery…holiday camp or hell-hole?

The entire question of civilian imprisonment caused a major furore back home. The mass internments in Germany were the first on such a scale, certainly the most publicised and regarded by the British as a major infringement of human rights. Newspaper attention was heightened by the fact that many of the Ruhleben prisoners were, like Bloomer, well known public figures. Although there was a complete mixed bag of social types in the camp, there were certainly a lot of high achievers among them. Most had been in Berlin because of what they were good at, whether it be sealing big export orders, riding winners or teaching rich Germans to play a decent game of golf. Yet the newspaper coverage that at first drummed up sympathy for the 'Ruhlebenites', as they came to be known, slowly turned public opinion away from supporting the prisoners. As horrific news came back regularly from the Western Front, the eye-witness reports that came in from visitors to Ruhleben, at least from mid-1915 onwards, described a society in which men lounged in deckchairs watching cricket, regularly received parcels of goodies from the homeland and enjoyed most of the services and entertainments that any country town or large village would have been proud to offer. Ruhleben provided the perfect material for cruel newspaper cartoons and cheap music hall jokes and therein lies the central enigma surrounding that band of men held captive right at the heart of enemy territory. So which was it, heaven or hell?

One thing must be made clear right from the outset. The civilian prison camp of 1914-18 was certainly not the Nazi concentration camp of World War Two. The German officers and guards could be rude, ignorant and stupid, sometimes very harsh, but never descending en masse to the levels of appalling cruelty associated with Nazi Germany. But that is not to say that life was a picnic. Ruhleben Camp in its early days was an extremely unpleasant place to be and it was only the talent, spirit and sheer hard work of its internees in making it into something more palatable that ultimately led to the 'Life of Riley' jibes that they had to suffer.

The truth is that right from day one the Ruhlebenites sought to improve their lot. It quickly became evident to them that the German staff had no real idea how to run a camp – after all, they'd had no training and no practical previous experience. If Ruhleben was to become at least bearable, then all the drive and initiative for change needed to come from its inmates. And that is precisely what happened. Those inclined to business began to open 'shops' in their lofts and boxes: 'Chapman's Boots' in Barrack 8 was the place for all footwear; and when they needed a clean, 'Sunny Smitty' of Barrack 10 was the 'Best Shoe-Black in Camp'; and if they started to rub a little, that was no problem, as a visit to George Teger in the Grandstand for 'a first-class pedicure' was always available for those that required it. Not that the services were confined purely to the foot department. The men opened shops for all manner of goods, set up a library and a theatre, ran classes for every subject under the sun, and arranged musical recitals, poetry readings and debates. They implemented their own system of internal government, with elected barrack 'Captains' and committees, fines for misbehaviour and awards for special achievement. To keep everyone up to date with what was going on, they printed a daily broadsheet and, from June 1915, issued a regular camp magazine of remarkably high production standards. As for anything happening in camp that they didn't like, protests were swiftly organised; the quality of the early food was widely condemned and the catering manager, blessed with the particularly appropriate name of Herr Griese, came in for universal stick. A noisy 'skilly riot' by a band of young sailors eventually ensued and a delegation of 'Captains' visited the camp commandant, insisting that he sampled the 'pig-swill'. The swift result was that 'Old Greasy' was ordered to modify his menu and 'skilly', at least, was 'off' for the duration.

Yet for every plus or pleasure there was also indignity and discomfort. Petty camp rules enforced by surly guards restricted men's movements and activities, sometimes for no logical reason. The fact that the food had 'improved' did not mean it reached 'cordon bleu' standard. Many of the shops and services offered were a sort of parody of the real thing, just as the street names given to the muddy thoroughfares throughout the camp were a 'tongue in cheek' attempt at feigning normality – Bond Street, Piccadilly Circus and Trafalgar Square. What resulted from summer 1915 onwards was a unique and curious mixture which, over 80 years later, reads like a cross between squalid prison and learned university campus, 'gold rush' frontier town and public school, or tumbledown shanty settlement and early Butlin's holiday camp. What is certain is that none of the good things which Ruhleben came to offer internally was the result of anything else but the dogged spirit, ability and determination of the internees. Yet that was something that the papers of the day seldom recognised.

What they printed instead was that one man received festive parcels containing no less than 15 Christmas puddings – but was it his fault he had caring family and friends back home? And what of the dysentery and flu epidemics, mental breakdowns suffered by some of the less resilient souls, and the sheer mind-numbing boredom and torment inevitably brought on by day upon day of seemingly interminable imprisonment? None of these was made truly clear to the public back home until internees' memoirs were published after the war; and most of those fell on deaf ears as the people who read erudite memoirs are generally not the same people who hang on to every sensationalist word of the popular press.

So where does Steve Bloomer fit into all of this? In 1966, when the German World Cup squad set up their training camp near Ashbourne, Derbyshire, a feature writer with the glossy magazine *Derbyshire Life* decided that was an appropriate time to run a short piece on 'Bloomer's War':

"Steve Bloomer, by the way, was interned for the whole of World War One but did not suffer any great hardship. He was, I believe, allowed to carry on playing football with his fellow internees."

It is that type of bland, indeed crass, reportage which truly creates an entirely wrong impression. In consequence some have said that Bloomer was 'lucky' in avoiding the armed conflict, being saved from front-line action and the nightmare of the trenches by dint of his fortunate geographic position at the outbreak of hostilities. That too is a ludicrous conclusion. Steve was almost 41, several years beyond the upper age limit, when the call to arms was answered by hundreds of thousands of patriotic volunteers in late-1914. Although many under-age and over-age men did manage to sign up, the chances of someone as well known as Bloomer managing to negotiate the recruitment procedure undetected seem extremely unlikely. So, had Steve Bloomer been in Derby in August 1914, a continuing role in the temporary football which ensued from 1915 onwards might well have been his niche, or, barring that, perhaps a useful civilian occupation or a part as a figurehead in the football-led Forces recruitment drive which was implemented. Let it be clear, Ruhleben for Bloomer was no blessing in disguise. Yet the *Derbyshire Life* reference to football being played in the camp is a valid one. Indeed, it is that part of Bloomer's Ruhleben which has entered into folklore.

Sport the saviour
Bloomer himself, speaking to reporters after his release, put matters into a more realistic perspective:

"Don't think that there wasn't suffering and hardship. It was no picnic and there were more dinner times than dinners in Ruhleben. Some of the stuff they gave us was hardly fit for pig-swill and we have the Germans to thank for nothing except scandalous treatment. In fact the reason so many of us remained alive is summed up in five words – food from home and sports."

And, not surprisingly, football was one of the sports which the Ruhlebenites took to with gusto. Within a few days of entering the camp, an organised kickabout occurred and Steve got his first 'namecheck'. The game was played on a small mud pitch between the stables because at that time the open expanse of grass in the middle of the racecourse itself was firmly out of bounds. Yet the match aroused considerable interest. Ashton-under-Lyne jockey Joseph Shatwell, retained to ride in Germany throughout the summer at the time of his own capture, referred to it in a letter home on 9 November 1914:

"Yesterday we had a football match in the presence of some 2,000 spectators, Jockeys versus the Rest. The jockeys were defeated by 10 goals to 2, a real disgrace, but Steve Bloomer of Derby County was playing for the rival team so that accounts for the heavy defeat of the horsemen."

Although there were many hugely successful businessmen in Ruhleben, men who in the council chambers or golf club might carry all before them and be universally recognised in their own High Streets, relative anonymity was the initial lot of many of the internees. In time those men would make their mark, but for Bloomer and a number of other sportsmen their names spread throughout the camp like wildfire and undoubtedly gave something of a boost to what was to become a varied programme of organised sport. After much lobbying by the Barrack 'Captains' for use of the racecourse, initially flatly refused, the great breakthrough occurred in March 1915 when permission was finally given and the camp magazine reported that 'the sporting spirit of the Britisher was evidenced by the magnificent roar of approval which greeted the news'.

A 'Football Association' was set up under the elected secretaryship of John Cameron, a former Spurs player and manager who was coaching in Dresden at the outbreak of war, and leagues were organised. Each barracks had at least one side and the fixtures drawn up scheduled up to eight games a day. The FA back home sent footballs out, goalposts were erected on 'a morass of a pitch' and the big kick-off took place on 15 March 1915 when the 'Lageroffizier', Baron von Taube, puffing on a fat cigar, graciously agreed to set the game in motion as Steve captained Ruhleben FC against the Rest in a representative game. From that moment football never looked back. The ground and facilities were gradually improved and football, at least for those that liked it, became a central activity in camp life. Bloomer captained Barrack 1 who, in surely the shortest league programme ever, had won the Premier League by 8 May without dropping a single point.

Fred Pentland, who had played with Steve both at Middlesbrough and for England, paid tribute to his old mate in the opening edition of *In Ruhleben Camp* magazine:

"What couldn't I write of my old comrade and friend Steve Bloomer, captain of the league winners. Such generalship, such unselfishness and such keenness for the success of his side need no words of mine to praise. A toast to 'Steve…Good Luck Old Sportsman'."

Even in captivity it seems Steve was 'doomed' to adulation. This was probably a two-edged sword which gave him an army of immediate 'friends' but a certain degree of pressure and lack of privacy and personal space. He soon became known around the camp simply as 'Steve' and, among a number of catchphrases which quickly caught on, "Hold it Edwin", apparently one of Bloomer's regular exhortations to one of his playing colleagues, became a camp favourite whenever caution needed to be exercised.

What comes through strongly in all of the many Bloomer stories related by camp internees is that Steve was popular, patriotic, modest and dignified in his behaviour both on and off the sports field and, above all, led by example. Some recent sports books have reported that he 'was largely instrumental in organising the football leagues in the camp'. That in itself is not correct. Along with other fellow professionals Sam Wolstenholme (Everton), Edwin Dutton (Newcastle) and Jack Brierley (Spurs, Middlesbrough and Liverpool), Steve was a great participator but not much given to being on committees or getting involved in camp politics. Football was just one of many sports which were to develop once the playing fields were secured; tennis, golf, rugby and baseball were popular but cricket at 'the Oval' was the highlight of the summer months. In his own letters home, Steve confirms his talents as something of an all-round sportsman, touching as well on the matter of health and the hazards of participation. This one was dated August 1915:

"I have not been too grand lately but am picking up again now. Our games make us forget our troubles for a while and we had a great cricket match over August Bank Holiday, an 11 of the camp against 16. It was a three days game and I played with the 11. We scored 414 for seven of which I made 129 not out and the crowd simply went mad and gave me a rare reception. The 16 could only manage 160 and 180 so we won and you will see by my score that my knee is now all right again."

And again, in May 1916, a letter to Ernest Gregson, landlord of the Eagle Tavern in Green Street, Derby, maintained an upbeat tone while hinting at the sadness which constantly underlay the more cheerful side of camp life:

"Thankyou for the consignment of cigarettes. I am so grateful that my Derby friends don't forget to send me comforts, which I can share with those about me. I am pleased to say I am keeping well and we are having some grand weather. It is very hot and all that is troubling me is that I want to see good old Derby again. It is hard being kept here all this time but we are a merry crew, I can tell you, and we have some good times. We'll soon be starting cricket again and there are some really good Varsity men here; we play on a matting wicket – bit different to grass."

Steve was always very keen on his cricket and smashed the camp record on matting with a splendid 204, but, as Englishmen have found to their cost ever since, runs didn't always come so easily; batting at number three for the Rest against the Varsities, his score unfortunately matched his batting order. But failure with the bat was often matched by success with the ball; playing for Barrack 4 he bagged six for 15 and managed seven wickets against the elite Barrack 10, which housed most of the public school types and included Oxford history tutor J. C. Masterman, 'the best all-round sportsman in camp'. With that type of 'contact', the cricket club were able to secure equipment from England including a generous shipment from Lancashire County Cricket Club, and everything was done in a way to recreate as closely as possible a typical English scene deep inside enemy lines.

Steve's profile remained high and his general sporting prowess was regularly reported in the camp magazine. He even achieved success in the unflatteringly named 'old-age handicap' sprint on sports day, running off scratch but still scorching home first in 9.6 seconds. (Before anyone reaches for the Olympic record books, I should say it was a 75-yard race!) The fact that he was known and liked in the camp certainly did his general welfare no harm and he was able to move barracks several times to 'better quarters' although he never reached the dizzy heights of Barrack 10, who had their own 'club' in a wooden pavilion with white-coated waiters serving drinks and, much to the mystification of the German guards, a regular delivery of English newspapers, some on day of publication!

And so life went on as the years slipped by. Serious sociological and psychological studies have been carried out on the way the men behaved and were affected by their position, and despite some of the more pleasurable elements of camp life it seems that universally the men would certainly have preferred to be elsewhere. Many reported great feelings of guilt at not being able to help the war effort directly, although a small number were later to write that it was the 'most amazing experience' of their lives. But the overwhelming desire was to get out. Applications for release on grounds of ill-health were made regularly and sometimes granted, and the early release of men over 45 was eventually sanctioned. Steve was both too fit and not quite old enough to benefit from either of these options, so he had to stick it out almost to the bitter end.

He seems to have coped well and the banter and communal life he had been used to as a footballer must surely have stood him in good stead. He was able to endure the suffering but at the same time make the most of a degree of freedom and comradeship that most of the men would not have experienced since schooldays. With that in mind perhaps the years in camp are most neatly summed up by the following quote from one of the prisoners:

"In Ruhleben we were all brothers. Our solidarity and comradeship showed itself every day and we made a life for ourselves out of nothing. We were surely happier than the German guards and did our bit in upholding the spirit of the Britisher in adverse circumstances. There were terrible times and good times and all those who experienced them will always share a kinship and never forget. Make no mistake that boys became men in Ruhleben…but it is far more pleasant for us to recall the better days when we went out to play cricket and football, and men became boys again."

Release to Holland
Throughout 1917 and 1918, lobbying for release of the 'Forty-Fivers' gathered apace and more and more prisoners were allowed to leave the camp. Bloomer was given some news in April 1917 but it was of the cruellest kind; his daughter Violet, a milliner, had died at Portland Street of Bright's Disease, a kidney complaint. She was only 17. Steve later wrote of this in a letter to his friend Frank Middleton, a former Derby County outside-left:

"…but, dear Frank, I am anxious to get home, for since I have been a prisoner I have lost one of my dear girls, the second one, just 17. You know what a blow that would be to me but I am trying to bear up as best I can."

There was better fortune for Steve when the lines of demarcation for the 'Forty-Fivers' became less rigid. He had his 44th birthday in January 1918 and in March finally got the news he had waited for. He was to be released to neutral Holland, first being 'cleared' through The Hague but then allowed to travel as he pleased although still officially 'interned' and subjected to some reporting procedures and controls; on no account was he permitted to travel back to England. Steve recounted those early days of relative freedom with some evident relief but a hint of trepidation and bitterness:

"I left Ruhleben for Holland on 22 March 1918. They put on a farewell football match and gave me a rousing send-off… the party we had will always be memorable. The scene outside the gates as we boarded the train was quite a surprise… there seemed even less food on the outside than there was in the camp and German mothers with hungry children crowded round begging for bits of chocolate or biscuits. Those men that had anything to give were as generous as they could be despite our treatment at the hands of the Germans. News of our arrival in Holland had got out and when the train pulled in there were thousands there cheering. Much to my surprise a lot of them seemed to know me and there was such an enthusiasm for football there as I had never imagined – and cricket too. This was due to the constant example of the thousands of our British boys out there, who displayed a sporting instinct far more pronounced than in any other nationality. I stayed in The Hague for just over a month and found that there was even less food than in Germany, although what we got was much better quality. Parcels from home, though, were prohibited, and much missed. When I first got in among a crowd of people and traffic I was a bit nervous but soon got used to it. After having all that time penned up in that hell-hole you can imagine my feelings. Only ourselves know what it was like…I had nearly three-and-a-half years of it, and although they tried to break my spirit they couldn't. I only wish I had the chance to break some of theirs and I would do it gladly."

Not for the first time, the grapevine which invariably spreads its tendrils farther and wider for those with a degree of celebrity status, worked in Steve's favour. He was offered a coaching position with the Amsterdam club Blauw Wit (Blue and Whites) and moved there on 1 May. For the first time in almost four years he seems to have found a degree of kindness and comfort waiting for him. And always football, as another letter home to Frank Middleton in July 1918 confirms:

"Well Frank, here I am in Amsterdam and I am very glad to tell you I have got a good situation coaching and training a team and I am doing all right. I have some good players but they want tuning up a bit and I think I can do that for them…what do you say, eh? But I have one drawback – there is none of them what can speak English but we get by fairly well together as they are a very nice lot of young men and most of my directors can speak English very well, which is a great help to me. As for my lodgings, I am in some fine apartments staying with people as keep a chemist's shop. And fine people they are too. The father speaks fairly good English but the mother does not, and their only daughter, a young woman of 21, speaks it as good as me. We all get on fine and I am happy and comfortable and that is something after what I have gone through. It's a fine city, too, with plenty of life and go and many interned English who I have made acquaintance with. It's very dear though and I can't get an English cigarette for love nor money. Their own cigs are not to my liking but we manage."

Apart from its interesting content, that letter is a rare example of Bloomer's own hand and 'speech', completely free of the sort of editorial tidying up to which some of his newspaper pieces were subjected, and by and large grammatically correct and with a nice turn of phrase. The lodgings he refers to were at 4 Lelie Gracht just west of Dam Square, fronting one of the canals, very close to a property later made rather more famous than 'Bloomer's House' by one of its courageous young residents, Anne Frank.

In another communication, Steve confirmed he was still getting his kit on from time to time:

"I seem to be in great demand to play for clubs in exhibition games and I played in a night match just recently which kicked-off so late they used huge electric lights fixed on the great stands of the stadium. The ground in Amsterdam was only built in 1914 and holds 30,000…a truly magnificent sight. The field was lit up with a dazzling brilliance but I considered good football under such conditions impossible due to the dark shadows caused by the players and the ball. Every time I tried to dribble I lost sight of the sphere in my own black shadow and when it was in the air it cast a moving, slanting image on the ground which flitted here and there in a most bewitching manner. I seriously doubt if football matches at night will ever become popular."

And again to Frank Middleton, in summer 1918, Steve closes in poignant manner:

"Well old sport, it will be a good job when this terrible affair is all over but we must show them what John Bull can do first and let them see how battles is won and lost. I should like to express my feelings in stronger terms but you know my feelings old sport. Drop me a line when you have time as I shall be delighted to hear from you, always one of the very best of chums. I shall come over and see you shortly after I get home but now I must conclude and send you my very best respects and good wishes. From your old pal, keep smiling…Steve."

Survival and home

Just over three months later, all the battles 'had' been won and lost and at the 11th hour of the 11th day of the 11th month in 1918 the ceasefire armistice was effected and arrangements for mass repatriation of survivors began. The numbers dead were truly shocking but Bloomer had come through to live another day and so, too, had football. Insignificant though it might appear, the game has been cited by historians as a major morale sustaining force throughout the years of conflict. Although the League programme proper had been abandoned after 1914-15, Derby County gaining promotion back to Division One, the popularity of the game was such that it simply refused to lie down. Indeed, many of the lads who went to the Front did so with football in their hearts, and the newspapers of late 1914 were full of letters back home asking for footballs or sports papers and reporting impromptu games within earshot of the shells. And on the wider scale the 17th Service Battalion of the

Middlesex Regiment, known as the 'Footballers' Battalion', entered the folklore of the Great War, as too did the game in 'No Man's Land' between British and German troops during the Christmas Day truce of 1914. The 18th London Regiment and the 8th East Surreys, meanwhile, answered the ultimate call of duty by going 'over the top' dribbling footballs before them under heavy fire. All very symbolic looked at from our own safe distance, but it was all too real at the time.

Thousands of 'footballers' never returned from the war. For them there were no 'match abandoned' signs as they struggled through the mud of Passchendaele and the Somme, fields made not for the 'beautiful game' but pock-marked quagmires of desolation and despair where only the ugly game prevailed. And for some the utter futility and cruelty of it all lay in ambush right to the final minutes. Derby County footballer Lance Corporal George Brooks, of the 24th York and Lancaster Regiment, was killed by a shell on the very morning of 11 November just a few minutes before the armistice took effect while his wife and four young children prepared to celebrate his homecoming at 224 Harrington Street in Derby.

Steve was sensitive enough to all of these issues to count himself extremely lucky in returning home unscathed. On Tuesday, 19 November he was told that he was free to leave Holland and arrived at Hull docks with 2,000 others on Friday 22nd. Thousands were there to greet the ship but when Steve arrived at Derby Station at six o'clock the same evening, no one but the family knew he was coming. He stepped off the train to find his wife Sarah waiting for him with 20-year-old Hetty and 16-year-old Doris…but no Violet. Four years on, but it was, after all, 'over by Christmas'. His father Caleb, now almost 70, was there too, not to meet Steve Bloomer the football legend but simply to say, "Welcome home lad." He always did say football would get his boy into trouble.

FORTY-SOMETHING CROSSROADS 1918-1923

"England, I love you better than I know,
And this I learned when after wanderings long,
'Mid people of another stock and tongue,
 I heard again your music blow."
Richard Trench

"AFTER an absence of four years which, with the exception of a few months, has been spent in captivity as a civilian prisoner-of-war, Steve Bloomer arrived back home in England and Derby, the town of his adoption, yesterday evening. Today a representative of the *Derby Daily Express* had the pleasure of visiting him at his home in Portland Street and some of the first words he naturally uttered were, 'I am very glad to get home again at last.' It was with no little surprise that we found him looking so well, having come through it all with comparatively good health and strength, with his hair not grey and his 44 years pressing lightly on his head."
Derby Daily Express, Saturday, 23 November 1918

Back to 'Normal'

If Bloomer had anticipated that four years absence would reduce his celebrity status, especially now he had ceased to be a player, he quickly found out that this was not to be the case. Being interviewed by reporters on his very first morning home probably wasn't the ideal way to begin a reassimilation into 'normal life' but he handled it in good part and introduced himself again to a Derby folk as keen as ever on their football. The comments on his health put to rest the mistaken assertion, oft-related in recent years, that he 'arrived back in Derby a shadow of his former self, ill and emaciated'. That yarn, I believe, emanates directly from a quote in the local press saying exactly that at the time of his death, but it simply isn't true.

Years later Steve was to say that he believed the bronchial troubles which plagued him late on in life might well relate back to Ruhleben in origin, but at the time of his release his health was not a cause for undue concern. Bear in mind, too, that he had played regular football throughout his stay in camp, barring a couple of spells out with knee trouble and a case of minor frostbite in his precious right foot. In Holland, too, he had coached quite heartily and appeared in exhibition games and within a few weeks of his arrival back home he was again to lead a team out at the Baseball Ground. Hardly the sort of activity for an ill and emaciated figure. Bloomer himself said he came through it so well largely 'because of my life-long participation in athletic sports, the parcels we received from home and the kindly hospitality of the Dutch in my latter days of internment'.

If there were any 'shadows' lurking, they would surely be mental ones. Anyone who has spent even a short time away from family and friends in peacetime circumstances may know that perspectives can change and it can be difficult to pick up relationships again, but almost four and a half years away, in an atmosphere of hostility, must be another matter altogether. Many of the men who returned from the war expecting days of joyous abandon were sadly disappointed. Some experienced the break-up of relationships and family, while others found difficulty in generating the self-motivation, after years of orders, to get into the workplace and a routine job. Some men actually admit in their reminiscences to being engulfed by a deep sense of boredom after the 'excitement' of action. Steve Bloomer had to face all of these things in varying degrees. Even something as apparently straightforward as getting to know the wife and children again had to be worked at. In a wider sense, too, Steve entered a completely new phase of existence. For over 20 years as a professional footballer, his life was effectively one long fixture list. Always he was told where to be and what to do. Now for the first time in his adult life on English soil he was no longer a professional footballer. The impostor most feared by sportsmen the world over had come calling – that small but frighteningly meaningful little word 'ex' which now prefixed the great footballer's remaining days. 'Former' is so much nicer and kinder, I always think, but it amounts to the same thing.

Bloomer was once described by a leading FA official as 'a strange compound of the philosopher and the stoic', by which he meant that Steve was both a deep and analytical thinker and sufficiently wise to be indifferent to changes in fortune which might befall him; translated into Derbyshire that might well mean that 'he used his noddle, called a spade a spade and never let 'owt bother 'im.' Either way he needed to understand what he and others had been through, not over-react to it and get on with life afresh. There is every indication that Steve was down to earth enough to do exactly that.

Football itself shared a common status with Bloomer and all who returned from the war... it too had survived and was about to embark on a new era. In football history World War One was the first real watershed and thereafter people would habitually talk of the pre-war 'old game' and the post-war 'modern game'. The names of the many players, both amateur and professional, who had died, were duly recorded and commemorated and mechanisms set up to help support their families. One, Second Lieutenant Donald Simpson Bell, formerly of Bradford Park Avenue, was posthumously awarded the Victoria Cross, the only League player to receive that honour, for heroics on the Somme in 1916.

While Bell and his like could not start again after it was all over, football eventually would. Back in the early stages of conflict, the 1914-15 season had been played normally and Derby County again won a Second Division championship to regain the place in the top flight they had lost in Steve's last 'season too far'. Thereafter, though, the Football League was suspended for the duration (the Scottish League continued throughout) and clubs played only regional or friendly games as they wished, with much guesting of players being permitted. The West Brom trio of Jesse Pennington, Hubert Pearson and Claude Jephcott, along with Aston Villa's Tommy Weston, all donned Derby togs in wartime but never appear in 'official' records because they were not permitted to be 'signed on' in the usual sense.

As football trundled slowly on in its temporary state through the 1918-19 season of Steve's return, with Derby playing in the four-team Midland Victory League, he must surely have wondered whether there would be a part for him in the future of the club. If he had needed any encouragement in that direction as Christmas 1918 approached, he need only have taken a short stroll out to the rather plusher reaches of Derby, towards Littleover village…indeed he probably did. There he may have seen a familiar and dapper figure, long overcoat and trademark bowler hat comfortingly still in place, setting off for work from his suburban villa at 104 St Chad's Road, just a few hundred yards from the base of Steve's very first schoolboy team, St Chad's choir. Jimmy Methven, Steve's erstwhile team-mate and manager, was still in the hot-seat. Methven had worked for most of the war at Rolls-Royce and, besides administering the works leagues there, which he reckoned was 'more troublesome than running the Football League itself', he had continued to hold the reins at Derby County and steered the club through the four seasons of uncertainty. Methven's presence was very likely a great comfort to Steve – one has to imagine that 'Logie' might be able to use his undoubted powers of persuasion on the directors to find a place for his old partner, however small, in the Derby County soon to be resurrected.

Life goes on

Bloomer's way of handling the early days after his return was not to hide himself away but to get out and about to renew old acquaintances. On 5 December, just a fortnight after his return, he spoke on the electioneering platform in support of Alderman Albert Green, Mayor of Derby in 1915, in favour of a Coalition Government. Green had represented his local ward as a Democratic Conservative for the past eight years and this suggests that, as an inside-right, Steve's political leanings mirrored his station on the field of play. Certainly his wife Sarah became an active worker and fund raiser in the Conservative Party for many years. There was something more to this, however. Alderman and Mrs Green had been one of Steve's regular 'parcel' suppliers during his internment and he was keen to thank them publicly. Green was born in 1874, an exact contemporary of Bloomer. Always a keen sportsman, and a champion racing cyclist, he had attended St James's Road Board School at the same time as Bloomer, so Steve might well have been helping out one of his old football playmates. At any event it was a rousing occasion in St Joseph's School Hall. While the Alderman gloried in 'having brought that proud man the Kaiser down to the dust', Steve related the tale of his own war and finished to loud applause as he told how 'every effort had been made to break our spirits, but the men proved themselves too hard to give in to that'.

This, his first official public appearance since his return to Derby, suggests that the time he spent in the company of educated men in the relatively learned confines of the camp at Ruhleben might have improved his confidence and leadership. It was certainly unlike the old Bloomer to volunteer for public speaking duties...perhaps he joined the debating society there, or maybe not as the case may be!

Realistically Bloomer's natural stage was altogether different – a place where long speeches could be left in the dressing-room and the occasional shout of "Hold it Edwin" could do more damage to the left flank than any amount of electioneering. On Saturday, 7 December, Steve captained a Best of Derby's Wartime League side in a charity match for the FA's Footballers' Families' War Fund in front of 6,000 at the Baseball Ground. No one could accuse the Derby Town Band of having a limited repertoire. *See the Conquering Hero Comes* wasn't quite considered appropriate, but as Steve emerged once more at the head of the pack to give that ball a 'hefty kick skyward' the band, no doubt rehearsing for New Year, excelled themselves with a rousing rendition of *Auld Lang Syne*.

No matter that the Derby lads were beaten 2-1 by the 1st Newark Royal Engineers (containing nine League players), it was the spirit that counted. Scenes like these were repeated throughout the country and, along with the cricket and village fêtes which would follow in the summer, took on a symbolic and very 'English' significance which said 'despite it all, we have come through'. That same spirit still prevails today. The press reported that 'Steve was accorded a most flattering reception from his old friends', and moreover 'the whole occasion itself was just like a pre-war scene'. This desire to regain familiar ground, whether real or imagined, was universal and as strong in football as in any element of life. During that game Bloomer, just short of his 45th birthday, 'showed one or two of his old touches' and was soon in demand for other games, appearing in a Newcastle shirt guesting for them against Sunderland, again in a charity game. Laudable as it was to be helping to raise money for others, Steve had to look out for number one too. He needed a job and the only job he really knew was football. Fortunately the League was about to resume afresh.

Season 1919-20...The big kick-off

"Today the good ship Derby County once again weighed anchor and set sail on the high seas of the First Division and the hope of all those who have the best

interests of the club at heart is that a pleasant journey is in store and that it will steer clear of the rocks and shoals which beset the course of a first-class football club."
Derbyshire Football Express, 30 August 1919

As normal service was resumed by League football for season 1919-20, Steve Bloomer was taken on board by Derby County in a supportive role. He had played the odd game with what existed of the reserve side in the season previous but now took on the role of 'player-coach' to the Reserves as the importance of having a squad heightened with the resumption of the League. Although his time coaching in Germany and Holland had been massively curtailed, he had shown sufficient interest in the instructional side of the game for the club, almost certainly prompted by Methven, to give him a chance to bring on the youngsters. The Reserves played at that time in the Central Alliance, then a motley affair comprising some of the second strings of the major sides intermingled with non-League clubs, but the importance of the competition's status was secondary to its role as a means of developing home-grown talent for a Derby County still hampered in the transfer market by ever-present financial constraints. Bloomer had always enjoyed ball work in training and shown an interest in working with young players, so there was every reason to believe it may be his niche. Effectively he was resuming the role he had already played informally back in the latter half of 1913-14.

Steve would undoubtedly be eager to concentrate his mind on something concrete again after all his troubles; on top of everything his father, Caleb, had died in June 1919, aged 70, not exactly a shock but nevertheless something his oldest son would have preferred to be without. An event which probably was unexpected in that summer of 1919, although we will never know for sure, was that Steve (45) and Sarah (44) discovered they had a late addition to the family on the way. There had been such a loss of life during the war that many couples felt an almost dutiful need to replenish the stocks of society, but whatever the Bloomers' motivation, deliberate or otherwise, there was no denying the news. It is pure conjecture but it is easy to imagine that Steve would have favoured a 'chip off the old block' after three girls. At any rate he had provided proof positive that he had lost none of his 'old powers'.

At the same time as he took up his coaching role, Steve began, in September 1919, a series of columns in the *Derbyshire Football Express*. These were at first fairly modest and irregular affairs but were so popular with readers that they were to become an eagerly awaited weekly highlight which was, as they say, to 'run and run'... for the next 12 years! Bloomer's interest and enjoyment on the journalistic side was very evident but there was a financial consideration too; pay for the Reserves' role was limited and the newspaper work provided extra pocket money. It is possible that Steve also took a part-time civilian position at this time with British Cellulose, later British Celanese, and possibly as a groundsman, but no documentary evidence either from Steve or anyone else exists. That in itself brings the theory very much into question but it is one that has been mooted as it is known that he played the odd game for the Cellulose works football team in 1920. There is equally no evidence that money was yet a problem… with the cash from his Derby and national testimonials to draw on, along with the contract severance pay he is said to have received from Berlin Britannia at the time of his wartime arrest, it seems likely he could ride out the leaner times at least for the present, although wartime price rises must inevitably have eroded the savings.

He was certainly not desperate enough to have to grab indiscriminately at any opportunity going, as his refusal of a rather interesting offer just three months into the season illustrates. Steve himself related the yarn to the press in November 1919:

"I have just received an invitation to go and be the Olympic coach for the Polish football team. The Polish emissaries' intentions were for me to go out in February 1920 to select 20 players from Warsaw, Lemberg and Cracow and to coach them to provide a team to represent Poland at the Antwerp games in 1920. It would be a six-month contract."

It was a flattering offer which showed the cachet still attached to Bloomer's name, even in Europe, and it might have led to other greater things. But he had been back in England barely a year and his response was understandable and also indicative of the rather dry self-deprecating sense of humour he was apt to display from time to time:

"I prefer to stay in Derby. They are still scrapping up there in Poland and I don't want to run into any more of that. I have had enough of war in Germany. Then there is the language. It was very difficult for me in Germany and in Holland, even though some of the directors and players there spoke good English, so how do you think I would get on in Poland? The Old Mother Country's good enough for me."

St James's Road Board School had a broad curriculum back in the 1880s but young Steve's options were copper-plate handwriting and traditional English nursery rhymes, not East European languages.

So Derby County Reserves it was. Until Christmas 1919 Steve played himself as captain and managed a few goals among the passing and prompting which he now generally confined himself to. In October he managed a couple against the Derby branch of the NUR at the Baseball Ground in a 3-3 draw which prompted a report full of outrageous puns from the local reporter:

"Steve was anything but a passenger to be left without a guard. He did some judicious shunting and was always prominent on the platform. On occasions he stopped in his tracks to show his delight of smart work by Spencer, Cooper and Needham by clapping vigorously."

If he needed any reminder of his age, it was present in that match, which included a Methven and a Needham, son and nephew of Jimmy and 'Nudger' respectively. Reports of the Reserves games under Steve's guidance reveal that he took a very conscientious and hands-on approach in a league far removed from the big-time he had been used to. In a game at Tonypandy, mid-Rhondda, the team set off on a Friday for the Saturday game and got as far as Cardiff before falling foul of a rail strike. The matter of getting to the match was eventually solved after much trouble, the team chartering a furniture van and all piling in the back. As for getting back, two vans had to be dispatched from Derby. Duly delivered, Steve sent his first batch of lads on the way but the second broke down halfway back. On Wednesday evening, a full six days after they set out, the van limped into Derby and Steve, like all good captains, was last off. The game, by the way, was lost 2-0. It sounds all very *Dad's Army* but Steve relished all that sort of thing. He certainly wasn't afraid to get his hands dirty, nor did an international reputation guarantee him an easy time of it.

After his 46th birthday in January 1920, the Bloomer name disappeared from the team sheet as he left the on-field stuff to the youngsters. By then he had been appearing in a Derby County shirt of one denomination or another for 28 years, and January 1920 can be regarded as his true retirement date from the competitive playing game. That month was also significant in the Bloomer household for other reasons...another girl, baby Patricia, made her entrance. Three weeks later, on 3 February, she joined her late sister Violet in Nottingham Road Cemetery. A young baby's death is always tragic and none more so for Steve and Sarah after their years of wartime separation. For Steve, particularly, it seemed to continue a run of bereavements which saw him lose both parents, his kid brother Phillip and two daughters, all by his 46th birthday, not to mention the numerous acquaintances that never returned from the war. Bloomer was never a great one for smiling in photographs; in the early years this was mainly down to having to keep stock still for sundry Victorian photographers, but in later photographs, too, there is often a sense of distance about his expression and an underlying sadness in his eyes which perhaps betrays the personal suffering which no amount of public adulation could ever wipe out.

That public adulation was certainly still with him in 1920. On Shrove Tuesday he joined the ranks of the Prince of Wales and the Dukes of Devonshire and Rutland by having the honour of throwing up the ball at the Ashbourne Shrovetide game. Billy Meredith, Stanley Matthews and Roy McFarland would later perform the same ritual but none of these great internationals could match the achievement of current Rams vice-chairman Peter Gadsby who, in 1965 when only 16, achieved the singular feat of actually 'goaling the ball'. Pub-quiz question masters take note!

As for the club's fortunes, the Reserves didn't pull up any trees and the first team finished 18th, winning four out of the last five games in a relegation escape act. It was very much a rebuilding period in which new blood was brought in as slowly the old guard moved on. Even on the training side, faces which had appeared in club photographs for years were seen around for the last time. Arthur Latham, for example, was succeeded as trainer by Sergeant Harry Curzon DCM, a well-known local boxer. Amid all the clearing out, only two of the real old stalwarts, Methven and Bloomer, hung on, and Steve even managed to add a last piece of silverware to his collection at the end of the season. On 10 April 1920 he turned out for British Cellulose against Crewton United in the Final of the Derbyshire FA Medals competition at the Baseball Ground, laying on the first goal in a 4-2 win. In spite of scepticism on the part of some in the crowd, the reports showed he could still handle it at that level:

"Despite the shakings of would-be wiseheads and the 'too old' murmurs, Steve is still a force to be reckoned with in that class. He made very few slips and although his speed is not what it used to be, the ball was usually disposed of to advantage and the first goal by Mitchell was the result of a fine forward pass by Bloomer."

Years later in their dotage, Mitchell and his team-mates would regale anyone who cared to listen, and some who didn't, about the time they 'played with Steve Bloomer'. If their audience had questioned the chronology that would be understandable, but rest assured those old footballing boys still had their marbles; their stories, albeit no doubt suitably embellished, were quite true.

Season 1920-21...On the fringe
Although Steve enjoyed the Reserves work, he was like most people in football – he would have preferred a part in first-team affairs. With someone of his calibre being around the ground, especially someone as opinionated as he, there is no doubt that he would offer advice to players and management across the board when asked but he wasn't able to do this in an official capacity. Jimmy Methven, perhaps feeling the strain, suggested to the directors at the start of this season that Bloomer be made first-team coach, effectively his number two, the sort of role filled so ably in Derby County's more recent history by Steve McClaren before his surprise move to Manchester United. Although they considered the proposal it was decided against at this stage, first because it would mean more outlay in salary terms and also because, at that period in the game's development, the discipline of 'coaching' was still a relatively new one and there was still scepticism about the real benefits of creating such a position for the first time in the club's history. So Bloomer remained in charge of the Reserves but some of his pre-season newspaper columns suggested he was itching to get to work at a higher level in ironing out some of the problems he believed were endemic in the game:

"Having been an inside-forward myself I am not going to suggest for a moment that I was infallible but it has more and more been impressed upon me as a mere spectator at first-class games that there has been a good deal wanting in the method and style of play of the inside-forwards and this has led to the sheer inability to get goals. If only players would realise that dribbling around a stack of opponents isn't always necessary when a simple pass would reach the required destination more quickly and just as well, nor is it necessary to shoot wildly over on sight when carefully picking the spot would do the trick. It's all a matter of using your brains."

It is evident Steve felt his experience was being under-utilised this season and when Derby were relegated to Division Two, he got his chance. The Rams won only five games in 1920-21, their worst-ever total, all despite the infusion of new blood in the signing of Harry Storer from Grimsby, Bill Paterson from Cowdenbeath and even the Egyptian inside-forward Tewfik 'Toothpick' Abdallah. Maybe the directors remembered a time when the return of Bloomer had taken the team back into the top flight. Whatever, in the close-season they created a brand new position and appointed him first-team coach in August 1921.

Season 1921-22…Boot on the other foot

It is one thing giving advice off the record but entirely another when you're asked to do it for real. Steve had been asked to put his methods into practice and the press felt it was a good move but only results would really tell in the long run:

"Steve is back in his old haunts, if in another sphere, and we think the club has done a good stroke of business in appointing him to a position to which he is well suited."
Derbyshire Football Express, 27 August 1921

Well-suited he may have been, but he found the one thing he couldn't do was put the ball in the net for his pupils. Theory into practice via the medium of players is, as many a manager and coach will readily agree, one of the most difficult jobs in football. Steve gave it his all alongside Jimmy Methven and took a high profile in the local press with a now weekly series of articles and a new illustrated feature, 'How to do it in Football', showing Steve in a variety of unnatural frozen poses trying to convey his methods. This earned him a degree of relatively mild leg-pulling from the *Football Express*. By mid-November the Rams had won six of 13 games, not too bad a return, and had managed 20 goals, again reasonable. But following a couple of narrow 1-0 victories the press wanted to know where all the goals were, running a satirical cartoon showing Steve's instructional strip while the onlooking 'Rams supporter' was seen to mutter: "Now if our boys would only get the hang of that shooting business, with a defence like ours we should soon climb up that table… eh Steve?"

In the event the forwards improved markedly to score 60, the second-highest total in the League, while the defence faltered in conceding 64, the worst record in the whole division, and Derby finished a disappointing 12th. That's why some clubs today employ a specialist defence coach. Bloomer knew how to unlock defences but that alone doesn't win football games. Working alongside Methven, Bloomer learnt the hard way. If he had aspired to a full manager's role, then this was the way to achieve that ambition but I believe Steve never quite developed the confidence, desire or man-management skills to go that far, at least on the domestic scene. If he listened to the advice of Methven he might well have heard: "Don't do it laddie." At any rate, Steve himself was later to say:

"Believe me, a manager's job is tucked in with thorns; he cannot move without one pricking him somewhere."

The press and fans were disappointed but the players, rather than Bloomer and Methven, got the blame. Attendances had dropped and the club were again heading for serious financial trouble.

Canada...close-season escape

The 1921-22 season had been a busy one, and not just on the field. Although Steve never did have a footballing son, he gained a footballing son-in-law when Hetty, 23, married speedy left-winger Alf 'Quicksilver' Quantrill who had moved from Derby County to Preston North End in summer 1921. The Indian-born Quantrill, with his undeniably pleasing features, was voted 'Best-looking player in the League' by *All Sports* magazine, quite a catch for Hetty and from all accounts one of which Steve fully approved. If he needed a complete break from wedding talk and his arduous first season as coach, Steve certainly got it.

In Ruhleben he had met a number of Canadian internees and still maintained contacts there. At the start of May 1922 he sailed from Liverpool on the Canadian Pacific liner *Minnedosa* to take up a summer coaching post in Montreal. Three months later, on 2 August 1922, he boarded the *Minnedosa* again and arrived back in England after 'a delightful nine-day voyage' on Friday the 11th. The *Derby Telegraph* typesetters made up the 'Bloomer's Return' heading that they had already had cause to use several times previously and would use again in the future; Bloomer always came back to Derby.

Like many travellers who cross the Atlantic, what he found on the other side gave him a tremendous lift and he came back full of it. As he no doubt told sidekick Methven: "It's football Jim, but not as we know it." He regaled readers of his column thus:

"After cramming three months of truly amazing and wonderful experiences of Canadian travel into the summer recess, I cannot say that I am sorry to be home again for, as the famous song says, 'There's no place like home'. Yet I would not have missed my Canadian coaching trip for anything as it has opened my eyes to the remarkable grip the big ball game has in our Colonies. There is not much football outside Montreal, Ottawa and Toronto, and it is all on an amateur basis, competing for favour with baseball and lacrosse, but it is rapidly gaining in ascendancy and the younger generation, especially the French-Canadians, are taking to it with great enthusiasm. My team was the Grenadier Guards of Montreal, composed mostly of English, Irish and Scotch players, not a military combination but including some ex-servicemen. They have just finished a wonderful season by winning the Quebec Cup and the League. Winter football is out of the question over there, when the country is blanketed in deep snow, so they play in the summer when it can get extremely hot.Just imagine what it was like playing in 88 and 90 degrees in the shade. Why, I sat on the stand watching with hat, coat and waistcoat discarded, my shirt wide open and my brow running with perspiration, while on the pitch the players ran around on hard-baked ground at a speed comparable to that in the English game, if not with the same science. They follow the results of our English League matches with great interest and every incident is reported in the papers. I expect the game will make wonderful strides in the next few years.

"The soccer public in Montreal treated me as well as anywhere I've ever been in my career. They even wanted to make me a Chief of the Indian Reservation outside Montreal, but the ceremony of being decked up in feathers, moccasins and leather habillments and of having to perform a war dance and strange initiation ceremony was too much for my natural feelings of modesty so I put the Red Indians off with the promise of becoming an Indian Chieftain if I go back next summer."

There is no doubt Bloomer made an impact wherever he went. The Canadians only knew him by reputation when he arrived but when he left they put on a grand 'Au Revoir' smoking concert for him at the Army and Navy Club, and the president of the FA, Tom Mitchell, spoke in glowing terms of the 'excellent work he has done and the great effect it has had in improving the game'. The Army and Navy Club, meanwhile, presented him with a gold signet ring as a gesture of thanks. It seems that Bloomer's somewhat modest, quiet and even bashful personality could, when expressed through the medium of football, be a real force for the good. What people getting to know him for the first time in his more mature years invariably noted was his enthusiasm and conscientious nature. On his return this was again to be put to the test with Derby County in the continuing capacity of first-team coach.

Season 1922-23...After you Cecil – the parting of the ways

On the very day he returned from Canada, the press reported that 'Steve was immediately busy at his coaching duties on the Baseball Ground'. Perhaps the extra edge to that keenness was prompted by a desire to impress his new manager. Jimmy Methven had developed a health problem with cataracts in his eyes and underwent an operation which didn't prove at all successful. All parties mutually agreed that it was impossible for him to carry on and in June 1922, at the age of 53, his 31-year connection with Derby County was quietly severed and, sadly, this fine club servant became partially blind. His job was advertised in July and four candidates were interviewed while Bloomer was in Canada.

If he was ever going to get the job of Derby County manager, a possibility rather than a probability, that was the moment, but I don't believe Steve wanted the job, nor do I think the directors would have given it to him. He was the last of the old guard left and, quite rightly, the club wanted to look firmly to the future rather than live on past glories. They appointed Sussex-born Cecil Bertram Potter, son of a Congregational minister. His name might conjure up the image of a somewhat delicate cove, the sort of chap who could well press wild flowers and inhabit the world of Bertie Wooster and chums, but in truth he was ambitious, enterprising, well paid and young, a successful former inside-forward with Norwich and Hull and player-manager at Hartlepools United. Although 33-year-old Cecil and 48-year-old Steve worked harmoniously enough side by side, Potter ominously began to build up his own team by bringing in two new men, trainer Laurie Edwards and assistant trainer Bill Bromage.

Steve described Edwards as 'a right good trainer' but in all his personal reminiscences never made any committed judgements on Potter. There is no evidence that they didn't get on, but no evidence either that they were bosom pals. Bloomer himself praised the spirit in the dressing-room under Potter's tenure and seems simply to have kept plodding on. There seems a strong possibility that he harboured the somewhat naive view that his own tenure with the club was secured by 'past association' and present 'commitment to the cause' but invisible undercurrents can strike without warning and with deadly effect. With the club in increasingly deep water on the financial front, and an arguably top heavy backroom staff, Steve might have sensed a strong degree of personal danger but, as this pronouncement from the start of season 1922-23 surely indicates, his focus was firmly on the welfare of the football club and he was apparently blissfully unaware that he was swimming with the sharks:

"I have been through a huge number of clubs' balance sheets since my return from Canada and the figures show that practically only two clubs out of ten made a profit last season. I have always been for players being paid what they are worth according to what gate they can draw, but in these hard times I feel they must appreciate the clubs' difficulties and 'stand their whack'. High transfer fees must cease, too, and the clubs must do what they can to cut down rigorously on expenditure in any areas they can."

Bloomer was genuine to a fault and this sounds distressingly like a case of shooting himself in the foot. Although he and Potter's 'boot room' created a good spirit and came within one game of taking the team to the historic first-ever Wembley FA Cup Final in 1923, Derby finished in their lowest-ever League position, 14th in Division Two. No-one blamed Bloomer and in fact a letter from supporter J. H. Widdowson described him as 'the finest coach in the country', but as Steve himself had warned, financial considerations had to be taken into serious account. At the end of the season the club were £10,000 in debt, and against that the board had to consider whether the coach's contribution, enthusiastic though it was, could really be justified. Bloomer's contract was not renewed. Thus ended his association with Derby County, at least as far as team affairs were concerned. It was in no way a sacking, but being 'let go' can be just as hurtful. Steve took it on the chin but was certainly disillusioned and felt that time would see his efforts with the players bearing fruit.

On the field he made the final break too, organising and playing in a charity match which raised £350 for the Mayor's War Memorial Fund. On the evening of 18 April 1923, Steve Bloomer's 'Old International' team played Derby County at the Baseball Ground. It was a unique and symbolic occasion which saw some of the giants of the Victorian game, men who had played almost since the birth of the League, line up against the young bucks of the 1920s who would take the game on and into the boom-time 1930s. It seemed to encapsulate the rapid progress the game was making and on that day the old boys put on one last collective show before the changing of the guard. Bloomer scored two at the official opening game at the Baseball Ground in 1895. This time, aged 49, he bowed out with one, a penalty. Six days later, on the day of the last home match of the season, he formalised his retirement as a veteran player with the following statement:

"Since playing in the 'Old Internationals' match I have been inundated with requests to play in other charity games but we old 'uns must call a halt some time or other! The arch enemy Father Time wins the battle in the end. I am no longer a youngster although my enthusiasm for the game is as great as ever. But it is not nice to go on to the field with a full realisation that one cannot do the things which came so easily in the days of our youth. I feel that the years of internment in Ruhleben in Germany have hastened the inevitable end and so I have decided that my last game in public has been played. I have not come to this decision without many pulls at my heartstrings, for the game has always had an irresistible fascination for me and it is with a pang that I realise my playing days are over."

Thus the 'Destroying Angel', the 'Incomparable Steve', dispatched the leather for the 'final' time and a week after this rather poignant and sombre announcement Bloomer took his seat as coach for the last time too. There was no animosity in the parting of the ways. Bloomer was always to be welcome at the club and would remain in the public eye and indelibly associated with it to this day, but the immediate reality in the summer of 1923 was that he was no longer on the payroll. The reality of age, too, was made all too evident to Steve when Hetty and Alf introduced his first grandchild to the world, predictably a girl. Pat, named in memory of Steve and Sarah's own departed child, was born in September. Would there be room for a 'grandpa' somewhere in the game's future?

In the event it didn't take long for football-related offers to come in, but none of them were from first-class clubs. Instead Steve took up a role sponsored by the *Derbyshire Express* as a sort of roving scout-cum-coach to local sides. Nowadays it would probably be given a fancy title, perhaps County Football Development Officer or Youth Academy Director. As it was, his brief was to watch local games, pass on tips to the 'junior' players and write in detail about a spotlighted local game each Saturday. It was a role he would eventually develop and hugely enjoy for a number of years but in the event he had barely started it before a more lucrative offer from the bigger boys was presented out of the blue. Just a few months earlier, Bloomer had discussed the incidence of personnel working abroad and at that time he said:

"I have not been on the Continent since returning from Germany. I had enough of that with the hospitality of Fritz at Ruhleben. Besides, if I was to go, who knows, another war might break out!"

All resolutions can be broken, though, and, if Bloomer believed in portents, an unexpected surprise after one of his junior games in October 1923 might have given him a clue that adventure and travel were in the air:

"One of my vows was that I would never leave 'terra firma' in an aeroplane but after the Alvaston and Boulton v Breaston game, a friend tempted me and bang went my promise. We had a seven-minute joy ride in the Avro plane which has been visiting Derby. When it banked steeply I lost my cap, which made a pretty nose-dive into the River Derwent."

Just a few weeks later, in November 1923, there was rather more than seven minutes at stake and the jesting had to stop. After five years in England, Steve Bloomer had an important decision to make.

AN HONORARY BASQUE 1923-1925

"At twelve noon,
The natives swoon,
And no further work is done,
But mad dogs and Englishmen,
 Go out in the midday sun."
Noel Coward

"**B**Y THE time these lines appear in print I shall be treading the soil of a country I have often heard about but which it has never been my luck to visit… 'sunny Spain', the land of bullfights, nuts and siestas. No doubt the news will come as a vast surprise to my many friends in Derby and district, just as it is a surprise to myself. When I went to Melbourne last Saturday to view the Melbourne and District Cup tie between Melbourne FC and Melbourne British Legion I had no idea that within 36 hours I should be out of England. Of course, I had knowledge that there was a coaching appointment going in Spain, but things were so much 'in the air' that I did not dream of the matter coming to a head so quickly. However, when I returned home after the match there were instructions for me to leave right away for Irún, a town near Bilbao, Spain, and there I am to coach the players of Real Irún Football Club for the ensuing two years at least."

A brave decision

On 3 November 1923 that was how Steve announced in the Derby press that he had accepted yet another coaching assignment abroad. After his ill-fated first experience in Germany in 1914 it wouldn't have been entirely surprising if he'd clung firmly to dear old 'Blighty' for the rest of his days, but his more pleasant experiences in Holland in 1918 and especially in Canada in the summer of 1922 had perhaps coloured his perception of the overseas opportunities which were available to the more adventurous spirit.

Notwithstanding that, the plain fact of the matter was that Steve still needed to earn a living. It was all very well being a national celebrity, still revered at this time as the greatest goalscorer England had ever known, but, as many 'celebs' before and since have painfully discovered, fame alone seldom pays the bills.

With no firm football management or coaching offers on the domestic front and without the lucrative options of the likes of *Question of Sport* or *Match of the Day*, Steve had to keep an open mind. At least Spain had stayed neutral during the Great War and maybe he felt it was a pretty safe haven. Had the position been in Germany or Northern Europe it seems more likely he would have declined the offer. His description of Spain before his departure, too, betrays the somewhat idealised image Steve had of the relatively far-flung and innocent Iberian peninsula, which surely helped to make up his mind.

The decision whether or not to accept the post was also eased by his knowledge that others who he knew intimately, and whose opinions he trusted, had already prospered there. Fred Pentland, Steve's England and Middlesbrough playing colleague and fellow internee at Ruhleben, had become Athletic Bilbao manager in 1921, after coaching in France. He and Steve had the sort of kinship which only their intense shared experience could have forged and it was almost certainly Pentland who first alerted him to the Irún vacancy. Even closer to home was Dumbarton-born wing-half Ted Garry, who Steve had captained for three seasons at Derby including the triumphant promotion campaign of 1911-12. Garry was coach at San Sebastian, only ten miles from Irún, so Steve knew there would be friendly faces close at hand.

Even so, it might seem unusual for Steve to have 'gone for it' in such an impulsive way, but overseas travel was something that many Englishmen of the era were taking to with a vengeance. Men born in the heyday of the British Empire were not afraid of dotted lines on maps. The ordinary working man, it is true, did not travel for leisure in any significant number, but among the skilled trade and professional classes the Continent had lured more than a few to up sticks to see what Europe could offer.

Considering Steve's football background too, his lifestyle had always been geared to 'packing a bag' and, as he reminded those who might have felt worried for him, he was an old hand as far as Europe was concerned and positive enough in attitude to grasp the opportunity in the right frame of mind: "In my playing days with Derby and Middlesbrough I did a lot of close-season continental touring, visiting nearly a dozen European countries during the early summer months, and remember, it is always well to be an optimist in most things, and sport in particular, for it is a well-known axiom that he who goes on the field with downcast spirit is already beaten."

It was armed with that sort of experience and positive energy that Steve considered the options that lay before him and no doubt those were the very sentiments he expressed to his wife Sarah when they discussed what he should do. Not knowing precisely how things might work out, Sarah was not to be part of the package, so if he said 'si' to the Spanish offer, Steve was to go it alone, coming back for visits in the close season. We can only imagine what sort of domestic discussions took place in the evening of Saturday, 27 October 1923 but there were no reports of domestic disturbances in Portland Street that night so the great debate must have run a reasonably amicable course before the hasty fond farewells.

It was a brave decision from Bloomer because he had no real conception of exactly what awaited him – the people, the team, the town, the food, the weather, the language, all the fundamentals of his daily existence were entirely unknown quantities. Weighing up the good times he had enjoyed abroad against the horrific ones he had endured, it would surely have been easier to say 'no', but Steve, not for the first time, displayed the opportunistic and courageous qualities in life which he had so often shown on the field of play. He responded to 'the call' quickly and without a backward glance. It was a two-year contract, a regular salary and a major challenge, none of which he enjoyed at the present time in England. Four months short of his 50th birthday he once again caught 'the train to uncertainty' and left Derby for Spain.

Spanish football in 1923

The appointment of Steve Bloomer was a real coup for Irún and a boost for Spanish football at an important time in its development. It was true that, apart from his two years stint as coach for the Rams, Steve had a limited track record on the non-playing side, but it was in his deep knowledge and experience of the game that his true value lay. Added to that, the sheer charisma of his name was a factor not to be underestimated; Steve was still a household name in England but his fame had also spread throughout Europe, becoming synonymous with everything about the history of the English game which the Spanish and others were keen to emulate. Perhaps only Bobby Charlton, Stanley Matthews and Pelé have commanded the same respect and ambassadorial influence since.

By definition the Spaniards had no one from within their own ranks who could possibly have matched Steve for involvement in football at the highest level over a period of 31 years. Quite simply, the Spanish game was much younger than the English in terms of its development and had yet to attain the levels of all-round technical competence and organisation which had been achieved in England only after 60 long years of trial, error and progression. While many of the first-class English and Scottish clubs were formed in the three decades before 1900, most of the Spanish clubs were formed after the turn of the century and a significant number didn't see light until after World War One and into the 1920s. Only the grand old 'senoras' of the Spanish game had played in the 19th century. Recreation Club Huelva (1889), started by British immigrants, was the first of the recorded Spanish clubs to be founded and was something of an early exception. They were followed by Athletic Club de Bilbao (1898) and Futbol Club Barcelona (1899). Even future giants such as Real Madrid (1902), Athletic Club de Madrid (1903) and Sevilla (1905) were mere infants against many of their British counterparts. In truth, in 19th century Spain, the only 'sports' able to raise excitement and interest in the nation's hearts and minds were horse-riding, fencing, pelota or the bull-fight and, as Spanish football historians were later to describe, those who sought to play or follow football were thought to be either disloyal or suffering from a touch of the sun.

"There was a madness outside, a madness that was to grow quickly and in time was to envelop all Spain, and its name was 'Futbol'. But at the time we didn't know it and at the turn of the century 'futbol' was just an insistent clamour from a strip of skeleton-white ground outside the bull ring, a noise that swept gustily through the lattices of the nearby bars and disturbed those within. To these customers, 'aficionados' of the great Corrida, football was nothing and footballers were shameless youths, daring to run through the streets behind a ball in their underwear... and probably mentally diseased."

How times change, although most of the Spanish players still wear vests under their shirts now, and I have always wondered about some of their bruising central defenders. Seemingly inevitably, the game described just a few years into the century as 'a virulent force to which few men are immune', worked its potent magic on the Spaniards just as it has on almost every nation in the world. Their first 'championship', organised initially on a regional basis, was contested in 1902; the Spanish Football Association was founded in 1913 and Spain took to football with a passionate zeal. They entered their national side in the 1920 Antwerp Olympics, having never played together before; and they were a sensation and finished runners-up. Although their professional Football League proper did not begin until 1928, by the early 1920s football was hugely popular in most areas of Spain. Realising they had a lot of catching up to do, many clubs favoured the import of British manager-coaches, a trend especially notable in the northern Basque region in which Irún is situated. Indeed that is a trend which has prevailed to this day, fuelled by the strong regional identity of the Basques which has always led them to respect their own people first, then the English, then anyone else in the world, with the rest of Spain bringing up the rear. It's regional pride gone mad, but that's the way it is. Such is the esteem in which English managers and their methods are held in the history of the Spanish game, that their legacy has stamped its mark on the very language of 'Futbol' itself. Whenever the super-rich 'futbolistas' give their post-match interviews or the powerful newspapers make or break careers, their colloquial word for the boss, no matter what his nationality, is still 'el mister'.

It was against that historical background that Steve went to Spain. As far as football was concerned, to coin a modern phrase, he had 'been there, done that, got the T-shirt' before many Spaniards even knew what a football was. For him it was almost akin to going back to his days at the County Ground in Derby in the early 1890s, where men were beginning to learn the rudiments of football with no real tradition of excellence behind them. But, unhampered by all the tedium of developing rules, because England had already done that for them, the Spanish men took to playing football with the natural flair and passion we now know they have. In Irún, interest had first manifested itself with the formation of Irún-Foot-Ball-Club in January 1902 which evolved by 1907 into Irún Sporting Club; in 1908, rivals Racing Club de Irún first took to the field and were blessed with the patronage of the king in 1913 to become 'Real' Racing de Irún. Inevitably in such a small town, a merger of 'Sporting' and 'Racing' subsequently ensued and the result on 9 May 1915 was the formation of Real Union Club de Irún, who played their first game on 29 June just outside Fuenterrabia at their quaint Amute stadium, former home of Sporting since 1910.

A 6-1 win over Real Sociedad de San Sebastian in that opening game was the prelude to a growing fervour in the town over the next few years which saw the club win both its regional and national championship by 1918. But the season before Bloomer's appointment, their pride took a severe blow described by the club president as 'shameful' when hated local rivals Real Sociedad took the regional championship and it seemed possible that the small-town Irún amateurs might be losing permanent ground to the bigger city clubs. However, there was some rare talent waiting to be developed by Irún's new manager-coach and if the wily old Steve could harness it there might yet be a chance of winning the gleaming trophies which would restore the club's tarnished honour.

Postcards from Spain

Steve left Derby on Sunday, 28 October 1923 and at least he could leave with his head held high as Derby had beaten Southampton 1-0 at the Baseball Ground the day before with a goal from Harry Storer. He decided to travel through France by train rather than risk the Bay of Biscay crossing – "I am not a good sailor and, though I have made many sea trips to Ireland and the Continent I have never yet come through without a touch of sea sickness." At the end of a 36-hour journey lay a completely new phase of the Bloomer life in a town which contemporary travel guides described as having 'nothing interesting except a pretty harbour and an entrance commanded by castles that might put a Devon man in mind of Dartmouth'. Of its twin town, Fuenterrabia, the guide proceeded in even less encouraging vein, labelling it 'a picturesque little town, but dirty and malodorous.' But beauty is in the eye of the beholder and the Spanish experience promised to be very different from the day-to-day familiarity of home.

So how did Steve fare? We are fortunate in that, having plenty of time sitting alone in his hotel, he sent back regular reports, postcards and letters which chart his progress as it unfolded, lamenting the lack of opportunity in England, relating his views on the state of the game, the achievements on the field of play, and difficulties and frustrations off it. Not to mention his tentative relationship with Spanish food and language, made more challenging still by an unusually 'interesting' local cuisine – 'kokotxas… a valued delicacy, glands from the cheek of a hake' – and an entirely separate regional language favoured by many in the Basque country. Might it all be too much for a 'meat and two veg' man from Derby? Welcome to Spain 'Mister Bloomer'.

Season 1923-24

In November 1923, Bloomer wrote the following introductory 'article' about his new life, addressing his 'Dear Friends' thus:

"Having just accepted the appointment as coach to the Real Football Club of Irún I am now domiciled in this small customs station town in the Pyrenees, where football has called me. It is quite a small place of some 10,000 population situated just over the border from France in the province of Guipúzcoa and standing on the pretty mountain river Bidasoa. It is high up and all the Spanish continental trains and merchandise pass through the town, which is an important railway junction. It is but ten miles or so from the resort town of San Sebastian where Teddy Garry holds a similar appointment, while a little further west along the Northern coastline is Bilbao where my old partner Fred Pentland is coach. So you see I am among friends and not so far away from the old Mother Country.

"My departure was such a surprise to myself that I had no time to say goodbye to any of my old friends, but I intend to keep in touch through my regular submissions to the *Derbyshire Football Express* and a letter can reach me in 36 hours so if any correspondents will address their communication to me at my new quarters c/o 'Hotel France y Gare Norte', Irún, I shall be able to reply without delay.

"I have to say that I left England with some regrets for I had great hopes that it was awaking to the realisation that we old players can do good work in the homeland without having to seek foreign countries for a livelihood. I do not wish to appear egotistical but I claim that my two years engagement with Derby County is this season bearing fruit. Players cannot be taught in a day, but the teaching of two years can now be seen; if the team meet with ordinary fortune I believe they will be playing in the First Division next season so I wish them every luck.

"My journey down here was entertaining. I travelled as far as Paris with a gentleman from Leicester who was met at the Gare du Nord by a Parisian friend. I was introduced and the Frenchman immediately invited me to dine and wine with him. I spent four and a half happy hours with these two chance acquaintances and when they saw me off the French gentleman said, "Ah! They say here in this country that England never made a 'bloomer', what you call a mistake, but she did, she did…and we know all about that Bloomer!" I couldn't help laughing at the quaintness of it all and of my own small reputation as a footballer having become known in Paris.

"When I finally got here, the Directors of the Irún club met me and declared that the first thing to do was to take a trip into the Pyrenees, so of course I had to be in the fashion. We went on the same day as my arrival and, though tired, I was more than refreshed by the magnificence of the scenery. I have never seen anything like it. From what I have seen of the town and surrounds it can certainly lay claim to being beautiful. Next day I made the 90-mile trip to Bilbao where I had a long chat with Fred Pentland, who talks Spanish fluently and looks a real 'Don'. He appears to be a 'little tin God' in Bilbao and has a courtly way with him…the lessons he gave me on the manners and customs of the country were as amusing as anything I have heard for some time.

"I am settled now in my hotel where the landlord comes of an English father and a French mother. He speaks fairly good English and we get along together extremely well but there are very few other people who speak my tongue. That is the chief difficulty of coaching in a strange country but I am told Spanish is one of the easiest languages in the world to learn, and I have already had my first lesson!

"I have now seen my Spanish boys perform on two occasions and I can say that any managers looking for talent might do worse than make the trip to this quaint and picturesque country... I have at least four players under my tuition who are the real goods. The club itself is not quite as old as Bilbao or San Sebastian and their full name is Real Union de Irún, the 'Real' simply meaning royal, which shows that we are blessed with the patronage of King Alfonso XIII, who is himself a great lover of the game. I suppose the club name is what we would call Irún United and we play at our ground near neighbouring Fuenterrabia in the black and white of Derby County!

"The 'Championship' here is different to ours. Each province runs its own league and the eight winners play off 'home and home' in a 'knockout' for the solid gold King's Cup, the gift of Alfonso. This is a great incentive to the Spaniards and from what I am told they make up for their lack of experience by an enthusiasm which is intense and hardly ever seen in England now except on Cup Final days, so we will see what we can do."

Despite his obvious disappointment at having to leave England, perhaps a hint of bitterness too, Steve gave every impression in these early letters back home, all written in his first two weeks, that he was determined to enjoy himself and keep a positive attitude. He is understandably curious about many of the differences he perceives and shows an intelligent interest in his surroundings and in the history and future progress of Spanish football, albeit evidently firmly set to preserve an 'Englishman Abroad' attitude to all that Spain might throw at him. Once settled into a day-to-day working routine with the pressure of trying to win matches, he wrote much less often but still regularly enough for his progress throughout the 1923-24 season to be fully assessed, and candidly enough for his inner thoughts, feelings and personality to be truly expressed. Read in conjunction with reports from the contemporary Spanish press and the official club records in Irún, a vivid picture of Steve's Spanish exile emerges. As for the outcome of his first season, 'El Bloomer' himself continues the tale through March to June 1924.

"I have been in Irún now for four months and I certainly have plenty of time to think out here. I heard about Billy Meredith making a comeback for Manchester City against Brighton in the last 16 of the Cup...he'll soon be 50 and I must admit a pang of envy flashed through me as I thought of Billy still being able to take part in the famous competition. As for me, well, like a Shakespearean character was wont to do, I have got into the habit of talking to myself so that I can hear

English spoken. The landlord here in the hotel is still the only man in the place that speaks our tongue and he can't keep it up for long. He says to me: 'Your language is so hard, so d-ee-f-ee-cult, while ours, ah!, senor… these long letters home you write would sound like poetry in our beautiful language.'

"Football is making rapid headway here, with crowds ruling up to 25,000 and sometimes well over 30,000, although above all the Spaniard loves to patronise a winning team. Bull fighting is gradually losing its hold in the north-east and south-east districts where the round ball game is played with such enthusiasm…the bull-fights commence in a month or two and I intend to see one, though my friends tell me one visit will be quite enough!

"We are now just into April and my side is doing quite well on the football field and we may have a chance of winning our championship, although training the players out here is surrounded with difficulties. My own boys are all 'in work', some in very good positions, and it is not always they can be freed to train, but they are so enthusiastic that two or three hours in the evening is nothing to them. I am down at the ground all day, for there is always a chance one or two of them will come down as they are as keen as mustard. When players turn up in odd ones there is the chance for personal coaching and they will listen and watch most carefully and their patience in perfecting tricks you show them is inspiring. But it is not easy work…there is still the language difficulty, which I am now gradually overcoming, and the impulsiveness of the Spanish character. However, such obstacles are there to be overcome. I train the boys on orthodox English lines but with far more ball practice and far less sprinting than in England. Their ball control is wonderful but their chief failure is in teamwork and too great a desire to shoot at inappropriate times. But they all take their football seriously and if it was permissible and feasible there are a number I could send back who are capable of holding their own with the best of the English League in craft and ball control, although they could never stand our climate of course. With Irún, the stars are Rene Petit, a centre-half who is a student, and Gamborena, a right-half who has played for Spain's Olympic games side. They are both good enough for any English League club…

"…Easter in Spain is now upon us and we are deciding the 'championship', with eight clubs in the running, each effectively the champions of their particular province. My club has won its own championship and already in the deciding games we have met Sevilla in home and away matches, drawing 1-1 at Seville and winning 2-0 at home. I was absolutely thunderstruck when I saw the excitement our games with them created… what would English fans think were they to find League clubs engaging lines of soldiers to line the enclosures to keep the crowds in order and stop them encroaching? Yes, football has taken a hold such as no one in England can imagine and the bullfight is now a very poor second in popular favour. We are now in strict training for meeting Barcelona in the next round, the semi-final, again 'home and home'…

"…Well, the warmer weather is with us and I have been sleeping under a mosquito net for weeks and the boys have been improving and improving as the days get hotter. I have heard that the Welsh FA, Everton, Birmingham and Newcastle may all be touring Spain in the summer and I can promise them a warm time and that both the mosquitoes and the players' form will trouble the tourists a good bit! At the end of April we overcame Barcelona 1-0 at home in front of our record crowd of 10,000 or so, but lost 2-0 away in front of 40,000. The rules decreed a third game at a neutral ground and we won 6-1 in San Sebastian to take us into the Final where we will now play Real Madrid."

Real Irún's victories over Sevilla and Barcelona were stupendous achievements for the romantic but unfashionable team of amateurs and they were duly marvelled at in the Spanish press, but the crowning glory was reserved for the Final at Real Sociedad's famous Atocha ground in San Sebastian, just ten miles down the coast right at the heart of Basque territory and surely not relished by the visiting stars from Madrid. Steve might have wondered whether his 'Finals' jinx was about to strike yet again, despite the fact that Archie Goodall was well out of the way…shortly before the big day the club's leading director and former player, Don Baldomero Martinez, died and the team decided to play the Final in all black in his memory.

On Sunday, 4 May 1924 most of Irún decamped to Atocha and the old ladies and children left behind in the town gathered around the telephone exchange and club house waiting for news. It came after 23 minutes… right winger Echeveste had put Irún ahead after a scramble, and so it remained, Irún 1 Madrid 0. The King's Cup, fairly overflowing with local pride, came to Irún. Having beaten the might of Spanish football, and non-Basques at that, the locals and club officials were simply beside themselves. Stirring letters and speeches were duly delivered which made even the *Derbyshire Football Express* seem low-key and unbiased by comparison and one adulatory reporter promptly elevated the manager to a status that even Bloomer had never been blessed with before – 'Saint Steve'.

The team's train was cheered by villagers all the way back to Irún and the saintly one might well have recalled distant echoes of Tutbury '92 as the 'banda Municipal' played them into town. Only the conveyance was different – 'autos' drove the team, holding the trophy aloft, to a celebratory 'fiesta' which continued 'long into the night'. No doubt the manager permitted himself a richly deserved glass or two of wine or the local speciality 'sidra'. Only six months after trading 1920s Derby for 1920s Spain, Steve had helped to restore valued esteem to his proud club and region in his first full excursion into management. His contribution was gratefully acknowledged by club secretary Jose Eceizabarrena in a rousing address to 250 reporters and club representatives from all over Spain, lauding the team's efforts and saying 'to Mister Bloomer is owed much of the glory'. A new club song was composed in honour of the win and the local and national press heralded the victory as 'both a triumph for football and for amateurism at a time when money and commercialism are threatening to take over the game'. Certainly the Irún club epitomised much of the 'Corinthian' spirit and there was an undeniable essence of 'Englishness' about both their sportsmanship and style of play during 1923-24, coupled with a reminiscently 'Derbeian' fanaticism in their support, which had 'Bloomer' and his old friend 'Johnny Bull' stamped all over it.

Taking a little time out to relax and meet old friends, he stayed on for part of the summer to see the English touring teams struggling against his own Irún and other leading clubs. Into the bargain Steve blew the gaff on the secret of Spanish team selection. Keen to put one over on the inventors of football, clubs with fixtures against English sides were not averse to pulling in ringers from other Spanish sides, so a number of the English teams 'shamed' in defeat had actually fallen to opposition not far removed from the Spanish national side!

Suitably refreshed and sufficiently rubicund to shed his 'Paleface' tag, our man in Irún packed up his halo and returned to England to renew acquaintance with Sarah, family, friends, his home town…and cricket. A pleasant couple of months ensued and before leaving again for his second Spanish campaign he took time out to wish the Derby County lads better luck for the new season; they had missed out on the predicted promotion in 1923-24 on goal-average…by just one fiftieth of a goal. He even sneaked into the 1924-25 team photograph, which has caused some confusion to Rams historians, who have sometimes cited him as Derby coach for that period.

At the start of September 1924 Steve again packed his bags in upbeat mood but as many exiles before and since have experienced,once the novelty of the first year has passed then the negatives can begin to surface. His letters home from the 1924-25 season begin to suggest that things were starting to pall a little, that a degree of homesickness was setting in, and that discomforts and irritations he had tolerated first time round were gradually weighing more heavily on the Bloomer heart.

Season 1924-25
In September 1924 came the following:

"As I write these lines I am back again in the land that many romantic writers have called 'sunny Spain'. Well it 'can' be very hot here, but no doubt the lure of alliteration over-ran the judgement of men who have made use of this pretty phrase; while it may be true there are parts of Spain which are invariably sunny, it has been my lot to have to live in a region where rain is as common as it is in Manchester. Another campaign in exile, though, has few terrors for me now, for I am beginning to be a hardened campaigner.

"I am luckily enough again installed in my modest and quiet hotel where the proprietor speaks good English and sees to it that my food is as near the English style as possible. That is one great consideration… the Spaniards like a lot of olive oil with all their food, and I hate it! So I have again given instructions for it to be cut right out of my menu, though at the ground I am laying in a stock of it for there is nothing finer for massage than pure olive oil. I have chances again here in Spain of reflecting on many things. I am like all exiles... my thoughts turn to the home country; there are many times when I can see the crowds rolling up to all the grounds I have played on and I can see the scenes almost as if I were among the people. This sort of thing becomes second nature to those of us who have to leave the homeland, but we English are the best of all the nations when we are up against it, as I found in Germany during the war...

"...So I am making another effort at coaching the Irún players, who are making an attempt to win the 'championship' of Spain outright. If any club wins King Alfonso's trophy two years running it becomes their own property and Irún means to cause their good King to put his hand down and provide a new cup! It is a big task but there will be many disgruntled people if I do not bring some good luck in the effort...

"... the football here really is the fastest I have seen, the chief reason being that the grounds are harder. Despite the rain we get, the conditions are very different in the hotter months. As an illustration let me point out that along the touchlines of Spanish grounds there are receptacles of running water where every now and again the players can plunge their heads in or have a drink; they have a 20-minutes interval and, believe me, they both need and deserve it, for after three quarters of an hour of hard football their faces are as red as fire. Just try to imagine how some of our players would fare when the heat is so terrific....they would fade away.

"As 1925 begins I hear the offside law debate is still raging and there may be changes afoot. Out here I can view these things with a very detached frame of mind without any garbled stories floating around and it helps me to see things in their true perspective. As an experiment I tested my theories on my own players in practice games using a 40-yard line inside of which you could not be offside; it encouraged some marvellously open play but then offside is a tremendous bugbear to Spanish players and spectators. The players seem not quite to grasp the smaller points of the game and are liable to overlook them altogether as they regard them as relatively insignificant... the ball, the goals and the other fellow are the chief ideas out here. So the offside amendment would help considerably. Most offsides here seem to happen by accident through the full-backs simply wandering upfield and not getting back, but still the crowds shout 'stop your dirty tricks.' It can cause great problems for the referees... in a match at Barcelona, a town official in the crowd ordered the police to arrest the referee and then took over himself, resulting in a cricket score for Barcelona. That is a rare incident but it shows the problem of the rules, the unruly crowds, the power of the town officials and the poor refereeing which prevails over here. It is all a very difficult problem for a Spaniard."

It isn't necessary to consult a mood psychologist to infer that Steve's increasingly 'Basil Fawltyesque' observations suggested he was beginning to find some of the idiosyncrasies of the Spanish game and lifestyle tugging at his nerve ends. He had no problem with his own players because he set the standards, but for someone who had played the game at the level he had, some of the naive enthusiasm in the wider Spanish game which he had admired so much in his first season seemed to have transmuted itself in his eyes to nothing more than bumbling incompetence and a blatant disregard outside of Irún for many of the values of football which he held so dear. Steve was a professional through and through…some of the players, officials and systems he was being asked to work with or against were definitely not.

There was no hint of animosity from Steve or the club… just a creeping feeling that the second year of his original contract would, as initially agreed, be the last. Irún did not manage to trouble the royal goldsmiths to fashion another cup that year, rivals Real Sociedad being crowned champions of Guipúzcoa and the big boys from Barcelona seeing to it that the King's Cup went to Catalonia. That is not to say that Irún had no further glory that season…an invitation to play friendly games against Real Madrid in the Spanish capital over Christmas 1924 resulted in astonishing wins for the minnows of 3-0 and 7-0, hailed in the press as 'sensational'. That giant-killing act was extended to the worldwide scene on 2 April 1925 when Irún met the touring Argentinian side Boca Juniors at Amute. The famous team from Buenos Aires had already accounted for Barcelona and Madrid but Bloomer's boys saw them off 4-0, leaving the dumbfounded Argentinians acclaiming Irún as 'capable of holding their own with the best in the world'. As a result of that victory, the club achieved celebrity status well beyond Spain and Bloomer's last games at the helm were on their tour of Switzerland in April 1925, where they beat Servette, Young Boys and Berne all in the space of four days. Spain was so proud of the club's ambassadorial achievements that the National Assembly presented them with a 'sash' for National Sporting Merit, the only football club to have received such an honour.

That singular event coincided with the end of Bloomer's agreed two-year contract and it was surely a mutually appropriate time for a return to English shores. Steve left for England during the summer, his last interview with the Spanish press neatly and diplomatically summing up his thoughts at that time: "These boys are born ball-players. There is nothing more to do. My work here is done."

He arrived back in England all the wiser for the experience, yet for all Irún's achievement few people back here ever became aware of the part Bloomer played in those brief halcyon days when the amateur 'black and whites' carried the banner of Continental football into the main arena. Modest to a fault, Bloomer seldom talked about this interlude in his life in which he had 'practised his methods' for two seasons in the most important decade in the history of the Spanish game.

At the start of the next season a buoyant Irún moved to their new ground, Stadium Gal, the Spanish professional league was inaugurated in 1928 and by the end of the 1920s football had developed to such a degree that their national side were accorded the opportunity of meeting England. A mile-long queue formed in Madrid four hours before the game – long gone were the days of 'mentally diseased youths chasing a ball in their underwear'. All the old bull-fighting sages would have given anything to get in. Some 30,000 spectators saw England go two up by half-time in torrid heat. Then the Spanish goals and the delirious pitch invasions began to surge. On 15 May 1929, Spain, managed by Fred Pentland, won 4-3, the first time any Continental country had ever beaten the nation who invented football.

There is no intimation whatsoever that Steve Bloomer alone was responsible for the upsurge in Spanish football's popularity, or that historic result, but he unquestionably played his part in developing the game there, and most important, its reputation beyond Spain, to the stage where that result was possible. As for Irún, they won the 'championship' once more in 1927 and played in the First Division for four seasons when the national Spanish League began in 1928 but thereafter they were relegated and had to seek re-election a number of times. Quite simply, 'professionalism' was the death knell for the glory days of the club; all their best players went to Real Sociedad, the Madrid clubs or other moneyed giants. They had a yo-yo relationship with the League structure for many years thereafter and were subject to voluntary relegation to the relatively minor reaches in 1979 due to severely depleted finances, where they now play in what is effectively Division Four in the 17-division structure of the Spanish pyramid.

The club's stirring story has ensured that they are viewed romantically in Spanish football history – a quaint and once-great club, perhaps 'the Accrington Stanley of Spain'. Their splendid 400-page definitive history was written in 1991 and the name of Steve Bloomer has taken its modest place in the chronology. The club is currently redeveloping the Stadium Gal and plans to open a heritage museum and archive room; when two intrepid Spanish-based Derby County fans recently made Bloomer enquiries there, they happened upon an affable club official trying to make something of a room which was in some state of disarray:

"Oh yes," he said, "we have such a long and proud history, and all of those precious times preserved here in these piles of boxes, right back to the earliest times. Only one small problem… I don't know which seasons are in which boxes…they are all mixed up… and Mister Bloomer, well he could be anywhere. Then, of course, there was the unfortunate mishap of the little flood which damaged some of the files…who knows?… perhaps he might be washed away for ever…"

Hearty banter was duly exchanged – and there lies the romance of the amateur game and the undeniable charm of Spain. In ten years time the museum might be open. Flushed down the plughole or not, there are still a few gnarled old men in Irún who remember those balmy days, but not for much longer. Scores of English motoring tourists still enter Spain through the frontier town. Perchance if you find yourself there soon enough, a diversion back to the 1920s might be worthwhile; and if you can get a walnut-faced local to nod sagely, eyes misting, and say: "Ah, si, Mister Bloomer… Irún…Campeones," then you too can nod in agreement, buy him a drink to stir his memories, and reply: "We know all about that Bloomer!"

AN OLD 'UN HOLDS COURT 1925-1935

"Comest thou with the veteran's smile,
Who sees his day of conquest fled,
But loves to view the bloodless toil,
 Of sons whose sires he often led."
James Hogg

“**I** AM more than delighted to be in my home country for the opening
of season 1925-26, a campaign which will inevitably mark a new epoch
in the history of the great game of football. Laws have been altered,
drastic reforms have been decided upon and the sowers now await to see what
the reapers will bring in."
Derbyshire Football Express, 29 August 1925

Roaring Twenties

That was how Steve reintroduced himself to the football followers of Derby on
his return from the land of 'nuts and siestas'. His Spanish journey had been a
marvellous experience from both a football and travel perspective but there is
no doubt, despite the lack of employment offers from any of the top clubs, that
he was pleased to be back on home territory in a decade when so much was
going on in the game. Steve had been advocating a major rewrite of the laws for
several years, but especially the offside legislation, and the change to that most
idiosyncratic and irritating of rules was finally implemented in 1925 to that
which has prevailed in essence to today. Initially, as teams struggled to adapt
their defences to the new regime, there was a glut of goals, 6,373 being scored
in the League in the first 'new' season compared to 4,700 in the last 'old' season.
Even by the 1930s, defences had not come to grips with forwards making the
most of their new-found freedom; in season 1930-31, a staggering 7,000 goals
were scored and records began to tumble.To a record goalscorer and old sage
of Bloomer's pedigree, such changes, whatever their effect, provided ample
material for debate among fellow football students, of which there were many.

Bloomer was not one of those football people who inexplicably declare a
complete disinterest in the game the moment it ceases to pay them. In fact just
the opposite; he was an avid follower of everything that was going on. He read,
he watched, he talked to people, he talked at people, he analysed, theorised,

condemned, proposed and enthused all at the same time, and above all he appeared in the press. In truth he probably bored some people to death, certainly those who had no interest in the inner workings and rationale of football, but there were sufficiently large numbers who did share Bloomer's passionate zeal for him to assume the role of guru to the huge following that the game had built up afresh since the war. In his playing days he had always been a thinker on the pitch, now he became a veritable professor off it. That he loved the game and cared deeply about its welfare is crystal clear. It was a consuming passion; and there was a lot to go at. Coming under the microscope with the offside question were increased wages and transfer fees, more technically-based training regimes, betting and bribery scandals, tactical adjustments, experimental floodlit games, the advent of radio broadcasting and the pools, numbers on shirts, the import of foreign players, suggestions for World and European tournaments and sundry other relative minutiae. All these real or potential developments occurred in the 1920s and early 1930s and signified a complete break from the 'Dark Ages' of football in which Bloomer had enjoyed his playing career.

Effectively football entered its third age – pre-war, post-war and now 'modern'. In general society, too, life was changing apace, as the aeroplane, faster trains and more widespread car ownership facilitated travel, the 'talkies' came to the cinema and stark new elements in domestic and industrial design created landscapes and surroundings entirely unfamiliar to anyone born in the Victorian age. Those of Bloomer's generation might well have been engulfed by it all, indeed some were and never adapted to the 'new way of things'. But Steve knew enough about football and life to 'go with the flow', at least some of the way, embracing the new where he thought it improved matters and upholding the traditional when he felt a valid case existed. Of course, someone who likes to debate and chew the fat needs an audience and an audience is only generally attracted when they feel the lecturer knows his stuff – and that was where Steve scored in a big way, as he carried his reputation before him; agree with him or not, his views had to be respected. He had done too much in the game to be ignored.

It was against this exciting and challenging background of change, both social and football, that Steve arrived back in England in late summer 1925. Photographs show him at 51 looking robust, tanned and apparently raring to go and in the next seven years, while the ambush that was to be debilitating ill health still laid largely hidden, he held court to whoever was interested and gave every impression of an 'old 'un', freed from the daily pressures of coaching and management, having a darn good time. This period of Bloomer's life as 'observer' largely comprised two elements, his position as a community coach and his role as a regular newspaper columnist; his employer in each case was the *Derby Daily Express* and the work was paid. Although by no means lucrative, it was sufficient to meet Steve's modest needs as he continued to live a comfortable but simple enough life at his home in Portland Street. Towards the end of the 1920s he supplemented both these roles by again going on to the Derby County payroll as a 'general assistant'. Each of his three jobs might best be related in turn.

Coach to local lads

Steve first took on this role in late August 1923 and had hardly got into full stride before the Spanish offer came along. He made enough impact in that short time, though, for the job to be immediately resurrected at the start of season 1925-26 and effectively, from September 1925 onwards, he simply took up the reins where he had left off. The idea of bringing on local players and spotting potential talent tied in quite closely with what was going on at a higher level. As is the case now, football clubs didn't always have the money to buy star players from other clubs and the idea of 'growing your own' was a very attractive one. Derby County were more financially strapped than most and the local newspaper first made the suggestion, once Derby had dispensed with Bloomer's coaching services, that he might be profitably used in the local football scene. The scouting role in truth was a secondary one; although Steve might well have had a financial arrangement with the club in the case of successful introductions, there were too few of these around and his prime role was to watch games, pass on coaching tips and offer his observations in his 'Bloomer as Coach to Local Lads' column which ran every week in the *Football Express* during the season. The games he went to see were invariably Saturday games and although they were sometimes morning kick-offs, many were afternoon and at this time he was not able to watch Derby County as regularly as he would have liked. Sometimes he dashed back to catch the second half but it was local, and sometimes schoolboy, football which became Bloomer's priority viewing in the second half of the 1920s. Steve himself explained his role and what he got out of it:

"When the editor of the *Derbyshire Football Express* invited me to assume the role of talent spotter and public coach among the many junior clubs in and around Derby, I accepted the position with some eagerness because I long ago realised that all great players begin their careers in junior circles. The expeditions have come to be a real joy and everywhere I go I receive nothing but the greatest kindness and consideration on all hands. I am told that my work has done real good and that the juniors have looked eagerly for my visit to the various matches. I know this personally from the letters and visits I receive from young players and only last week a youth called at my house asking advice, and I was glad to give it.

"So when I first gave up the work to go to Spain I did so with great regret. All I can say is that football to me has ever been a sport, recreation and loving hobby and if the series of articles I have been able to pen have done some little good to foster the game among junior clubs then I am well repaid. The sole aim of my role was to develop local talent in a way in which it had never been developed before and from what I have seen of junior football in Derbyshire I can say that our senior club can find many players of undoubted ability in this district... they just require spotting."

One might well say 'twas ever thus; how many Derbyshire-born 30-goals-a-season men have the Rams plucked from local obscurity since then? Ilkeston-born Ray Straw did it for one glorious Third Division North season in 1956-57 before he found it much harder in the Second Division and Derby let him go to Coventry; and Derby-born men Tommy Powell and Jack Parry, although not prolific goalscorers (though Parry scored 24 in 1955-56 before being injured), became great local favourites. But as for that one golden striker who must surely be out there somewhere...believe us 'Steve', we are still looking!

The match reports make interesting reading and reveal much about Bloomer's philosophy of the game. They were presented not as ball-by-ball accounts but effectively as analytical critiques, picking up on points of good or bad individual and tactical play and suggesting ways of improvement. Those given a good write-up must have been pleased as Punch but Steve was also apt to shoot from the hip on occasions and could be critical in a headmasterly sort of way almost to the point of ridicule: "Vickers must learn to use his left foot if he is to have any future..." "Wingfield seemed to forget he had an inside partner for he persisted in trying to beat all opposition by sheer dribbling powers where a pass was the royal and easy route to success..." "Collins in goal looked terribly nervous and inexperienced as he completely turned his back for the first goal..." How many hearts Steve must have broken in this way one can only guess. Was Vickers ever to regain the confidence to mix freely in polite society? Would they never let Wingfield forget his beastliness? Was it true that Collins was picked up in the desert en route for the French Foreign Legion? On one occasion Steve was actually taken to task over his 'criticism' by an irate team manager; his reply, though, was unequivocal...he saw 'little point in always painting a rosy picture' and in any case 'the comments are designed to help by being acted upon in a practical way'. Maybe Steve didn't fully realise how sensitive some people can be to criticism simply because, in his own career, he cultivated an immunity to it and had his own foolproof way of dealing with paper talk. A contemporary tribute to Bloomer which appeared in the *Sporting Life* is revealing in the first of those directions:

"Here is a player who has left a mark on the records of the game which will prove to be indelible. For two decades he has played football that has been the real football, free from embroideries but rich in genius. Like all true artists he never once worried about placating the gallery. If they appreciated his play, well and good; if they failed to appreciate it, also well and good. He has always been on the field to play football to his own conception of the game, not to worry unduly about what is being said of him. Always he has been impervious to the cheap criticism of those who do not know and content with the praise of those who do."

It might be Raich Carter or Igor Stimac being talked about here...Bloomer, too, trod the thin line between self-belief and arrogance just a little dangerously at times but when you 'know' you have the ability, then why worry? Steve's own comments about the press are even more apposite:

"I have played more than a few indifferent games myself, games which I have sometimes wished for the chance of playing over again. But when I was a player I never once read a report of a match or of a criticism of myself. By cutting out the newspapers so completely I saved myself many a tortured moment...no player likes to read about himself playing poorly because all players know when they have not done well and to read about it afterwards is only to rub salt into the wounds."

Steve's own articles, it is true, were for the entertainment and instruction of the several thousand readers of the *Derbyshire Football Express*, but if he expected the 22 young players under the Bloomer spotlight to exercise the same extraordinary level of restraint in ignoring the press as he had done, then he was very much mistaken. Of course, the lads read them. So Ivan Sharpe's observation: "Our Stephen was a tyrant...he said what he thought," certainly applied to the written word too, but so did Sharpe's qualification of that comment that "he always meant well". The fact is that Bloomer was a perfectionist in matters of football and in applying the same demanding criteria to the assessment of others as he did to himself he could appear overly dismissive and at times hurtful. But that was the man and I would venture to suggest that he'd have gladly spent any amount of time with the Vickers, Wingfields and Collins of this world if they'd come to him for a private word and a coaching session.

At any rate the 'criticisms' never became anything but an occasional minor issue and Steve continued his 'Junior Coach' role until the end of the 1931-32 season. Become two-footed, master instant control, always think fractionally ahead, take your time, and use your brains... those recognisable 'Goodallisms' were his own adjuncts to success and now became his constant watchwords to the juniors; sound advice, and one has to ask how many professionals, even in the current Premiership, can lay claim to five out of five on the 'Bloomerometer'. Steve certainly had ample opportunities for putting his theories to the test, perhaps at some personal cost. Over a period of nine seasons, interrupted only by his Spanish time-out, he watched and reported on well over 200 junior games throughout the county; he never owned or drove a car and often chose to walk, an activity he enjoyed, to local venues like the Meadows, Darley Fields, the County Ground or Parker's Piece, and when he got there he stood on often damp or soggy ground in all sorts of weathers before the walk back. Knowing in retrospect that he was later to suffer from severe bronchitis and asthma, one has to wonder whether these 'pleasant excursions' didn't later take their toll.

Whatever the case, Bloomer's work was regarded as progressive for its time, a sort of forerunner of the 'Youth Academy' work so fashionable now, and there is no doubt, in linking a big name to the smaller scene, it helped to create an ongoing weekly interest in local football which has always been a strong point to this very day. Even now, among any group of old boys sharing a pint, there is invariably someone able to recollect the footballing days of their youth as if they were yesterday…names, incidents and goals are all lodged away and as age creeps relentlessly on the memory may diminish and the goalscoring yardages increase from 20 to 30 then 40, but beneath the frail exteriors of old men the young footballer's spirit lives on. Many of those who Bloomer cast an eye over have long since passed away but there are a few still soldiering on in their late 80s and 90s who were watched by Steve in the late 1920s… and I know one or two who, even 70 years after the event, are still proud to tell of the day 'Steve Bloomer gave me a good write-up' and still have the yellowing cuttings to prove it.

There is an axiom that says it's good to give something back to any system you once benefited from. Steve Bloomer's work with and for young footballers who would seldom rise anywhere near his own dizzy heights was exactly that. It is something for which he was heralded at the time, although never since, a side of his love of the game which was neither glorious or financially lucrative but one with which he could be well satisfied and one which linked him to a whole new generation of football people. That is one of the very reasons for Bloomer's longevity in Derby men's memories…they may never have seen him play, but he saw them play, he once threw the ball back to them, they nodded to him, spoke to him even, read his reports, and maybe wrote the odd 'Dear Steve' letter. And those things alone are sufficient for men throughout the decades since to have said with a confidential air and a twinkle in the eye: "Oh yes, I knew Steve Bloomer."

Perennial pundit

"Well here we are again ready for another eight and a half months of the big ball game with all the multitudinous topics, discussions and controversies that it will surely bring in its wake. I am just as keen as ever on writing each week some of my notions on the game and of co-operating with my readers by touching upon just those matters they are interested in. This may be taken as a general invitation to readers to write to me and ask me questions. My post-bag was a heavy one last season but it certainly brings all of us closer together, and that's the main thing."

Bloomer's introductory note to the 1929-30 season was typical of his annual message to readers since he began a regular general football column, again in the *Derbyshire Football Express*, in August 1921. True to his morals on the subject of players and the press, he had done little of a journalistic nature during his playing days, partly through lack of natural confidence in that direction, and also because players then hadn't fully entered the popular domain, but mainly because he felt that playing the game and writing about it did not make for comfortable bedfellows. There were certainly some opportunities in the late-Victorian era. John Goodall, for example, wrote his own book, *Association Football*, in 1898, while still a regular member of the Derby side, and some leading players were more apt to sound off in the press than others. Bloomer, for his part, kept fairly stumm. He did contribute an entertaining and informative six-page piece entitled 'The Forward Game' to the lavish Volume One of *Association Football And The Men Who Made It* in 1905 and that was a piece which showed some signs of the developing analytical approach which Bloomer was later to apply to his study of the game to such good effect. It also contained a suggestion that he felt a little uneasy in the role of scribe, finishing the piece by saying that 'this little effort claims no literary merit other than that which was learnt at an elementary school.'

Thereby hangs a tale; although Bloomer was by no means an academic in the true sense he was undoubtedly a thinker and believed in self-betterment. He was one of the first breed of working-class lads to benefit from a structured learning programme in the 'three R's' and he left school at 12 with a literacy standard that might well embarrass many of the 'console kids' who are his modern counterparts. He first started to contribute to periodicals just as his playing days were closing with a series of articles for *The Boys' Own Paper* in late 1913, entitled 'The Young Footballer In The Making', telling his young readers that 'it has been a very pleasant time to me, trying to put into words most of those little points in the game with which I have become familiar after many years experience'. The cynic will undoubtedly chime 'well he would say that', but Steve's sentiments seem genuine enough. Although there was undoubtedly some editorial input and control to the pieces, I do not believe they were all entirely ghost-written by any means and the fact that he later went on to regular contributions is testimony to his popularity with readers and to the fact that Bloomer thoroughly enjoyed expounding his theories in written form. Four years in Ruhleben certainly didn't harm Steve's educational and cultural development and after his release he made his debut as a columnist in the local press at the start of the 1919-20 season.

While other contributors to the Derby papers preserved their anonymity behind the corniest of pseudonyms, Bloomer's own name was too valuable a publicity tool to be played down. So he took his initial place alongside 'Bullioph' (hockey), 'Plunger' (swimming) and 'Clodhopper' (athletics) simply as 'Steve Bloomer...The Prince of Goalscorers'. During that entire season, though, and the next, his contributions were sporadic, amounting to no more than half a dozen pieces. That is responsible for the sometime quoted misconception that 'after his retirement from playing, Bloomer wrote the occasional column for the papers'. In truth, nothing could be a greater understatement, for when he began regular pieces in 1921 he continued to make weekly contributions during the football season right until the latter end of season 1931-32 and his autographed Steve Bloomer sign-off became an integral part of the design fabric of the *Derbyshire Football Express*. Bloomer wrote about all the football issues of the day, contributing around 1,500 words a week for what became 'Steve Bloomer Writes'. He delivered roughly the same for his 'Coach To Local Lads' piece and on occasions extended himself to three pieces an issue by reporting on Derby County's matches directly 'Through Bloomer's Eyes'. An appropriate cumulative calculation shows that the lad from St James's Road School put his name to in excess of 750 pieces and well over one million words in the Derby press over a period of 11 full seasons; that was more akin to a second career than 'an occasional contribution'. Inevitably the press in other parts of the country reported a selection of Bloomer's views, and some were directly syndicated to other papers, which brought a good degree of feedback. Bloomer developed an entertaining and chatty style and to read his pieces today is the closest we can get to hearing him speak. It seems this new string to his bow came as rather a surprise to Steve himself:

"When I first undertook my series of articles shortly after my appointment as coach to Derby County I had no idea how many football enthusiasts took the game so seriously as to go to the trouble of writing to a newspaper. It has often seemed remarkable to me, too, that having ignored newspapers so completely during my playing days I should now be writing regularly."

What the newspaper wanted in exchange for Bloomer's fee was entertaining, well-informed and thought-provoking material which would build up a loyal readership and enhance circulation figures; he didn't let them down. Even when employed by Derby County, some of his writing was pointedly forthright but when his formal connection with them had been severed in 1923 he declared his intention to be 'more frank and open than ever before now that I have the freedom from not being connected with any one club'.

Although most of his views were very sound and he seemed to have a knack for knowing exactly what was needed to resolve particular ills in the game, he occasionally put forward outlandish schemes for reform and while more often than not 'on the mark', he blazed spectacularly over once in a while. Inevitably he sparked occasional controversy but, as Bloomer explains in 1931, for the most part it was healthy debate:

"In ten seasons of writing I have only ever received three letters in my postbag which came directly from men employed by clubs. Most come from supporters genuinely interested in the game and its issues but I provoke the occasional strange one. Recently I spoke out against the prevalence of rough play, which didn't please everyone. One of my correspondents says: 'Who wants rough play wiping out? Nobody. Just listen to the roars of the crowd when a player knocks another down and that will show whether people want football to be made into a game for 'ninnies'... Yours, 'Shut Up!' "

Strong stuff indeed! Bloomer generally held his corner, though, especially when his antagonists maintained anonymity. One of the things that comes through strongly from the writings is that there is really very little in our present game that is 'new' despite the fact that we are forever being told that football has changed out of all recognition. Off the pitch that may be so, but on it all the old chestnuts were there back in the 1920s. Referees and linesmen were seen as a malady and as a remedy full-time paid officials, goal-line judges, independent timekeepers and a referee for each half of the pitch were all advocated. Match-fixing came under close scrutiny, as did the fairest way of properly penalising scoring-opportunity fouls on the edge of the box. Some of the remedies offered might well have mileage today…in the latter case one of Steve's readers suggested a referee be 'given the power to restrict a defensive wall to only three men at his discretion'. Bloomer backed that one and I would too – it would make defenders think twice, that's for sure. Quite frankly one could fill an entire book with 'Bloomerisms' alone, but a random sample must suffice to set the tone.

Steve the prophet

February 1931 – Just too many games: "I have thought about this for a considerable time and know it won't please everybody, especially the sacrificial clubs, but it has been obvious to me that there are too many clubs in the League and that the season is too long. I believe it would be to the advantage of the game as a whole, clubs, players and spectators, if the number of clubs in each section of the League was reduced to 20. Also I believe it would be a good idea if there was a recognised opportunity for stronger clubs outside the League to win a way into it by means of competition in one or other of the healthiest among the various lesser organisations. These things may come some day in the not very distant future and those concerned with the conduct and government of soccer would not regret it I'm sure."

*The Premier League was reduced to 20 clubs from 1995-96 and direct promotion from the Conference League to the Football League was introduced in 1986-87.

Bloomer bloopers

March 1930 – A dim view: "The recent experimentation in floodlit games has left me rather cold. The whole idea of playing football under artificial light is rather fantastical when it comes to considering it as a development in League football. Apart from being a novelty way of celebrating a special occasion, perhaps, the matter has no other importance. Spectators who heard of the night match at Mansfield last Saturday need not let their imaginations run riot as to the football of the future or of having to wait until 10 o'clock at night for the papers to come out with all the 'League Finals'. That day will never come."

*Bloomer was not alone in this view. Although floodlighting on the Continent and in the United States became commonplace before World War Two, the Football Association resisted the innovation and it was not until 1956 that the first official League match under lights, Portsmouth v. Newcastle United at Fratton Park, took place. Nowadays night games are favourites with the fans and the standard of lighting at stadiums of the quality of Derby's Pride Park and Middlesbrough's Riverside is second to none…except when they fail on opening night!

March 1931 – Clashing views: "These are days of standardisation so why not standardise colours to be worn by Football League clubs to do away with a lot of squabbling that arises from time to time over who should change and when.

I propose the League should lay it down that in all cases the home teams will play in red and visiting teams in blue, although perhaps I am treading on dangerous ground. I know that thousands of football followers have a conscientious objection to their favourites playing in other than their familiar raiments."

*Too right…leave our raiments alone! Club colours have become an enduring part of the folklore of the game and the home and away replica shirt market, like it or not, is now worth millions of pounds. Bloomer, incidentally, never had the opportunity of 'kissing his club badge' in the demonstrative manner of some modern goalscorers. Derby County Football Club did not introduce a shirt badge until 1923 and even then it failed to become an established feature. Barring the 1925-26 season they mostly wore badgeless shirts right up to and including the 1946 Cup Final triumph and adopted their old Ram's head logo only from 1946-47.

September 1928 – Come in No.8: "Wasn't it two years ago that there was a widespread discussion as to whether Association players ought not to wear distinguishing numbers on their backs to coincide with the number marked in the official programme? The 'stunt' – for a stunt it was – died out, and I for one welcomed the early natural death of the idea. So imagine my surprise and astonishment last week when the Arsenal and Chelsea clubs announced their intentions of numbering their players for last Saturday's game. To my mind they have acted most indiscreetly. Had this idea ever been introduced in my playing days I should have refused to wear a jersey with a number on it. As an inside-right I would have been No.8. The contention is that crowds cannot identify players but that is an insidious doctrine that will do untold harm to the game if it is allowed to get a hold. Every good player has a name and a personality and to say: 'No.8 is a clever player,' well, bang goes all that personality, the romance, everything a player has strived for and gained, and all because some people that go to football matches when they feel like it do not know the players intimately enough to identify them on the field. I preferred to be known as Steve Bloomer, not No.8."

*Shirts were numbered in the 1933 FA Cup Final for the first time, from 1 to 22, but the familiar 1-11 numbering became compulsory in England from 1939. In 1993 the English Premiership introduced players' names and squad numbers to the back of shirts, which might have placated Bloomer part of the way. Of all his protestations about the game this was probably his wildest aberration of all.

Random rantings
1927 – Who is the fellow in the black?: "If the present standard of League referees is the highest that can be reached then I am sorry for the referees and for the selectors, but not nearly so sorry as I am for the teams that have to submit to

such control week after week... as for the 'flagwaggers', I believe the League made a big mistake when it provided the linesmen with these small flags because it gave them an exaggerated idea of their own importance by implying they must make themselves seen. Moreover, a flag is a sort of toy, made to be wagged, and that is probably why they are wagged so often."

*Views such as these were apt to get Bloomer into hot water with officials. John Lewis, a leading referee in Bloomer's playing days, was moved to a stern 'reply' on occasions, and local referee Reuben North, a fellow *Football Express* columnist and for 16 years a Football League linesman, approached a state of near apoplexy at Bloomer's 'flagwagging' jibe, saying: "Once again I must cross swords with Mr Steve Bloomer as to me his opinions are simply astounding..." Bloomer was later to have hands-on experience at officiating. In the early 1930s he used to referee games himself on Duffield Rec, cadging a lift from George Thornewell, former Derby and England winger, landlord of the White Hart in Duffield village at the time. The paper loved all the banter, of course, friendly or indignant. Readers then as now lapped up controversy with relish.

It would be wrong to imagine that Bloomer was a crank when it came to suggestions for improving the game. Most of the time he was clinically well-informed but, like all of us, his emotions got the better of his judgement now and then with spectacular results. At any rate his second career as a columnist and pundit thoroughly entertained his public and kept the Bloomer name well under the spotlight long after his active involvement in the game ceased. These days it would undoubtedly have given him a television or radio career if he'd wanted one...just imagine what sharp-tongued banter might have ensued if miserly defender Alan Hansen and arch goal poacher 'Steve' could have worked together.

Bloomer re-signed by Derby County
After Derby County finished an unlucky third in Division Two in both 1924 and 1925, manager Cecil Potter left the club, fully intending to stay out of football. In the event he was lured back to replace Herbert Chapman as manager of Huddersfield and took them to a remarkable third successive Football League championship in 1925-26. Derby, meanwhile, entered a new phase with the appointment of George Jobey whose subsequent 16-year reign, despite a lack of major trophies, was to rank as one of the most successful in the club's history, starting with promotion back to the top flight in 1925-26, his first season in charge. In the remaining years of the 1920s, names which are very familiar to current Derby County followers began to arrive at the club: Harry Bedford, Sammy Crooks, Harry Storer, Tommy Cooper, Jack Barker and Jack Bowers to name but a handful. Bloomer, too, was re-signed by Derby County during the 1928-29 season, at the age of 54, but as this is a serious biography rather than a fairy story, it must be said that this was in the capacity of 'general assistant' on the

groundstaff. During the earlier part of the decade it seems likely that Bloomer had supplemented his coaching and journalistic incomes by drawing on accumulated savings, but by 1929, as Britain itself entered a deep economic depression, he possibly needed more in the way of hard income as the savings dwindled.

Later pictures of Bloomer at the Baseball Ground in overalls, and accounts of him sweeping the stands, have brought a reaction from some quarters which basically says… 'how tragic for a great star to end up like that'; true, there is a certain poignancy and irony in the scenario but it is not such an unusual occurrence in football circles. More to the point there are hundreds of ex-players who have fallen on much harder times in their later years, living dejected and rejected lives in complete poverty, totally excluded from club affairs, and there is every reason to believe that Bloomer was delighted simply to 'be involved'. With an effective 'access all areas' pass to the Baseball Ground, it seems from a number of accounts from players of the time that Bloomer became a sort of revered talisman, rather like the factory cat who roams as he pleases, becomes part of the scenery and is indulged by all and sundry. It wasn't all dirty work, either. He enjoyed the football 'circuit', attending Wembley Cup Finals and international games and on occasions travelling with the team, as for the match at his old club Middlesbrough on 29 November 1930 when 'I thoroughly enjoyed the game and spent the weekend in Darlington staying with my old friend Alf Common, now mine host of a licensed house'.

A number of contemporary football magazines described Bloomer at this time as 'spotting' for Derby County and neither the scope or exact time span of his role has ever been accurately documented. It does seem likely that his duties were part-time and embraced all manner of assignments, at least in the earlier stages, from forking the pitch to watching games and representing the club at presentation evenings and supporters' functions. Steve himself put it in a nutshell in stating his position in 1930 as 'now helping the County in the hundred and one little things that have to be done'. Inevitably there are a number of anecdotes from that period; Ralph Hann, who joined Derby in March 1932 and was later to be club trainer until the arrival of Brian Clough in 1967, remembered his first encounter with Bloomer:

"Shortly after I arrived at the Baseball Ground as a 21-year-old, Bloomer was pointed out to me sweeping the stands and I couldn't believe that a former star was reduced to that after so many legendary performances for the club. I got to know him quite well and although he was only one of the ground staff he was treated with great respect by all the players. When I first met him I must admit to being in awe and wondering how he gained such a reputation for phenomenal shooting when he looked hardly big enough to kick the ball."

Most re-told of these yarns, though, is the rather more romanticised one from Derby half-back/inside-forward, and later manager, Harry Storer. As a Rams player since 1921, Storer had been coached by Bloomer and knew him well but had particular reason to recall one of their last meetings in late 1928, shortly before moving to Burnley:

"Bloomer was in his 50s and employed on the Derby groundstaff. We were chatting together and standing with our backs to a group of players having shooting practice in the goalmouth. Suddenly a ball was mis-hit in our direction, hurtling towards our backs, and one of the players shouted: "Duck!" I did, but Bloomer turned quickly, sighted the dropping ball and, perfectly balanced, volleyed it into the net. We were all left speechless. He was about 40 yards from goal."

A symbolic tale rather than a truly amazing one, for lots of 50-somethings are still kicking footballs daily on the training grounds, but it serves admirably to encapsulate the latent awareness and enigmatic charisma which had ever been Bloomer's trademarks.

The urge to kick a ball is never lost as long as the legs hold up and one wonders if the odd incident of this type might well have inspired Bloomer to one last effort on the field of play. Despite his categoric 'retirement' pledge after the 'Old International' game in 1923, he 'accepted without hesitation' a request to turn out again at Belper for one last fling on Wednesday, 30 September 1931. Aged 57 he pulled on the striped shirt of Belper British Legion for a charity match in the town where so long ago his grandfather had once gone in search of nailmaking work. Herbert Strutt School provided the opposition in a match which raised £10 towards the Christmas treat for war orphans and children of the unemployed. The game itself, played in front of almost 1,000 spectators, was a light-hearted affair and, inevitably at inside-right, Bloomer entered into the spirit by responding humorously to the Derbyshire touchline wags with audible asides to his team-mates and a positive refusal to subject himself to the indignity of donning his international cap during play, before scoring a penalty in a 4-3 defeat. The press reported 'there's life in those old boots yet' and described his last-ever goal thus:

"A Bloomer drive from outside the area was handled and he took the resultant penalty; Steve walked casually up to the ball and almost apologetically put it straight into the top corner of the net."

There are worse ways of signing off, but of far more significance than the match is what it says about Bloomer's constitution at that time. That he should appear on a football pitch at all, and play for the full 90 minutes, shows his health was still holding up and match photographs show him cutting a pretty trim figure. Coupled with the fact that he was still working at the Baseball Ground, and continued to do so until the mid-1930s, the oft-quoted 'fact' that his health 'had gone' in the early or late 1920s is shown to be erroneous. Those days lay ahead yet, but in the meantime Bloomer had used his time since returning from Spain to the full. In fact he appeared vigorous enough to be offered a chance to return there, testimony as well to his popularity among the football fraternity in that country:

"In December 1931 I went to Highbury to see England play Spain and renewed my acquaintance with old Spanish friends at their hotel. The mercurial and excitable Gamborena from Irún spotted me first and I was made to feel like the Prime Minister. I met all the players and officials and was made so welcome that afterwards I almost wished I had accepted one or other of the offers I had made to me that day to go back to Spain. As it was, I had to confess to them that I was getting a trifle ancient for giving demonstrations of my conceptions of football. What with my Spanish and their English, we struggled a bit but still got along famously. I was puzzled by their performance…after I'd sung their praises all week they lost 7-1!"

While his reputation as a celebrity was still intact, Steve evidently acknowledged that the clock was advancing inexorably, as family and personal happenings had a habit of confirming; oldest daughter Hetty had presented Steve and Sarah with their first grandson, Alan Quantrill in 1927, and Steve gained another son-in-law when daughter Doris married cathedral chorister and would-be licensee Cyril Rawlins Richards at the newly-appointed Derby Cathedral; in 1929 they presented Steve and Sarah with another grandson, Steve Richards, named after his 'grandpop', as they called him. Hetty Richards, a second granddaughter, was to arrive three years later. But it wasn't just births that marked the march of time. Funerals of old colleagues, too, became an increasingly regular habit. Derby goalkeeper and fellow baseballer Jack Robinson died suddenly in 1931 from pneumonia, aged only 62, a reminder again to Bloomer that ongoing advances in medical science had yet to eradicate many potentially preventable early deaths.

In employment terms, too, Bloomer was reminded that all good things must come to an end; the early 1930s were times of great austerity, widespread unemployment and cut-backs in all walks of life. Market forces decreed that Derby could not sustain two rival daily newspapers and in early 1932 the *Derby Daily Telegraph* 'incorporated' the *Derby Daily Express*, and their *Football Special*, the legendary *Green 'Un*, absorbed the *Derbyshire Football Express* for which Bloomer had written for so many years. The *Telegraph* had enough trouble in keeping their own payroll on board so Bloomer, understandably, was dropped. 'Major Jinks', 'Mark Eaton', 'Wardwick', 'Derby Boy' and the ubiquitous 'Man With The Hat' took Derby sports journalism into a new era and Steve's final columns appeared at the end of January 1932, just past his 58th birthday. Freed of the responsibility of watching local games, Bloomer became a regular at the Baseball Ground again and the press reported that he had succumbed to the latest craze among the players by taking up golf at the old Markeaton Golf Club. He continued his groundstaff duties and gave every impression of poddling along quite nicely in a state of semi-retirement. What a tonic it would have been if Derby could have landed the League and Cup during this period. In the event it was more agonising near-misses as the championship runners-up spot they secured in 1929-30 was followed by a narrow Cup semi-final loss in 1932-33.

As the seasons passed as surely as ever, Bloomer's health held up sufficiently for him to continue to be active, but supporters' and players' memories from the mid-1930s onwards begin to describe him as 'an elderly gent' and in a well-known photograph of the 'old 'un' holding court to a group of players, believed to have been taken early in 1934 shortly after his 60th birthday, 'Steve' is certainly showing signs of wear. Nor was the financial future quite as healthy as it once was. That he had little money was made publicly evident from a special contribution he made to the *Derbyshire Advertiser* in 1934 to celebrate Derby County's Golden Jubilee:

"Just under 12 months ago I was tempted to describe the 1933-34 Derby County team, on their early form, as on a par with the finest of my own time and they have never had so many internationals on their books as they have now. Nothing would give me greater pleasure than to see the present generation of Rams do what we old 'uns failed to do – that is to win either the championship or the Cup...or both. If I had any left of my two benefits with the club, a total of £400, I would give it and more for that joy. Play up Rams!"

That rallying cry, appropriately enough, constituted the very final paragraph of Bloomer's formal press contributions. The game had not made him rich financially but he had cultivated and maintained a love for football and Derby County which never waned; and as the 1934-35 season closed he still had other sustaining elements in his life, which he cherished dearly. The statistics showed him still to be record League scorer in British football; he continued to enjoy the longstanding company and comforts of wife Sarah and their Portland Street home; and, by and large, he still had tolerable health. Besides, 61 wasn't old. But life, like football, is 'a funny old game' and so often it's the later stages when everything slips away. Within three years, one by one, each of those three constants were to be taken from him.

IN THE CLOSING STAGES OF THE GAME 1935-1938

"Do not go gentle into that good night,
Old age should burn and rave at close of day,
Rage, Rage, against the dying of the light."
Dylan Thomas

"**M**RS SARAH BLOOMER, wife of the famous footballer, died suddenly today at 42 Acacia Avenue, Sale, Cheshire, the home of her son-in-law, Alfred Quantrill, while Steve Bloomer was at their home in Portland Street, Derby. Aged 61 and a native of Derby, Mrs. Bloomer was taken ill three weeks ago and went to stay with her daughter, Mrs Hetty Quantrill. She appeared to be recovering but suffered a relapse and the end came suddenly. Mrs Bloomer was an active worker for the Conservative cause and a member of the Pear Tree Ward Conservative Association."
Derby Evening Telegraph, 9 April 1936

Farewell to Sarah

The 1935-36 football season had started like any before it and as Steve might have contemplated what it would bring by the time of its close, the one outcome his punditry could not have predicted was the death of his wife. Throughout the progress in Bloomer's career and all the ups and downs it inevitably brought with it, Sarah had been one of the few stabilising constants. Long before the days when 'footballers' wives' became somewhat unfairly stereotyped, Sarah was a solid and sensible home-making type right from the wedding day in 1896. While Steve always kept his football and home life entirely separate in his relations with club supporters, very rarely referring to anything 'personal' in his newspaper columns or interviews, there is every supposition that he valued the home comforts which his marriage and family life gave him through what we would now call 'the old-fashioned type of set-up'. Steve had always been used to being 'provided for' on the domestic front and there is no evidence that he was a dab hand at either cooking or house work…accusations of chauvinism would be rife now, but 'new men' were a rarity in Bloomer's day and his marriage was typical of the times. It was quite normal that Steve should not be expected to hold the fort and look after Sarah during her period of illness and convalescence, and equally clear that he was what we would now term 'a man's man', someone who had always played with the boys and was comfortable in male company.

But that didn't mean that he would find Sarah's passing easy to cope with and her death led the 'Old International' into a new and final stage of his life. Sarah was buried in Nottingham Road Cemetery on Wednesday, 15 April, the funeral party convening at the Great Northern Inn in Junction Street, where daughter Doris Richards and her husband were licensees. From all accounts the Bloomers' marriage had been a happy one, sustained despite sometimes long periods through which they were parted; at least there were never rumours of troubles outside the usual undulating parameters which any marriage goes through and they were together for just a few months short of what would have been their ruby wedding anniversary. Sarah was known by generations of Derby County personnel and a wreath was sent on behalf of the club. That the couple's relationship was a close and harmonious one was encapsulated by the ever-astute Jimmy Methven. In just a few short words he said as much about Sarah Bloomer as any lengthy tribute ever could:

"Without a doubt the finest partner Steve ever had was Mrs Steve Bloomer".

Farewell to home
It is well documented that many men of the old-fashioned breed find life particularly difficult after losing their wives. All the things that have been taken for granted for so long suddenly come into a sharp and revelatory focus; cooking, washing, ironing, and the simple pleasure of company...substitute sources for each of these domesticities need to be found. Either that or new depths of hitherto hidden talent and independence from within. For the first time in Bloomer's life, 35 Portland Street, the home Steve and Sarah called 'Cromer', probably as a reminder of their own favourite holiday spot, became a quiet and lonely place. Bloomer had few hobbies outside football and an active participation in sport and, now that age increasingly excluded him from that, time began to hang more heavily than ever before. Gardening, so often the supposed saviour in such circumstances, wasn't an option... 'Cromer' only had a small yard. What Bloomer did have was an army of 'friends', some genuine and others no doubt of the hanger-on variety. He still helped out at the Baseball Ground where friendly words were only a nod away and out of hours 'the local' was a ready antidote to lack of company which many men before and since have discovered to be a valued pleasure. Steve was sufficiently sociable and well enough known to be able to go into any hostelry in Derby and not be alone for long, but of course he had his own special favourites where he still delighted in displaying his competitive edge, one of his erstwhile taproom cronies describing him as 'a mean dominoes player and a shrewd hand at whist'.

That fondness for the culture and company of the public house has sometimes been misinterpreted as something more sinister; at least one book on the history of Derby County alludes to Bloomer's personal status at this time as 'apparently with a drink problem', but that was vehemently refuted by his surviving family as 'besmirching his name'. What it all boils down to is the old chestnut of the vast difference between being a 'regular pub-goer' and 'having a drink problem'. Fairer, then, to accept his family's genuine assurances than the odd dubious apocryphal tale from someone whose grandfather 'told me he had a friend who used to know someone whose brother-in-law drank with Steve Bloomer…' More certain is that here was a man increasingly left with only his memories, a man who had immersed himself completely in the culture of football to the exclusion of other potential pastimes, a man who realised that no number of instalments of fame and talent can serve as an insurance against loneliness and a man imbued with essentially Victorian values being asked to look after himself domestically for the very first time. Many such men, including scores of professional sportsmen, have found such circumstances too difficult to cope with and have fallen on 'hard times' which have led to undignified and painfully poignant ends. Bloomer was fortunate in having family close by who were sensible and caring enough to understand what was for the best. At the age of 62, shortly after Sarah's death, he left his home of 26 years and went to live with his daughter Doris, her husband Cyril and grandchildren Steve and Hetty, at the Great Northern Inn. This was a move to a completely different part of town in the area known as Rowditch, the only one of his eight Derby addresses which lay beyond kicking distance of the Baseball Ground, but far more important it was a move towards greater comfort, security and company at a time when Bloomer was to need it most.

Farewell to the record

Even as Bloomer had entered his 60s he was still regularly referred to in the press as 'the holder of the British record of League Goals scored'; those 352 strikes had for over 20 years kept him at the head of the ever-growing rank of football personalities even as the game's history lengthened relentlessly, and it was a record of which Bloomer had every reason to be proud. A subtle but notable change to the tagline had been forced in October 1935 with the substitution of 'English' for 'British' as a prolific Scotsman had taken the British record. Celtic's Jimmy McGrory officially took Bloomer's place in the statistics books with his 353rd goal but it was then 'discovered' that Motherwell's Hugh Ferguson had already surpassed it with 362. That didn't trouble McGrory, who simply proceeded to pass Ferguson in December 1935 with a hat-trick, then go on to finish his career in 1938 with an astonishing record of 410 League goals for Celtic and Clydebank since 1923 and in just 408 games. Even Bloomer could not compete with an amazing strike rate of more than a goal a game and no one since has been able to match that 'rate' although England's Arthur Rowley later beat the total, from far more games, with a final haul of 434 League goals.

Despite losing the British crown, Bloomer's English record was still intact until after Sarah's death although it became clear that it, too, would soon be taken from him. Everton's Dixie Dean was talented enough to be free-scoring in any environment but when the offside law changed in 1925, he had taken full advantage of the temporary, albeit prolonged, defensive insecurities to regularly plunder goals at a rate never before witnessed in the English game. His single season, and surely never to be beaten, record of 60 in 39 League games in 1927-28 was an obvious prelude to cumulative achievement. Shortly before his record fell Steve acknowledged the inevitable with fulsome praise for Dean but a sensible considered judgement of the relative circumstances:

"Ever since the offside law was altered teams have been remodelling their systems and their styles and some of them have not yet developed the killing process to the full standard. Of course I have to be careful when discussing this subject of goals and their relative value in my day and now. I am not a little proud of my own English record but I have a conscientious objection to being regarded as a boaster. It took me a long time to collect my 352, but I can assure everybody that there could be no suggestion of jealousy if another player were to go beyond that. There is obviously a great likelihood that Dixie Dean will eclipse my score and I say: 'Good luck to him.' He is without doubt a fine player and I shall not be moved to indignant protest when he is hailed as the new holder of the title of highest scorer ever in English football. It is not in self-defence, therefore, that I mention here that goals are unquestionably 'cheaper' than they used to be and I would as little think of trying to compare the merits of my own and Dean's or anybody else's record as I would of comparing Hannibal with Napoleon or Foch. There is no fair method of comparing the different goalscoring generations and such comparisons are too apt to create misunderstanding, misapprehensions and pinpricks of jealousy. So let each generation have and hold its own treasures as long as it may."

Despite his magnanimous initial stance in this statement there is no doubt by the end of it that Bloomer felt pangs of regret in losing the record in 'unlike' circumstances and was particularly irritated by some of the less well-informed press comment that accompanied yet another Dixie headline. Bloomer never minded losing in the wider sense but he always despised anything that smacked of sheer injustice. Imagine England's own triple Wimbledon champion, Fred Perry, being alive today and being told by a young tennis journalist that Tim Henman would have thrashed him off court. That is entirely true because of changes in fitness, technique and equipment but it does not diminish Perry's status as Britain's finest ever 'modern' player. So Bloomer is quite right in condemning comparison over time. A more realistic maxim is that any man or woman who is the best of their era at any sport would be the best of whichever alternative era they might have been born into given all the prevailing circumstances and opportunities. The final line of Bloomer's statement almost sounds like a cry for help: "Don't discard me yet, don't forget what an old man once did when he was young."

Certainly the loss of something apparently as trivial as a record would have accentuated any negative feelings Bloomer had about 'getting old', but he maintained his dignity well enough in the face of mounting media attention. With two games of the 1935-36 season left, Dean still needed four goals to equal Bloomer's record but typically took everyone by surprise in grabbing a hat-trick against Birmingham in the next game. Despite injury in that match he played on to leave himself just one goal short of equalling the record. With a degree of misplaced haste a pressman at the *Liverpool Echo*, Leslie Edwards, thought it would be a good stunt to get Bloomer up to Goodison Park for Everton's final game of the season, at home to Preston, when the record might well fall. Edwards duly arranged it all and Steve travelled up to Liverpool on Saturday, 2 May 1936. The *Liverpool Echo* man, though, had failed to do his homework; on the day before the game he listed Dean at centre-forward in his pre-match column but the great marksman, tough as he was, could not turn out due to injury. The collar-bone was fractured and there was no way he was ever going to make that game.

In the event Bloomer could have stayed in Derby to watch the Rams Reserves romp to the Central League championship in front of a record 10,000 crowd at the Baseball Ground. As it was, just a few weeks after his wife's death at a time he might well have been disinclined to travel, he stepped off the train in Liverpool to be met by a sheepish Edwards accompanied by Dean with his arm, entirely to Steve's surprise, trussed up in a sling. Was it any wonder Bloomer had sometimes lost his patience with generations of impulsive pressmen? Nonetheless Steve bit the bullet, enjoyed the attention and a 5-0 Everton win and was interviewed at length by the Liverpool press; in any case he knew all about the frustrations of broken collar-bones… 'Peggy' Lord had seen to that many moons ago. Bloomer was both generous and genuine in his praise of Dean's abilities and for that the *Echo* described him as 'a great sportsman'. Meanwhile, Dixie himself did his level best to soothe the situation and the two greatest English goalscorers to that day had a friendly heart-to-heart:

"I apologised to Steve in the dressing-room after the match, then we left the ground and had a few beers together. I sent him home to Derby with a bottle of Scotch under his arm because he'd taken the trouble to come all that way."

What a contrasting pair the two of them must have made propped against a bar; Dean tall, burly, virile, wavy-haired and dark…Bloomer small, wiry, slightly stooped, and pale by contrast. Yet what an unspoken goalscorers' kinship they shared. And by one of those strange sporting coincidences, even more than that; they were both working class boys from a family of six and both were talented baseball players, Dean having won medals with Caledonians in the National Baseball League. If Steve had to lose his record to anyone, Dean was as good a man as any and he eased Bloomer into second place at the start of next season; on Wednesday 2 September 1936, against Sheffield Wednesday 'the Fabulous Dixie' scored his 353rd goal to relieve 'the Incomparable Steve' of something he most definitely secretly cherished.

Football prevails

Despite the personal losses he suffered in 1936, Bloomer's interest in football was unaffected and he continued to be a familiar figure at Derby County home games during the 1935-36 and 1936-37 seasons. What a huge relief it must have been to him that he hadn't been tempted to have another dabble at the Spanish game in Irún, for that town was subjected to a fortnight's siege and merciless fighting in late August 1936 before falling to rebel troops on 4 September and being largely destroyed in the process. Had Steve been caught up in the Spanish Civil War he must surely have developed a complex about the effect of his presence on European stability. At any rate today's Irún, substantially rebuilt, differs greatly from that known to Saint Steve.

In contrast, Derby was far more peaceful. As for the club itself, the Rams had established themselves under the continuing stewardship of George Jobey as a top half side playing attractive football, but in both League and Cup terms they were still the nearly men. Many Derby people who lived into the current decade, and some still alive today, remember their boyhood spectator days and having Bloomer pointed out to them by knowing fathers or benevolent old sages. Bemrose School pupil Tommy Powell was one who most games 'saw an elderly gentleman standing outside the players' entrance with his back to the wall, looking very unassuming dressed in top coat and cap'. He recalled: "It wasn't until someone told me to ask for his autograph that I discovered his identity."

That particular schoolboy, of course, went on to become an immaculate contributor to Derby's side in the post-war era. It is curious that boys born over a decade after Bloomer's last-ever League game should covet his signature but that is a measure of his reputation in football and the town. Another fan remembers having his autograph book signed by Bloomer after a game, and he cherished it even as a pensioner. In April 1997, Ken Burrows remembered:

"I was 12 at the time and after the game my dad usually went into the Baseball Hotel for a pint, bringing me a lemonade outside. On this particular occasion he took my autograph book back in with him and ten minutes later returned with my album and Steve Bloomer. The great man shook my hand, asked me about my school football and hoped that one day I'd play for England. I didn't, of course, but I still remember that day…I had heard so much about Steve Bloomer and I don't think anything in my life has ever given me a greater thrill. I'm 73 now and I still have my prize autograph and still follow Derby County."

Bloomer always had a soft spot for the young 'uns but could be less tolerant with those who ought to know better, namely the players. Although he had always avoided the trap of insisting that the old days were superior, there is evidence that his patience with modern football began to wear thin as he got older and he certainly showed some frustration during games themselves. An 81-year-old still with a Derby season ticket in 1999 clearly remembers Bloomer the fan:

"In the 1930s as a lad I used to stand in the paddock right next to the players' tunnel. Bloomer was pointed out to me and I recall that to one of my tender years he simply looked an old man. I suppose he could have gone in the directors' box but every week he stood in the same spot right by me, leaning on the gate that used to be there next to the tunnel. What I remember most was how he used to chunter during the game. Peter Ramage, the inside-left, seemed to come in for most of the stick."

Maybe Bloomer thought he knew a thing or two about inside-forward play. It was during 1936, too, that Bloomer made his last public appearance on the Baseball Ground… as a referee. Since 1932 Derby had been home to a curious form of football entirely of the town's own invention. Derby Railway Veterans met Crewe Railway Veterans in an annual fixture for a silver trophy played under modified rules. All players were to be 65 or over and only allowed to walk! Bloomer refereed the games in May 1933 and 1934 at the Municipal Sports Ground and those in 1935 and 1936 at the Baseball Ground. Saturday, 9 May 1936 was thus Bloomer's real 'swan-song' on the ground where he had performed so many heroics. Reports of the match, played in front of 1,000 paying spectators, confirm that 'late in the game Steve could not resist the occasional kick at the ball in favour of the trailing Crewe men'. The home side won 2-0 despite the Crewe winger Collier 'walking splendidly and shooting just wide with a cross-shot.' It was obviously a triumph of experience over youth…the Derby team's combined age was 748 but the Crewe youngsters could only muster 742 years between them. It was all marvellously tongue-in-cheek and Bloomer was under instructions that 'all players who run will be disqualified'. Surely the rules should have read that 'all players who run will be congratulated'. As far as I am aware this brand of football is unique to Derby and it continued up to the war. There is a significance in the fact that Bloomer never refereed this game again. Derby's own famous veteran referee, Arthur Kingscott, who died in June 1937 and is commemorated in Sawley Church, wielded the whistle for the game in May of that year, and England international Sammy Crooks the year after. Quite simply, by May 1937, Bloomer's health was no longer up to it, even for a slow motion game.

Ill health strikes

That Bloomer's health deteriorated late in his life is well-known, but the chronological placement of this has often been misconstrued. Although he may have shown tendencies towards asthma and bronchitis for a number of years, by the start of 1937 he had yet to reach the stage where he had succumbed to ill health to a degree where it affected his activity and became a serious issue. Indeed, during the 1936-37 season he was still on the Derby County payroll as general assistant although his attendances were probably on a more casual basis. Young player Tim Ward, arriving at Derby early in 1937, recalled: "There was an old man in his 60s walking round the pitch with a fork, his physique concealed by baggy overalls. One of the players told me to kick the ball to him, so I did. The man barely raised his leg but kicked it back without breaking stride. So what, I thought, but the other player smiled and said: 'Now you can tell your grandchildren you played football with the great Steve Bloomer.' "

Research would suggest that Bloomer's bronchitis worsened from May 1937 and photographic evidence from around that time shows him with increasingly drawn features. A year after attending Sarah's April 1936 funeral, he attended another sombre April occasion. In 1937, Bloomer was photographed at the funeral of his old international colleague Billy Bassett and the resulting picture of him in funereal garb might well have struck those of a superstitious nature as something of a doom-laden sign. If such things really did run in threes then Bloomer might well have pondered what April 1938 would bring.

In the curious way that things sometimes have of coming to a rounded conclusion at an appropriate time, Bloomer spoke publicly to the people of Derby and surrounds en masse for the first and last time in the spring of 1937. At 9.10 pm on Wednesday, 31 March, Steve was a guest with Sammy Crooks on a BBC Midlands Radio broadcast covering Derby County's history. In a lively debate with Crooks, the ever more reflective Bloomer pulled no punches in stating that '...the forwards today are all wrong; the five we had in my day were far superior to the combination of today'. Not surprisingly Sammy stood his corner but was diplomatic in stating that 'it is all a matter of opinion in which the old and new school will remain divided'. The 20-minute programme was heralded as a great success and is the only known recording of Bloomer. Perchance some local enthusiast, maybe Derby's well-known radio retailer and sound engineer Vic Buckland, might have recorded it to survive somewhere to this day, but the official line from the BBC is that it has 'probably never been saved, but who knows, some of those early broadcasts do survive in our uncatalogued archives, but finding them is a different matter'. Tantalising stuff.

Barely a month later, news that Bloomer was ill began to filter into the local press and by the autumn of 1937 a national paper ran the story under the headline "Greatest Soccer Star is 63...ill." Although Bloomer was quoted as saying he had 'been ill for five years and not worked during that time' all the evidence suggests that this was a simple press error which should have read 'five months'. What caused Bloomer's bronchitis and asthma will always be a moot point but spending so much time out in all weathers watching football may not have helped. Nor would his lifelong smoking habit. Long before the anti-smoking lobby achieved wider influence, cigarettes were considered acceptable, indeed at times positively fashionable, even for sportsmen. Even into the 1950s, *Charles Buchan's Football Monthly* carried advertisements in which Stanley Matthews, no less, extolled the virtues of Craven A cigarettes!

It should not be imagined that Steve was bed-ridden and entirely debilitated as this is certainly not the case, but his doctor saw sufficiently bad signs to advise Bloomer strongly to avoid the oncoming British winter by going abroad. That was typical of the medical advice of the time but, right or wrong as it may have been, it probably seemed academic to Bloomer. Sitting as he did below his portrait in his room at the Great Northern, reading glasses in place to devour the daily papers, he might well have surveyed the holiday advertisements with some scepticism. Steve Bloomer had troublesome bronchitis but neither he or his family had enough money to pay for a worthwhile break on sunnier shores.

Recuperative cruise

Although Bloomer may not have realised it, he had a second family which collectively had sufficient clout to make things happen; that was Derby County. Immediately the news of Bloomer's plight became public, a group of local businessmen with Derby County connections set to work on donating and raising funds with a view to sending the ailing Bloomer on an extended cruise holiday. A leading personality in the group was Derby County manager George Jobey along with club director Ben Robshaw and local men-about-town Dick Mooney and Tommy Stephenson. There was some persuasive talent among that quartet of go-getters and they set to with a vengeance, writing hundreds of letters and securing good press coverage. The results were excellent... donations came in from many of the League clubs and supporters in Derby and all over the British Isles. The total reached the then substantial sum of £558, sufficient to send Bloomer on a quality cruise to Australia and New Zealand which would completely span the coldest and dampest of the English months.

He was to leave England in late-November and arrive in Sydney, Australia, just after Christmas. There he was to stay for a month with exiled Derby man Frank Ballington, a relative of Ben Robshaw, before sailing on to New Zealand and back again via Sydney to reach England in March 1938. Cruising was a very fashionable pastime in the 1930s and there is no doubt this represented a splendid opportunity for Bloomer to see something more of the world, but holidays can be incongruously exhausting too and there must surely have been some trepidation as Bloomer made plans to sail. The generosity of his 'football family' in that respect put him in a rather awkward position – once they had raised the money and suggested the itinerary for the trip, Bloomer had little option but to go with the flow. Whether it would do him good in the long term only time would tell.

Steve left Derby Midland Station on Friday, 19 November 1937, travelling with the Derby County team set to play at Portsmouth the next day. He had a chance meeting on the station concourse with an old England colleague, Fred Spiksley of Sheffield Wednesday, arriving in Derby for the races. The two had not met since the war and one imagines Spiksley getting quite a shock because Steve looked genuinely ill, his gaunt features and hollow-eyed stare giving him a worryingly fragile and vulnerable appearance against the robust health of the young Derby players and 'Bon Voyage' well-wishers. Steve's daughter, Doris, was certainly worried for him. Knowing that his journey was scheduled at just over four months, she was in tears as she waved goodbye from the platform while the train steamed slowly away. It must surely have crossed her mind that she would never see her father again. Even the newspaper headline 'Goodbye to Steve' had a whiff of finality about it.

Both the press and Bloomer, though, ever the old hand on such occasions, maintained a suitably upbeat stance. While the local paper expressed the wish that 'this great old player has a happy holiday and a speedy return to health', Steve expressed his gratitude to his benefactors thus:

"I am very grateful to the organisers and contributors to the testimonial fund and I am sure the sea trip will do me the world of good and put me on my feet again. I have not been at all good just lately and I will be glad to get away from the damp and fog of the winter here."

Bloomer took the boat train from St Pancras and boarded the luxury P & O liner *Otranto* at Tilbury, sailing on Saturday, 20 November while Derby were being hammered 4-0 by Pompey further down the coast. The 20,000 gross tonnage vessel, in operation since 1926 and the second of that name, provided every comfort for its 1,100 passengers and Bloomer, travelling alone, was able to settle in and get to know people in relaxed surroundings. In a letter from the Mediterranean, Steve expressed some relief that he was getting to know the ropes:

"I am already feeling the good effects of the journey, and I have gone through the menu nearly every time to my surprise. Although I am not renowned as a good sailor, I have only missed one sitting. It is pleasing too that there are so many people who seem to know me."

If that latter fact sounds curious for someone who hadn't kicked a competitive ball for 23 years, just imagine sharing your dinner table on holiday with Stanley Matthews, who retired 34 years ago…you might just recognise him, or Bobby Charlton, Geoff Hurst and a host of far more minor players of yesteryear. Football followers have long memories, even for relative nonentities, and it is no surprise that someone of Bloomer's stature found company easy to come by. Ports of call at Gibraltar, Palma, Toulon, Naples, Port Said and Colombo took him into new European territory and new continents before he enjoyed 'a real good old fashioned Christmas on board… absolutely champion', and arrived for a month's stay in Sydney on 29 December.

Nice as it was to enjoy company, Steve's account of his trip also suggested the other side of the coin when anonymity might have been a more restful option. There was just a suggestion, too, that knowing the season was in full swing back home, he was missing his football!

"Everybody was very kind to me and so hospitable and I was pleased to meet people in Australia and New Zealand from around Derby and Belper way who are living out there. In Sydney, Auckland and Wellington, the Football Associations wanted me to lecture but I had to say I didn't feel up to it. It was a pity, though, that football was out of season for I should have liked to have seen some, although I saw a few grounds."

Steve sailed to New Zealand on 26 January on board another P & O liner, *Oronsay*, and made the return journey home on that same vessel, which docked at Tilbury in the early hours of Friday, 25 March 1938. After having enjoyed 'good weather practically all the way there and back' the ship was held up in the Channel for 24 hours due to fog and it arrived back to a cold and damp English welcome which was potentially ominous for someone with bronchial troubles. Early signs, though, were good for Bloomer. When he was met at Derby Midland Station by director Ben Robshaw on Friday evening, he was much fuller in the face and far less strained looking than he had been four and a half months earlier, and seemed in buoyant mood:

"I enjoyed every minute of the trip and it has done me a lot of good. I feel a great deal better than when I went away…I was really in a poor way then. But although it was a wonderful experience I am glad to be back to see my daughters and grandchildren… having not seen football for five months too, I hope to see Derby County in one or two of their remaining games and I am determined to get to the Cup Final."

As he installed himself once more into the familiar surroundings of 19 Junction Street, Bloomer's family and the people of Derby had every reason to share that optimism but, as all football followers know, the closing stages of the game can deliver the cruellest of blows.

Final whistle

Health is a fickle customer. The day after his return, while Derby County were winning 2-0 at Leeds United with goals from Ronnie Dix and Sammy Crooks, the newly rejuvenated Bloomer was taken ill at home. Whether it was a change in climate, or perhaps a delayed type of exhaustive reaction to what had been an incredible schedule, we will never know. What we do know is that Bloomer started to struggle more severely with bronchial trouble again, but there was every reason to believe that medication would turn the tide. Three weeks later, though, on the morning of 16 April, he had another more serious relapse and as his breathing became more laboured, his eight-year-old grandson Steve was hastily dispatched from his grandpop's room to fetch medical help. Now nearly 70, Steve Richards remembers that trauma still:

"The fastest I ever ran was to the doctor's house on the morning Steve Bloomer lay dying at my mother's home…but it was too late."

If it is true that our lives pass before us in the final moments, how much harder it must have been for Bloomer than the rest of us to edit the highlights; which of his special goals might he have recalled, which of the many countries he'd visited or the hundreds of fellow professionals he'd played against? Or perhaps he saw the broken bodies of Ibrox 1902, thought of England and recalled the stench of Ruhleben Camp on the day of his arrival. Or maybe his mind filled with the good times of games played and won, friends made, baseball, cricket, fishing, Spanish almond blossom…and young lads on the parks of Derby playing their hearts out to impress the old 'un just that once. Surely, too, he must have reflected on Sarah and the girls, his brothers and sisters, father and mother… and Derby County. We can only guess… perhaps he was just a small boy again shooting at sticks.

Steve Bloomer was a tough man who had overcome many obstacles but the opponents ranged against him that morning, later written into their allotted spaces by Eric Johnson MRCS, were the hardest of them all. Stephen Bloomer, male, 64 years, retired professional footballer, finally met his match in the face of myocardial failure, asthma, bronchitis and myocardial degeneration. He never did get to see Derby County again, or the Cup Final...how strange that having seen or played in a game every week in season for 50 years, he should not see a single match in his final six months.

It was a Saturday, the day when he had always been so much more alive than any other; but on this Saturday there was no chaff and banter, no cartwheels and lusty cheers, no triumphal band playing in his honour and no way out of the dark tunnel that faced him. Instead, an elderly gent with a life full of memories closed his eyes on the world for the final time...the 'Incomparable Steve' was dead.

LEGACY AND LEGEND 1938-2010

The last whistle has sounded, the great game is over.
O was ever a field left so silent as this;
The scene a bright hour since, how empty it is;
What desolate splendour the shadows now cover,
The captain has gone, the splendour was his.

He made no farewell, no sign has he given
That for him never more shall the big ball roll.
Nor the players he urged on, from his strong heart and soul
Strive again with his skill as they always have striven
Not again will he hear when the crowd shouts 'Goal!'

But somewhere...somewhere his spirit will quicken
With victors and vanquished. For now he has cast
In his lot with the Olympians of old who outlast
This human encounter, this football so stricken
That it seemed for a moment to die as he passed."
Thomas Moult

"THE *TELEGRAPH* announces with regret the death early today of Steve Bloomer, one of football's greatest personalities and the finest inside-right in the history of the game. Although he was taken ill the day after his return from a recuperative holiday, his death was comparatively sudden and will come as a great shock to the countless thousands who knew him affectionately as 'Steve'. He lived to see his League record broken by Dixie Dean but there has been no successor to achieve the magnetic personality of Steve's diminutive figure, pale face and twinkling feet. He was a man who performed his greatest feats in a most unassuming way, disregarded anything in the way of tribute and remained calm and cool in any circumstances. His name in England became a tradition and people spoke of the 'days of Steve Bloomer' when they wished to recall something worth remembering from their fast dimming past. After his trip to Australia many had hoped this grand old player would be set up once again for a considerable period and would enjoy the leisure he so richly deserved. Alas it was not to be. Peace to his ashes!"
Derby Evening Telegraph, Saturday, 16 April 1938.

Funeral and tributes

The *Telegraph's* reaction was typical of the respectful way in which Bloomer's death was treated by the press. All the national papers devoted some space to 'Steve's passing' and formal obituaries appeared in both the *Daily Telegraph* and *The Times*, but the reaction from all quarters, while tinged with obvious sentimentality, was above all spontaneous and genuine. Nothing was over-mawkish, nor were the column inches devoted to the news excessive. Locally, Derby County paid their own immediate tribute on the afternoon of his death, the team appearing in black armbands at home to Liverpool and letting their football do the talking in a 4-1 win. At grass roots level, in the few days either side of the funeral, many local football clubs and other sports organisations in Derby observed a minute's silence before their matches or meetings. Derby people are neither over-emotional or unduly demonstrative and such gestures showed the affection and respect that had built up in the town over the years.

The conduct and stature of the funeral, too, was indicative of those same sentiments. Steve's third April funeral in a row was this time his own. On the afternoon of Wednesday, 20 April 1938, Derby Cathedral was full to capacity and many people wanting to gain admittance were turned away and stood bareheaded outside. Thirty Derby County players past and present followed the coffin, the young bloods represented by future Derby manager Tim Ward and the old brigade by former boss Jimmy Methven. There were names, too, which might strike a note of surprise now, among them future legendary Arsenal manager Bertie Mee, then a mere Derby Reserves winger.

Clusters of onlookers lined the route of the cortège from Junction Street into the town and when the Provost of Derby, the very Reverend P. A. Micklem, had completed formal proceedings inside the Cathedral, gathered crowds saw a line of eight funeral cars proceed slowly to the interment at Nottingham Road Cemetery. Over 100 wreaths were sent, those from the FA and major clubs adorned with suitably coloured ribbons laid side by side with personal ones from family, friends, local sports clubs and Steve's favoured watering holes. As the hearse passed the County Ground on Nottingham Road, scene of a 'young, pale, almost ill-looking' lad's club and international debuts, the Derbyshire County Cricket Club players practising in the nets left their ground to line the road still wearing their whites. Steve was laid to rest with Sarah, Violet and Pat in a simple grave with no headstone and no mention of his football prowess, that entirely at his own last request, later subtly embellished by the patronage of local sports enthusiast and bookmaker Dick Mooney with a single stone football. The press described the day's proceedings as the biggest funeral Derby had ever witnessed.

A legend explained

Such a reaction might cause puzzlement to those who say 'he was only a footballer' and it is fair to record that whenever we talk about Steve Bloomer and the reaction he provokes 'among Derby people', those statements need more correctly to be qualified by saying 'Derby 'football' people'. It has ever been the case that for any one person enthralled by the great game there are, amazingly, more than one left entirely cold by the whole boring affair. Hence the apparent indifference of ladies of the persuasion of Maud Mugliston, whose 22 April weekly newspaper column 'A Derby Woman's Diary' made not a single mention of Bloomer's death but devoted several columns to the 'King of the Big Top', circus impresario Bertram Mills, who also had Derby connections and died on the same day as Steve. There are still plenty of Mauds and her male counterparts for whom football is nothing but worthless rubbish. It is that sort of supreme 'Who's Wayne Rooney?…What's offside?…It's only a game…' mentality, which is far more widespread even with today's media-saturation than we football fans might care to admit, that begs us to ask the question why any man who simply kicks a ball into the back of a net should be the subject of such strong affections. It's a conundrum football followers instinctively know the answer to but might not be able to articulate quite so readily. Indeed, lengthy academic treatises on the whole rationale of football 'fandom' have been written to try to explain why something like 'Bloomermania' could exist.

This is not the place to regurgitate those sometimes complex psychological and sociological theories. A much simpler way of understanding is to study the faces in a football crowd a split-second after their side has scored an important goal…the expressions can only be described as showing sheer joy, that extreme emotion entirely different to happiness and contentment and seldom experienced in everyday life. Yet there is that joy, bottled up by an essentially reserved nation, exploding in the spontaneous unguarded moments when a ball crosses a line between two white posts. It is arguably hugely irrational, but when it's 'your' team it does matter and millions of football people worldwide are similarly afflicted, none more markedly than in our own nation. Quite simply, Steve Bloomer was a purveyor of goals and as such a purveyor of that rare commodity 'joy' and a symbol of the extraordinary sporting prowess which 'ordinary people', successful or otherwise, secretly covet. That is why Jack Robinson and Jimmy Methven, both described as 'wonders of the football world' in their day, have never been revered and remembered at a level even remotely akin to that accorded to Bloomer…they didn't score goals.

There is more to it, of course. Bloomer was a truly entertaining charismatic player yet people felt they knew him because he had the common touch. He was a working-class lad who carried the hopes of any number of 'Steve wanabees' on to the field with him and he was just 'dangerous' enough off it to be seen as ordinary yet fascinating at the same time. Style, swagger and pluck are all words which the press have used in connection with Bloomer over the years but never once have dull, cowardice, elitist or boring got anywhere near the compositor's tray. Perhaps most important of all…when people met Steve Bloomer, most of them came to like him as a person as well as a footballer.

Thus it was that he achieved what we would now call the 'superstar' status in his own lifetime which was an absolute pre-requisite to his subsequent longevity in footballing halls of fame. Being presented with his portrait by the

FA in 1905 and later securing the England and League goalscoring records had made him famous; and making it past the pompous editorial committees of *Burke's Who's Who in Sport* to be included as one of just a handful of professional footballers in their opening 1922 edition, then being portrayed in one of the murals adorning the luxurious public rooms of the *Queen Mary* on her maiden journey in 1936…those are the sorts of trivial yet significant personal milestones which heralded Bloomer's lasting reputation down the years and provoked the affectionate response shown at his funeral. That all seems readily understandable in that distant pre-World War Two context, but why are people still talking and writing about him now, over 70 years on?

Memories…on ice and rekindled

World War Two, from 1939 to 1945, had a similar effect on football and the way people perceived its history as did World War One 25 years earlier. A suspension of official football activity for the duration of hostilities encouraged people with massively uncertain futures to look back to an earlier and 'better' age with which they were comfortable and familiar, despite its toughness. Bloomer's death just over a year before Chamberlain announced that 'this country is now at war with Germany' assured him an immediate place in the suspended memories of those who lived through the war, but that mood changed when it was all over; Derby County finally achieved something Bloomer would have loved to have witnessed, winning the first post-war FA Cup in 1946 under the managership of Stuart McMillan, son of Bloomer's former team-mate Johnny.

That long-awaited 4-1 victory over Charlton Athletic, still talked of as the greatest triumph in Derby County's history despite two subsequent League championships, created a new set of heroes at precisely the time people needed them most. Never was *Abide With Me* sung with more emotion than at that Wembley Final and there is no doubt, in the blissfully relieved peacetime mood prevailing from 1946, that the memory gears were shifted and people in general began to look forward from that date, not backwards. It was Jackie Stamps and the 'Boys of '46' that football folk talked about on their strolls down memory lane from then on, strolls which became increasingly necessary as Derby County slipped alarmingly into Division Two in 1952-53. Fans may have thought things couldn't get any worse, but they did, as under manager Jack Barker the Rams again finished bottom of their division in 1954-55, being relegated to the hitherto unexplored depths of the Third Division North. Again, regular doses of Raich Carter pills and Peter Doherty tonic were necessary to get Derby followers through the bad times and remind them of that all-too-brief post-war high.

Not that Bloomer and his age was forgotten entirely, but he was certainly put 'on ice' for the next 20 years or so. Both the 1950s and 1960s were supremely progressive decades in which youth took centre stage, nostalgia 'wasn't what it used to be' and everything new was hip. In Derby County terms that mood was epitomised by the whirlwind arrival of young management team Brian Clough and Peter Taylor in July 1967. Their 'new broom sweeps clean' approach to the football club's management even extended to removing photographs of the old days from the walls of the boardroom and corridors and Bloomer was, at least metaphorically, perhaps even physically, stuffed into the cupboard under the stairs to gather dust. Such was the continued march of 'progress' in society that this attitude prevailed in far more football clubs than Derby County and the amount of club records and other ephemera dumped into skips at that time can still bring out a cold sweat on the brow of the most hardened sports historian. At Derby, the young guns were first tolerated then worshipped as promotion to Division One in 1968-69 was followed by the club's first League championship in 1971-72. Another championship success under Dave Mackay and Des Anderson in 1974-75 cemented Derby's position as one of the teams of the 1970s and created yet more ranks of new young supporters for whom the past really was 'another country'.

Although the scientific principle which states that 'to every action there is an equal and opposite reaction' does not always operate in sociological terms, it was something that the old stagers of Derby subconsciously implemented by dint of an innate instinct that the past was worth valuing. Progress in both society and sport had simply been distastefully fast for many people, especially those born around the turn of the century, the sort of people who really had seen Bloomer play in their own childhoods, and who began once again to resurrect those days of yore as their own 'golden era'.

Certainly from the late 1970s onwards, a new nostalgia began to develop which manifested itself in a revived interest in local and social history fostered especially through local newspapers and publishing companies. Amongst the plethora of subjects so avidly scrutinised, football has ever been a favourite and one of the 'Kings of Football's Stone Age' began to receive his first real airings since his death in 1938. Although it is fashionable in some quarters to mercilessly pillory the 'I remember when it was all fields' lobby, there is nothing wrong with nostalgia so long as it's kept in its proper balance against the best elements of progress. There is a big difference between harbouring an obsessive interest in the dusty old cobwebs of the past and cultivating a healthy enthusiasm for the finely spun web of history which football clubs and their fans have become proud to celebrate. The real breakthrough in this second coming for Bloomer came in 1983 on the threshold of the club's centenary, when its history was first celebrated in detail by a book, *The Derby County Story*. On the cover among the colour photographs of Roy McFarland, Charlie George and their trendy mates aimed at ensnaring young supporters like myself, were curiously short-haired black and white figures including one singularly pale chap in international shirt and cap. Inside there was more of the Bloomer fellow and his startling deeds for the Rams. In that way a new generation born after World War Two was introduced to this two-dimensional, almost comic-book character, known as 'Steve', and that burgeoning cult of nostalgia developed apace right into the 1990s and beyond to a stage where football and sports memorabilia has itself become an important market niche in the commercial activities of any progressive club.

Bloomer had taken his fair share of opportunities in his time. This was an unexpected one which, if he took it, could take him into a third dimension right on to the year 2000 and beyond to achieve his hat-trick of centuries as a football star.

A legend revived

As the Derby County nostalgia industry continued to flourish through the 1980s and '90s, Bloomer images and anecdotes made ever more regular appearances in the local press. Derby fan Moz Curtin epitomised the new interest being taken in the club's early days by the younger supporters, naming his historically-based fanzine *Bloomer Shoots...Shilton Saves*; and interest in Bloomer wasn't just confined to Derby. Articles appeared in the *Black Country Magazine* and Cradley area newspapers effectively reclaiming their long-forgotten son and newly dubbing him 'Cradley's Cannonball Kid'. In such a climate the time was ripe for more permanent reminders of Steve Bloomer to be considered. But a catalyst was needed to make things happen. It came in the shape of a familiar figure, Bloomer's closest surviving male relative. When we last encountered Steve Richards in this narrative he was a small boy on a spring day in 1938, running faster than he had ever run before to the doctor's house. It may have been too late that day but it is never too late to be proud of your grandfather, hope that other people can share that pride and that permanent reminders of his achievements might be left for posterity. Steve Richards would have loved to follow his grandfather into football but by his own admission he just wasn't good enough:

"I was once given a trial with Derby County on the strength of whose grandson I was, but it didn't get me signed on. I wasn't much use and my grandfather knew that. He used to come up to Rowditch Rec and watch me and my pals kick a ball around. He never said anything but his eyes gave away what he thought."

Although young Steve didn't inherit old Steve's football skills, the newspaper work which Bloomer enjoyed so much in his later years did emerge as a family trait and he would surely have been proud of Steve Richards' long career as a sportswriter and national football journalist. Appropriately enough that included ghosting an autobiography in 1970 for another palefaced predator of the goalmouth, Leeds United and England's Allan Clarke, entitled *Goals Are My Business*; and at four successive World Cup tournaments from 1974 onwards, one of Steve's most pleasant jobs was to interview and present the views of a player universally acclaimed as the best inside-forward of all time...the great Pelé.

Despite mixing in such illustrious footballing company, Steve Richards' greatest admiration was for the grandfather he never had the opportunity of getting to know fully. Bloomer's death at 64 was premature from all sorts of perspectives... had he lived at least 20 years longer, his grandson would no doubt have asked him all the questions that an aspiring young journalist could muster and this biography might well have been penned by Richards himself many years ago. As it was, Bloomer left no scrapbooks, few photographs and only scant records of his life so that the personal insights gained by his grandson were frustratingly sparse. Over the years Bloomer even gave away his medals and shirts to well-wishers along with some of his international caps. He never saw Derby win the Cup or League, nor England the World Cup. Many of Bloomer's former playing colleagues and opponents outlived him…his valued mentor John Goodall died aged 78 in 1942, Jimmy Methven in 1953 at 84, and the 'Offside King' Bill McCracken was ever canny enough to sneak up all the way to 1979, finally being 'sprung' by advancing years at 96.

While these personalities had at least some opportunity in their genuine old age of making their presence felt to later generations, the feeling that Bloomer had to a degree been 'short changed' was never far from his grandson's mind. With knighthoods later becoming the order of the day for sportsmen of the ilk of Sir Bobby Charlton, Sir Stanley Matthews, Sir Geoff Hurst and Sir Tom Finney, it seems likely that a similar honour must surely have been bestowed upon Bloomer had he lived in another era. As it was, barring a plaque on the wall of the Baseball Ground by the directors' entrance, his home town displayed nothing of a permanent nature by way of memorial. By the early 1990s even the stone football from Bloomer's grave had been stolen. Steve Richards, by then in his 60s, determined to remedy the state of affairs and went on record as saying how important it was 'that Steve Bloomer should be remembered by future generations of Derbeians'. With him in that view were other surviving members of the Bloomer family; grandson Alan Quantrill, and granddaughter Hetty, who married and later divorced South African-born Derby County player, Cecil Law. Steve Richards marshalled the forces to provide a handsome new gilt-lettered headstone for the regularly tended grave at Nottingham Road Cemetery and a memorial seat nearby, and in Derby city centre itself, a permanent black and white marble plinth and plaque stands, entirely as a result of the efforts of Richards and family, in Lock-Up Yard, an ancient and well-used thoroughfare known locally as the 'fish market'. The unveiling ceremony on Monday, 28 October 1996 was attended by many football personalities including current Rams manager Jim Smith, but guests of honour were the many old players who gladly accepted their invitation to attend. 'Preston Plumber' Tom Finney renewed acquaintance with Middlesbrough's 'Golden Boy' Wilf Mannion and Bolton's 'Lion of Vienna' Nat Lofthouse, who finally beat Bloomer's England scoring record in 1956; Johnny Morris, inside-right and British record signing when he joined Derby County from Manchester United in 1949, was also present and, most appropriate of all, record League goalscorer Arthur Rowley.

While the city applauded the concept of a Bloomer memorial, it is scarcely possible to do anything these days without some sort of controversy and some locals condemned the plinth as 'inappropriately sited' and 'not grand enough'. True, in an ideal world, a life-sized sculpture in Derby Market Place or outside the football ground might have been appropriate, but planning, aesthetics, political and cost considerations simply didn't make that possible. Steve Richards made this clear in the press and said that Bloomer 'wouldn't have wanted anything grand'. Nonetheless, if ever anyone should ask the question 'what is the biggest fish in Derby fish market?' the answer is easy...Steve Bloomer, by a long way.

Most of the chuntering came from quarters which didn't understand the economics involved and the sacrifices which were made to get the memorial in place at all. The money to make it came partly from the sale of Bloomer's 19 surviving international caps, almost the only special reminders Steve Richards had of his grandfather's achievements, but he felt it more important to give 'something' back to the people of Derby than to see the caps eventually gather dust to no purpose in a more distant relative's attic or, worse still, to be sold for personal gain. At the Christie's football memorabilia auction in Glasgow on 26 October 1994, for which Bloomer graced the catalogue cover, the caps had been expected to raise at least £10,000; in the event they reached a relatively disappointing £8,050. Even supplemented by a £300 figure for a Brazil shirt signed by Pelé, the total after commission wasn't sufficient and Steve Richards and family made personal sacrifices of both time and money to reach the required target. Again some Derby people were critical of the fact that the Bloomer caps had been allowed to go out of the city at all, but, if neither the club nor local enthusiasts bid for them, there was no alternative. When the hammer fell the buyer was revealed as Carlisle United chairman Michael Knighton, whose explanation of his purchase should pacify any Derby fans still smarting with indignation:

"I was born in Belper in 1951 and brought up as a young lad in Loscoe. We were Derby County through and through and I was always football mad. I played for Heanor and Ilkeston Boys and Derbyshire at representative level and signed schoolboy forms for Derby County at 14 before joining the ground staff as a youth player at Coventry City. I hoped for great things but all too soon I had a serious injury and never played again. Steve Bloomer has always been a hero to me, which might seem strange considering the difference in eras, but there was a family connection which had always drawn me closer; my maternal great-grandfather was Willie Layton, who played for Sheffield Wednesday over 300 times in Bloomer's day. He played against Steve in the League and with him for the English League v Irish League in 1900. That connection, and my regard for the Rams and football heritage in general, was why I bought the caps. A few years ago I did offer them back to Derby County but they were right in the throes of moving and the time wasn't right. If ever they made a formal request then, of course, I'd consider it, even though I do cherish those Bloomer mementoes."

Although no moves were made by the club in that direction, another much bigger move ultimately opened up a further chapter in the continuing Steve Bloomer story. At the end of the 1996-97 season Derby County left the famous old Baseball Ground and began their next campaign at the magnificent new Pride Park Stadium, where Bloomer soon secured a rather unexpected presence. By 1998-99 the team were taking to the field to the rousing chorus of its newly-adopted club anthem, *Steve Bloomer's Watching*, written in 1996 by supporters Mark Tewson and Martyn Miller as a re-work of the Aussie Rules football song

Up There Cazaly, and recorded in 1997 with the help of Ilkeston-born actor and musical star Robert Lindsay, himself a keen Rams follower. When approached, the club readily agreed to promote and use it. That in itself has put Steve Bloomer's name back in front of all Derby County fans on a regular basis and the song has even had its own website on the internet. As Bloomer's memory became ever more pervasive, there was also activity closer to his roots, again driven largely by his grandson Steve Richards. In 1999 he assisted Dudley Council in their provision of a Steve Bloomer memorial plaque in Cradley close to his Bridge Street birthplace.

The publicity surrounding such activity brought Bloomer ever more into the countrywide public domain again, with a growing number of appearances in the national press. He was voted by the Football Writers' Association into the Football League's 'Top 100 Legends of All Time', appropriately enough in the company of John Goodall, and his photographic portrait chosen to appear at the National Gallery exhibition of 'British Sporting Heroes' in London. Only one major honour yet eluded Bloomer – some sort of permanent memorial at Pride Park Stadium. And in the fullness of time this too came to fruition. From 2003 a supporters' organisation known as the Rams Trust began pushing for a large bronze statue of Bloomer to be erected outside the stadium. A great deal of hard work was done over a number of years, but despite some encouragement from the club itself, the projected cost of £100,000 proved a step too far. In the event a compromise was reached, and finally on 17 January 2009 a splendid bronze bust of Bloomer by talented sculptor Andy Edwards was unveiled inside Pride Park. It stands behind the home dugout on a plinth made from bricks taken from the demolished Baseball Ground, a fitting link with the scene of so many of Bloomer's triumphs. So long as the statue remains, the *Steve Bloomer's Watching* anthem will carry a real truth.

All of this new-found exposure has greatly enhanced the recognition of Bloomer's name in football circles. Yet 'beyond the game' it remains a harsh fact that few people have heard of him. That seems a great shame, but illustrates again an earlier observation – that the history and culture of football, a game loved by countless millions, is pointedly ignored by countless more.

So where does all that leave us? Here was a man who overcame the difficulties of his humble origins, achieved excellence at his chosen sport, self-tamed the cocksure excesses of extravagant youth and embraced new responsibilities to become England's leading player of his time, highly respected by his fellow professionals and supporters alike. A man who never made great riches from the game he loved, but steadfastly continued to support it until his premature death and in doing so, and being a decent sort into the bargain, secured himself a permanent and respected place in football's history and in Derby's folklore. Above all an ordinary man, touched with that so elusive essence of greatness, who achieved so much in his chosen field and lived such an extraordinary life. Of course he was by no means perfect, but which of us is? He deserves to be remembered.

Perhaps it bodes well for continuance of that remembrance long into the future that the majority of youngsters in Derbyshire schools have already become acquainted with at least the rudiments of the Steve Bloomer legend. If this book has helped the process, then it will have achieved some of the objectives set out in my introduction.

I have not been able to reveal everything about the life of Steve Bloomer. Like most of us he retains some secrets. But if readers know him better now than they did before, and feel a closer affinity to him because of that, then hopefully the journey in his company has been worthwhile.

Although that journey is now at its close, there is no truly definable end to the Bloomer story. So long as people take an interest in football's history he will rank as an important figure of a certain age; his name will assuredly be spoken tomorrow by someone in Derby and even if, in centuries time, the game should cease to be played, an ancient historian somewhere will do the requisite digging into 'sports of the old world' and renew acquaintance with the 'Incomparable Steve'.

As for the foreseeable future, perhaps just 50 years from now when all the world's literature must surely be digitally downloadable on to a personal pocket-sized 'book-screen', is it too much to hope that some staunch traditionalist who values the pleasures of both real books and Association Football could chance to slide this very volume from its resting place? If so, might they also be moved out of sheer curiosity to visit the small grassed plot at Nottingham Road Cemetery which is an old footballer's final field? Perhaps as they look upon the names of Stephen Bloomer and family they will see not a scene of death but the evidence of a life; and they will feel no sadness but permit themselves a knowing smile and fancy that they hear carried gently on the breeze the triumphant strains of the Derby Town Band and just the faintest echoes of distant cheers that will never ever cease.

CAREER STATISTICS

Season-by-season Club Record
Derby County

SEASON	LEAGUE		FA CUP		OTHER		TOTALS	
	App	Goals	App	Goals	App	Goals	App	Goals
1892-93	28	11	0	0	–	-	28	11
1893-94	25	19	2	0	–	-	27	19
1894-95	29	10	1	0	1	1	31	11
1895-96	25	22	5	5	–	-	30	27
1896-97	29	24	4	7	–	-	33	31
1897-98	23	15	3	5	–	-	26	20
1898-99	28	24	5	6	–	-	33	30
1899-1900	28	19	2	0	–	-	30	19
1900-01	27	24	1	0	–	-	28	24
1901-02	29	15	7	3	–	-	36	18
1902-03	24	12	2	1	–	-	26	13
1903-04	29	20	6	5	–	-	35	25
1904-05	29	13	1	0	–	-	30	13
1905-06	23	12	3	0	–	-	26	12
1910-11	28	20	4	4	–	-	32	24
1911-12	36	18	2	1	–	-	38	19
1912-13	29	13	1	1	–	-	30	14
1913-14	5	2	1	0	–	-	6	2
TOTAL	474	293	50	38	1	1	525	332

Middlesbrough

SEASON	LEAGUE		FA CUP		TOTAL	
	App	Goals	App	Goals	App	Goals
Part1905-06	9	6	0	0	9	6
1906-07	34	18	2	2	36	20
1907-08	34	12	1	0	35	12
1908-09	28	14	0	0	28	14
1909-10	20	9	2	1	22	10
TOTAL	125	59	5	3	130	62

GRAND COMBINED TOTAL
600 League Games(incl. 1 Test)
353 League Goals(incl. 1 Test)
55 FA Cup Games
41 FA Cup Goals
655 League, Test and FA Cup games in all and 394 goals.

FULL England International Caps

9 Mar 1895	England v Ireland at Derby 9-0	.....(Bloomer 2)
6 Apr 1895	England v Scotland at Everton 3-0	.....(Bloomer 1)*
7 Mar 1896	England v Ireland at Belfast 2-0	.....(Bloomer 1)
16 Mar 1896	England v Wales at Cardiff 9-1	.....(Bloomer 5)+
20 Feb 1897	England v Ireland at Nottingham 6-0	.....(Bloomer 2)
29 Mar 1897	England v Wales at Sheffield 4-0	.....(Bloomer 1)
3 Apr 1897	England v Scotland at Crystal Palace 1-2	.....(Bloomer 1)
2 Apr 1898	England v Scotland at Glasgow 3-1	.....(Bloomer 2)
18 Feb 1899	England v Ireland at Sunderland 13-2	.....(Bloomer 2)
20 Mar 1899	England v Wales at Bristol 4-0	.....(Bloomer 2)
8 Apr 1899	England v Scotland at Birmingham 2-1	.....(Bloomer 0)
7 Apr 1900	England v Scotland at Glasgow 1-4	.....(Bloomer 1)
18 Mar 1901	England v Wales at Newcastle 6-0	.....(Bloomer 4)
30 Mar 1901	England v Scotland at Crystal Palace 2-2	.....(Bloomer 1)
3 Mar 1902	England v Wales at Wrexham 0-0	.....(Bloomer 0)
22 Mar 1902	England v Ireland at Belfast 1-0	.....(Bloomer 0)
3 May 1902	England v Scotland at Birmingham. 2-2	.....(Bloomer 0)
9 Apr 1904	England v Scotland at Glasgow 1-0	.....(Bloomer 1)
25 Feb 1905	England v Ireland at Middlesbrough 1-1	.....(Bloomer 1)
27 Mar 1905	England v Wales at Liverpool 3-1	.....(Bloomer 0)
1 Apr 1905	England v Scotland at Crystal Palace 1-0	.....(Bloomer 0)
18 Mar 1907	England v Wales at Fulham 1-1	.....(Bloomer 0)
6 Apr 1907	England v Scotland at Newcastle 1-1	.....(Bloomer 1)

*In this match Bloomer claims two, crediting the own-goal by Neil Gibson to himself.
+Some reports only give Bloomer four. Bloomer himself claims six.
The Ibrox Park disaster game in Glasgow on 5 April 1902, for which Bloomer was captain, finished in a 1-1 draw but does not appear in the official records. The game was replayed in Birmingham.
The accepted official record for Bloomer's international career is 28 goals in 23 games.

Odds and Ends

*Bloomer scored in his first ten internationals, notching 19 goals in the process, and only twice finished on the losing side in an England shirt.

*He is the only player ever to score six goals for Derby County in a first-class game.

*His 18 hat-tricks for Derby County is a club record and he is the oldest player, at 38 years and 261 days, to achieve the feat.

*Bloomer topped the Football League scoring charts five times and was top League scorer for Derby County on 15 'consecutive' occasions and twice for Middlesbrough.

*He is the third longest-serving player for Derby County; his 16 years 312 days has been bettered only by Jack Nicholas and Sammy Crooks.

*At 40 years and 19 days, Bloomer is the oldest forward ever to play for Derby. Only right-back Arthur Latham and goalkeepers Harry Maskrey and Peter Shilton have beaten him in the age stakes.

*Most clubs' scoring records have been broken a number of times since the early days; Bloomer is the earliest player from all the 92 League clubs whose record still stands and one of only two current club-record scorers to have played in the 19th century.

NOTES ON SOURCES

MANY different sources have been used in securing the information which makes up this biography. The following few notes may help clarify certain points for any researchers who have already undertaken Bloomer study, or intend to carry out further work in the future.

Career statistics given are those traditionally credited as being official so no additional 'goals' have been given to Bloomer even where there is a very strong case for doing so by reference to his own memoirs.

The extensive extracts from Bloomer's own reminiscences are quoted verbatim; the only departure from that is the very occasional correction of grammar, syntax or date where obviously incorrect or misleading. Also, again on very few occasions, passages written on the same subject but at different times, have been merged together, but never with any change of context.

Researchers choosing to consult Census returns, parish records, cemetery records etc relating to Bloomer and family will find some discrepancies in ages and spelling of names due to contemporary miscalculations, spelling errors or inaccurate transcription. These have been corrected/adjusted in the text; Steve's father Caleb, for example, is recorded on the 1881 Census as Calib and in 1919 cemetery records as Capil. Steve himself appears in the 1881 Census as Staren and his poor brother Phillip as Phallis. Most important and misleading of these, though, is the 1881 Census recording of Stephen's 'mother' as Alexandra, which has led other researchers to record that his mother Merab died before Stephen was seven years old. This is incorrect. A full investigation of this has shown that Alexandra is a phantom creation caused by the limitations of the Census data-gathering methodology, being a mis-transcription by the Census visitor from his original rough notes on to his official returns which now constitute the permanent record. The enumerator, Nottingham-born Samuel Mosley, made other such errors in his returns, evidently having great difficulty in reading his own hasty scribble when called upon to submit his neat copy a few days later…all family-tree tracers beware!

BIBLIOGRAPHY

General works

Football: Our Winter Game/ Charles W. Alcock; Field 1874.

*Athletics and Football/*Montague Shearman; Longmans, Green 1887.

*Football/*A. Budd et al; Lawrence and Bullen, 1897.

The Rise of the Leaguers/'Tityrus'; Sporting Chronicle, 1897.

*Association Football/*John Goodall; Blackwood, 1898.

*Association Football & The Men Who Made It/*Gibson & Pickford; Caxton, 1905-06. 4 volumes.

*How to Play Soccer/*contribution by Steve Bloomer; Spalding, 1906 .

*The Book of Football/*Various contributors; Amalgamated Press,1906.

Cricket and Football/'The Sportsman'; Sporting Life, 1917.

*Wickets and Goals/*James Catton; Chapman and Hall, 1926.

*The Story of the Football League/*Sutcliffe; The League, 1938.

*British Sport and Games/*Bernard Darwin; Longmans, Green, 1940.

*Soccer the Ace of Games/*Alec Whitcher; Southern, 1945.

*Soccer Calling/*Alec Whitcher; Southern, 1945.

*The Official History of the FA Cup/*Geoffrey Green; Naldrett, 1949.

*The Story of Football/*William Lowndes; Thorsons, 1952.

*40 Years in Football/*Ivan Sharpe; Hutchinson, 1952.

*A History of the Football Association/*G. Green; Naldrett, 1953.

*Soccer the World Game/*Geoffrey Green; Phoenix, 1953.

*A History of Football/*Morris Marples; Secker and Warburg, 1954.

*Soccer/*Denzil Batchelor; Batsford, 1954.

*Corinthians and Cricketers/*Edward Grayson; Naldrett, 1955.

*Soccer Nemesis/*Brian Glanville; Secker and Warburg, 1955.

*Football Through the Ages/*Percy Young; Methuen, 1957.

*Sixty Seasons of League Football/*R.C. Churchill; Penguin, 1958.

*Association Football/*Fabian and Green; Caxton, 1960. 4 vols.

*Don Davies: an Old International/*J.R. Cox; Stanley Paul, 1962.

*A Century of Soccer/*Terence Delaney; Heinemann, 1963.

*England v Scotland/*Brian James; Pelham, 1969.

*Edwardians at Play/*Brian Dobbs; Pelham, 1973.

*The People's Game/*James Walvin; Allen Lane, 1975.

Marshall Cavendish Football Handbook; Marshall Cavendish, 1978.

*The Goalscorers from Bloomer to Keegan/*T. Pawson; Cassell, 1978.

Soccer; a Pictorial History;Roger Macdonald; Collins, 1977.

*Dixie Dean/*Nick Walsh; Macdonald, 1977.

*Association Football and English Society/*T.Mason; Harvester, 1980.

*Cup Final Extra!/*Martin Tyler: Hamlyn, 1981.

*Football Wizard: the Billy Meredith Story/*J.Harding; Breedon, 1985.

*The Football Grounds of Great Britain/*Simon Inglis; Willow, 1987.

*The Football League 1888-1988/*Bryon Butler; Macdonald, 1987.

*League Football and the Men who Made It/*Inglis; Willow, 1988.

*History of Derbyshire County Cricket Club/*J.Shawcroft; Helm, 1989.

*The Illustrated Footballer/*Tony Ambrosen; Breedon, 1989.

*Football League: Grounds for a Change/*Dave Twydell, 1991.

*Sport and the Making of Britain/*Derek Birley; MUP, 1993.

*The Victorian Schoolroom/*Trevor May; Shire, 1994.

Armed with a Football/Andrew Ward;
Crowberry, 1994.
The Cassell Soccer Companion/David
Pickering; Cassell, 1994.
Aerofilms Guide to Cricket Grounds/W.
Powell; Dial House, 1995.
A Football Compendium/Peter J. Seddon;
The British Library, 1995.
Football and the English/David Russell;
Carnegie, 1997.

Club and local works
Fifty Years of Derby County, Derbyshire
Advertiser, 1934.
Let's Talk About Derby County/Tom
Morgan; Sentinel, 1946.
Gresley Rovers Centenary/Brian Spare;
Gresley Rovers FC, 1982.
The Derby County Story/Anton Rippon &
Andrew Ward; Breedon, 1983.
*Derby County: The Complete Record 1884-
1984*/Gerald Mortimer; Breedon, 1984.
There Was Some Football Too/Tony
Francis; DCFC, 1984.
Derby: An Illustrated History/Maxwell
Craven; Breedon, 1988.
*Derby County: The Complete Record 1884-
1988*/Gerald Mortimer; Breedon, 1988.
Black Country Folk At 'Werk'/Ned
Williams; Uralia Press, 1989.
*The Derby County Story Told in
Pictures*/David Thornton, 1989.
*The Derby County Story 1884-
1991*/Rippon et al; Breedon, 1991.
The Who's Who of Derby County/Gerald
Mortimer; Breedon, 1992.
The Great Days of Derby County/Rippon
et al; Breedon, 1993.
The Book of Derby County/Anton Rippon;
Breedon, 1994.
A Cradley Album/Peter Barnsley; Two
Gates, 1994.
Yesterday's Derby/Rod Jewell; Breedon,
1995.
Images of Derby County/Anton Rippon;
Breedon, 1995.
The Black Country Nail Trade/A. Willetts;
Dudley Libraries, 1996.
Cradley Castings Through the Years/Bev
Pegg, 1996.
The Baseball Ground 1895-1997/Jim Fearn

et al; DCFC, 1997.
Derby County Days/Edward Giles;
Interleaf, 1997.
The Derby County Story/Anton Rippon
and Andrew Ward; Breedon,1998.
*Middlesbrough: A Complete Record 1876-
1989*/H. Glasper;Breedon,1989.
Boro's Best/Dave Allan et al; Juniper, 1997.

Ruhleben Camp
The Ruhleben Prison Camp/Israel Cohen;
Methuen, 1917.
The History of Ruhleben/J.Powell &
F.Gribble; Collins, 1919.
In Ruhleben Camp/magazine June –
December 1915 (10 issues).
The Ruhleben Camp Magazine/ 6 issues
March 1916-June 1917.
Ruhleben:a Prison Camp Society/J.
Davidson Ketchum; OUP, 1965.
War Games/Tony McCarthy;Queen Anne
Press, 1989.

Spain
Album Nacional de Futbol/A.Karag, 1947.
Real Madrid Book of Football/Melcon and
Smith; Souvenir, 1961.
Cincuentenario del Real Union Club/A.
Karag, 1966.
The Football Grounds of Europe/Simon
Inglis; Collins, 1990.
*Historia del Real Union Club de
Irún*/Carlos Fernandez, 1991.
European Football Results Bulletin/Dave
Allan & Graeme Riley, 1993.

Newspapers, magazines and periodicals
*All Sports Weekly, Association of Football
Statisticians Reports, Association of Sports
Historians Reports, Athletic News, Belper
News, Bloomer Shoots...Shilton Saves,
Boys' Own Paper, Burton Mail, Daily
Graphic, Derby Daily Express, Derby Daily
Telegraph, Derby Evening Telegraph,
Derbyshire Football Express, Derbyshire
Advertiser, Derbyshire Life, Football Chat,
Fry's Magazine, The London Magazine,
North Eastern Evening Gazette,
Nottingham Evening Post, Ram Magazine,
Sporting Chronicle, Strand Magazine, The
Footballer, Windsor Magazine.*

INDEX